Liminal Sovereignty

Liminal Sovereignty

Mennonites and Mormons in Mexican Culture

Rebecca Janzen

Cover art reprinted with permission from the Mennonite Centre Archives

Published by State University of New York Press, Albany

© 2018 State University of New York

For information, contact State University of New York Press, Albany, NY
www.sunypress.edu

Book design, Aimee Harrison

Library of Congress Cataloging-in-Publication Data

Names: Janzen, Rebecca, 1985- author.
Title: Liminal sovereignty : Mennonites and Mormons in Mexican culture / Rebecca Janzen.
Description: Albany : State University of New York Press, [2018] | Series: SUNY series in Latin American cinema | Includes bibliographical references and index.
Identifiers: LCCN 2017049447| ISBN 9781438471037 (hardcover : alk. paper) | ISBN 9781438471044 (e-book) | ISBN 9781438471020 (paperback : alk. paper)
Subjects: LCSH: Mennonites—Mexico. | Church of Jesus Christ of Latter-day Saints—Mexico. | Christianity and politics—Mennonites—History—20th century. | Christianity and politics—Church of Jesus Christ of Latter-day Saints—History—20th century. | Christianity and politics—Mexico—History—20th century.
Classification: LCC BX8119.M6 J36 2018 | DDC 305.6/89772—dc23 LC record available at https://lccn.loc.gov/2017049447

10 9 8 7 6 5 4 3 2 1

I dedicate this book to the memory of my grandparents,
Abram G. and Gertrude (Wiebe) Janzen.

CONTENTS

FIGURES

ACKNOWLEDGMENTS

This book would not have been possible without the advice and encouragement of my family, friends and colleagues. My immediate family—Bill Janzen and Marlene Toews Janzen, Phil Janzen and Rachel Powers—have been very encouraging. Other members of the Toews and Janzen families, especially my aunt Clara Toews, have also been very supportive. I would also like to thank family friends Ghenette Houston and Brian Ladd, Steve and Gloria Houston, and Moira Toomey and Paul Siebert and Dave and Ally, and Jane and Ben Willms.

My friends in Bluffton, Ohio, who were instrumental to all aspects of my life and work, especially Karen Bontrager, Ryn Farmer, Marathana Prothro, Jackie Wyse Rhodes, and Emily Buckell. Their respective families made my time there joyful. I am thankful for the friendship also of Brad and Sarah Potts, Judy Lester, Amy Marshall, Elizabeth Kelly and Ray Person, Esther Yoder Strahan, Walt Paquin, Kate Spike, and Rudi and Ravonn Kauffman. Ross and Anna Kauffman and their daughter Nora are truly in a category of their own. I also am thankful for finding friends and community at Grace Mennonite in Pandora for continued friendship in Toronto, including Adleen Crapo, Paula Karger, Sara DeMoor, Geoff Wichert, and Marcia Boniferro. I finished this project in Chicago, with special thanks to Ryan Radebaugh and Nick Seamons, and in Columbia, SC, where my new colleagues and department made my move a happy one.

My colleagues in Mexican studies have also shaped this project. First, I would thank the lady locusts, Ilana Dann Luna, Sara Potter, Amanda L. Petersen, and Cheyla Samuelson. Emily Hind belongs there, as well as in my writing group with Carmen Serrano and John Waldron. Thanks also to Susan Antebi, Ignacio Sánchez Prado, Carlos Amador, Tamara R. Williams, Olivia Cosentino, Christina Soto van der Plas, Ariel Wind, Carolyn Fornoff, Dan Russek, Pedro

Ángel Palou, Jason Dormady, Bram Acosta, Sam Steinberg, Daniel Calleros, Brian Gollnick, Sergio Gutiérrez Negrón, Saúl Hernández, and others.

This project began as a presentation about Carlos Reygadas' film, *Stellet Licht* [*Silent Light*] at the 2013 LASA meeting in Washington, DC, at a panel organized by Eva Romero where I presented alongside of Vicky Garrett and others. It grew from that initial exploration to include an analysis of Mormons in Mexico. Thanks to my friends Brian L. Price and Benjamin Cluff, for telling me about the LDS tradition, and then introducing me to their family and friends in Mexico. Russell M. Cluff initially provided information about the colonies. In Colonia Juárez, my hosts Sam and Mona Cluff were incredibly generous with me. John and Sandra Hatch, Ed and Gayle Whetten, and LaVon B. Whetten were also helpful in my research. They introduced me to some Mennonites from the US—Phil and Jeanne Stover, who helped me contextualize the Colonias Juárez and Dublán. David Dalton made sure I knew about the other Mormons in Mexico.

My visits to Mennonite communities in Mexico were greatly facilitated by my dad—his presence on a first visit and, on a second visit, his *Kanadischapapiaoabeit* [Canadian citizenship paperwork]. He arranged for us to visit in Cuauhtémoc with George Reimer, Anna Martens, and Elena Krahn, and with Peter Rempel and his family, and, on my second visit, with Franz and Sarah Penner. We attended a Conference church in Blumenau, and an Old Colony church in Rosenort. On a later visit, I also met Cornelius Loewen and Helen Thiessen and their family, including their children Tony and Veronica, and their friend Angelina Peters. In Capulín, Gerhard and Susanna Neufeld showed me around their colony and introduced me to their family. They also drove me and my dad to the Sabinal colony to meet some of my family there, John and Maria Redecop, and Jacob and Eva Neudorf, and their families. Their kindness extended far beyond my limited understanding of Low German (I definitely know what *oba yo* means now). In La Honda, Zacatecas, I have many kind relatives. These include my dad's cousins Henry Bergen, and his family, Abe Bergen, and his family, and Sarah and John Thiessen and their family, and Anna Friesen and her family. I especially appreciated spending time with my second cousins Maria and Eva Thiessen, Anna and Peter F. Friesen, and Peter T. and Nancy Bergen and their kids. Also special were my visits with Hermann and Julia Penner and their daughters. In Nuevo Ideal, Durango, John and Helena Guenther welcomed me warmly, and Helena took me everywhere I could possibly have wanted to go. I met more relatives, and Anna Hiebert showed me many old family photographs. Laura G. Gutiérrez made sure I knew about the other part of Nuevo Ideal.

I gratefully acknowledge the generous support of the Plett Foundation, particularly the assistance of Andrea Dyck. The project has also benefited from the support of the C. Henry Smith Peace Trust and the Karl B. Schultz Award. I submitted the manuscript as the Kreider Fellow at the Young Center for Anabaptist and Pietist Studies at Elizabethtown College, and would like to thank its director and affiliates, Jeff Bach, Hillary Daecher, Cynthia Nolt, Steve Nolt, Edsel Burge, and Don Kraybill. The High Library staff, particularly its director, Sarah Penniman, and archivist, Rachel Grove Rohrbaugh, created a welcoming space for me to write and research. Thank you.

The following is reprinted with permission:

The cover artwork is reprinted with permission from the Mennonite Centre Archives.

An earlier version of chapter 5 was originally published as "Still Life/ Mexican Death: Mennonites in Visual Culture," in volume 19 (2015) of the *Arizona Journal of Hispanic Cultural Studies*, pp. 75–90.

INTRODUCTION

They Did Not Come to My Mexico

My great-grandmother and six great-aunts and uncles and their children emigrated from Canada to northern Mexico, along with several thousand other Canadian Mennonites, between the 1920s and the 1940s.[1] These immigrants lived on individual farms in the states of Chihuahua and Durango. These farms were grouped into villages, which were then grouped into colonies. To this day, some of my relatives live in colonies. They and their descendants aim to pursue their own educational systems and religious practices, preserve their Low German language and farm in tight-knit communities.[2]

They did not come to the Mexico I had learned about through my previous academic work on twentieth-century Mexican literature. When I traveled to visit them, I did not know what to say. There was often a language barrier. So, I listened and I watched. I noticed that the land, their land, the land I almost could have come from, shaped them. I was impressed with how they used their comparative isolation to preserve their religion, language, and family structures and carefully monitored their interaction with the world beyond their communities.

My work in Mexican studies has given me the remarkable privilege of meeting many Mormons belonging to the Church of Jesus Christ of Latter-Day Saints (LDS Church). I learned that there is a group of LDS people with roots in nineteenth-century Utah who live very close to several Mennonite colonies. In spite of theological differences between Mennonites and Mormons, the Mexican press and archives have confused the two groups; moreover, several academics have studied them alongside of one another.

This book, *Liminal Sovereignty: Mennonites and Mormons in Mexican Culture*, explores the question of belonging as it relates to these minority religious groups and Mexican nationhood: were they inside or where they outside of the understanding of Mexico after the 1910 Revolution?[3] When? Under which circumstances? It answers these questions by examining the ways that visual and print culture, here confined to photography, film, television, comics, and archival documents, represent the relationship between these Mennonites and the outside world, or Mexican society. It will compare them to understandings of the groups of Mormons who live in Chihuahua, represented in similar sources. I argue throughout this book that the perception of these two groups, who theoretically occupy a space at the edges of the nation, aligns with ideas of the Mexican nation, from *mestizaje* [racial mixture] at the beginning of the twentieth century to violence and death in the early twenty-first.

The book argues that these groups at the edges are an integral part of the nation. This emphasis on the state of exception comes out of Carl Schmitt's foundational work on the state of exception and Giorgio Agamben's recent interpretation of it. Schmitt famously stated that the "Sovereign is he who decides on the state of exception" (5).[4] That is, the entity in charge of the state is the one who is allowed to decide how, and under which circumstances, to enforce the constitution and the law that comes out of it. As political scientist Gabriella Slomp explains, for Agamben, "under normal circumstances, the state was still the primary entity . . . but under exceptional circumstances groups or parties that did not see the state as protecting their own way of life developed into political units" (59). These units could then threaten the sovereign, and challenge the application of the law. Agamben notes that the exception does not necessarily mean a dictatorship. Instead, it is "a space devoid of law . . . in which all legal determinations—and above all the very distinction between public and private—are deactivated" but that remains connected to the law and the legal system (50). The minority religious groups, who have developed agreements for exceptions to Mexican law, are exceptional in a different way— their communities temporarily suspend the rule of the law; in a context of a widespread suspension of the law, they are no more or less likely to be attacked or ignored than others.

This book focuses on Mennonites and Mormons from 1920 to the early twenty-first century in Mexican history and culture. In so doing, it will show how these groups fit into the Mexican exception and how Mexican concepts of nationhood have been flexible enough to accommodate them. Mexican visual and print culture presents two schools of thought about these religious minorities. One idealizes both groups, stating that they are hardworking contributors who better their regional and national economies. The other is that they are bad for the nation because they refuse to integrate with its schools, its language, or the entirety of its laws. The idealistic tendencies tend to surge in periods of economic growth or revolutionary optimism, while the critical tendency approaches in times of economic downturn and uncertainty. It also rises among concerns about the rights of indigenous people, which are often in conflict with the comparatively privileged positions of the Mennonites and the Mormons.

The Mormons this book discusses descendants from those who emigrated from the US to Mexico in the 1880s and eventually set up colonies in the states of Chihuahua and Sonora. It is important to note, however, that other Mormons in Mexico vastly outnumber these US-descendant Mormons. According to official LDS church statistics, there are 1.3 million LDS Mormons in Mexico ("Facts and Statistics"). Mormon colonies were and are the size of a small town surrounded by extensive landholdings used for cattle ranching, fruit trees, and crop farming. The vast majority of these Mormons left their homes in Mexico in 1912, and some of them returned to Mexico in the 1920s.[5] The Mennonites, for their part, emigrated from Canada to Mexico en masse mostly between 1922 and 1926. Today there are some Mennonites in Mexico who do not live in colonies, but they are in the minority. Both groups' migration patterns, then, and commitment to a level of separation from society mean that the surrounding government has had to expand some of its ideas to accommodate them. These groups have also had to change their understanding of their separation in order to remain in their host country.

EXCEPTIONALITY IN MEXICO

The two religious groups suggest that Mexico's status as a state of exception is not new.[6] Indeed, the religious groups settled in Mexico in order to live out their particular beliefs, and only came to Mexico upon agreements with the Mexican government that they would have freedom to do so. The LDS Mormons who live in what are today Colonias Juárez and Dublán are primarily descendants of people who bought land there as part of colonization companies in the 1880s and 1890s. A contract printed in the October 12,

1893, *Diario Oficial de la Federación* provides us with details of their settlement.[7] It allowed the Mormon-owned Mexican Colonization Company in the states of Chihuahua and Sonora to act as a land broker in those states as long as the land they purchased was not in a border zone (Secretaría de Fomento 3).[8] The agreement provided a flexible definition of the term family. It could be any group with one or two parents and their children; it could also be a group of siblings, as long as one has reached the age of maturity. This flexibility, which we see in other agreements from the time period, was likely meant to account for different constructions of family that resulted from illness and death. Conveniently for the Mormons, it allowed for polygamous families to register as independent family units without falsifying legal documents. According to Mormon historian B. Carmon Hardy's *Solemn Covenant: The Mormon Polygamous Passage* (1992), early Mormons struggled in Mexico. He explains that bigamy has always been forbidden in Mexico, and private polygamous marriages have also fallen outside of the intent of Mexican law (Hardy 173). Hardy adds that Mexican legal "intent" also allowed for adultery in the case of men; so, polygamy in Mexico was tolerable (174).[9]

In addition to this semblance of permission for an alternative family formation, the agreement does not force Mormons into a concept of Mexican identity. It acknowledges that the Mormons are not from Mexico and so it allows for exemption from military service and from federal and state taxes. They are only to pay municipal taxes and *impuestos de timbres y estampillas* [taxes on property loans or other forms of credit]. The agreement gives the Mormons a strong economic incentive for their agricultural pursuits. They will be allowed to import without restriction and will be rewarded for their economic contributions. It also gives them a tacit recognition for their own state; they are allowed to sign their own passports and avoid Mexican consular services (Secretaría de Fomento 3). The Mormons were expected to contribute to the region and would be rewarded by being able to act essentially as their own mini-state, pay limited taxes and have their own family formation. The LDS church officially abandoned polygamy in the late nineteenth century. Other religious groups that also claim the name Mormon continue to practice it, and I deal with them in chapters two and four, calling them non-LDS Mormons. These people continue to be granted unofficial exemptions from Mexican polygamy laws.[10]

The Mennonites, who primarily belong to the Old Colony Mennonite Church, today are spread out over the states of Chihuahua, Durango, Zacatecas,

Tamaulipas, Campeche, and others, were also granted their own exceptions that satisfied their particular religious beliefs. A letter signed by then-president Álvaro Obregón (1920–24), tells Mennonite leaders:

1. You will not be forced to accept military service.
2. In no case will you be compelled to swear oaths.
3. You will be completely free to exercise your religious princi-ples and to observe the regulations of your church, without being in any manner molested or restricted in any way.
4. You are fully authorized to establish your own schools, with your own teachers, without any hindrance from the gov-ernment. Concerning this point, our laws are exceedingly liberal.
5. You may dispose of your property in any way you desire. The government will raise no objections to the establishment among the members of your sect of any economic system which they may voluntarily want to adopt.

    It is the most ardent desire of this government to provide favorable conditions to colonists such as Mennonites who love order, lead moral lives, and are industrious. Therefore, we would deem it a pleasure if this answer would satisfy you. The aforementioned privileges being guaranteed by our laws, we hope that you will take advantage of them positively and permanently. (Redekop 251)

This preserved the Mennonites' freedom of religion and reassured them that they could come to Mexico.[11]

HISTORY AND CURRENT PRACTICES OF THE RELIGIOUS GROUPS

Mennonites and Mormons, as religious groups, both arrived in Mexico seeking religious freedom. The beliefs highlighted in these agreements with the Mexican government have led to misunderstanding by broader society.

Some scholars have already compared the two groups and highlights their unique features and similarities.[12] These scholars tend to focus on how the religious minorities protect themselves from the world. Glenda Miller's superb MA thesis in anthropology, *A Comparison of the Mennonite and Mormon*

Colonies in Northern Mexico (1990), situates both groups in their historical context. She conducted a range of interviews and observed community members, to argue that:

> both groups [are] products of utopian movements, of persecutions, of religious identities, and of migrations. To the extent that both groups see themselves as chosen people similar to the Israelites of the Old Testament, we can safely say their respective religions establish their world views and determine their social structures and social systems which allow them to pursue their religious goals in an increasingly secular world. (42)

Miller concludes that the Mennonites are an insular group with a survivalist mentality, and that Mormons, while maintaining strict boundaries, are more open to integration and self-improvement. I contest these assertions of separation and boundaries throughout my work.

These Mennonites are part of the Anabaptist religious movement and began during the Radical Reformation in sixteenth-century Europe. Some men felt that others who were reforming the Catholic Church, such as Martin Luther, were not going far enough. They reformed the Reformation by rebaptizing one another. Eventually, groups of rebaptizers began to be called Mennonites, after one of their early leaders, Menno Simons. In Mexico, the Mennonites trace their history to the Netherlands and to the migrations from there to Poland, part of which was later taken over by Prussia, and the migrations from there to Russia late in the eighteenth century, and from Russia to Manitoba, Canada, late in the nineteenth. At the time in the 1870s when about 8,000 moved from Russia to Manitoba, another 11,000 Mennonites from Russia moved to Kansas and Nebraska in the US. Unlike most Amish, Brethren, or Mennonites in the eastern part of the United States, they do not trace their history to Switzerland or southern Germany.

The Mennonites who moved from Russia to Manitoba in the 1870s belonged to three groups: the *Bergthaler*, the *Kleine Gemeinde*, and what became known as the Old Colony church. The official name of this last group was *Reinlaender Mennoniten Gemeinde* but they were commonly known as Old Colonists because they originated from the oldest colony in Russia. Of the three groups that settled in Manitoba, the Old Colonists were the most conservative. This meant that they were the most determined to follow a separate and more communal way of life: they wanted to live in street villages on a block of land by themselves and run their own affairs; they were firm in resisting all governmental overtures about teaching English in their schools; and they had strict dress codes and rules about the use of technology.

This separate lifestyle was not to last. Shortly after World War I (1914–18) the provincial governments in Manitoba and Saskatchewan passed laws making attendance at English-language public schools compulsory. Old Colony people paid heavy fines and sent delegations abroad to look for a new homeland. In 1921, they found what they were looking for in Mexico. Thus, starting in 1922, 6,000 Low German Mennonites from Manitoba and Saskatchewan moved to Mexico. They settled in exclusive colonies on the large blocks of land that they had purchased. They built villages and constructed houses, barns, schools, and churches. The first Mennonites left Manitoba for Chihuahua in March 1922, a movement that ended in 1926. The movement to Durango started in June 1924; there were seven more trains that took people from Saskatchewan to Mexico until 1926, and several small groups continued to migrate to Mexico until 1934 (Sawatzky, *They Sought a Country* 62).

Historians contextualize the Mennonite arrival in significant historical developments in the 1920s in northern Mexico. Martina E. Will's "The Mennonite Colonization of Chihuahua: Reflections of Competing Visions" (1997) provides a balanced explanation of the relationship between Mexico and its Mennonite minority. She explains that the Mexican government, under President Álvaro Obregón (1920–24), granted Mennonites multiple exceptions to various laws because of ongoing post-Revolutionary conflict in the state of Chihuahua and the desire to repopulate the north with subjects who would be loyal to the new president (Will 353–54). This implies that the Mexican government was hoping to integrate these people after some time had passed. Historian Daniel Nugent's *Spent Cartridges of Revolution: An Anthropological History of Namiquipa, Chihuahua* (1993) complicates this implication by pointing out an alliance between the government and wealthy landowners vulnerable to having their land redistributed through agrarian reform laws. Nugent explains that the Mennonites bought land at ten times the going rate in Chihuahua and that this large land purchase may have benefited the previous landowners, the Zuloaga family, and the government.

From the 1920s to the 1940s, Mennonites found it hard to live in Mexico. Some became very poor; crops that had worked well in Canada did not work so well in Mexico. At the same time, everyone in a given colony belonged to the same church; the church was led by a Bishop and a council of ministers; they regulated many aspects of life in the colony—farm tractors with rubber tires were prohibited, and the village schools were carefully controlled. Martha Chávez Quezada's 1948 undergraduate thesis—the earliest I am aware of—notes that Mennonites contribute economically to Mexico, and she praises the way the community cares for widows and orphans (80–81). At the same time, she observes that: "sería conveniente que a cambio de estas concesiones ellos aceptaran incluir en sus programas escolares el aprendizaje del idioma" ["it would be convenient that in return for these concessions they would include (Spanish) language learning as part of their educational programming"] (91). This wish is ongoing and represents one popular opinion about Mennonites in Mexico. Similarly, Santiago Fierro Martínez's detailed 1989 study about Mennonites in the Mexican state of Durango explains some of the Mennonite social fabric. He establishes that not all Mennonites are wealthy, the way their communities allow for some wealth redistribution, by leaving some land for cultivation by poorer people, and low-interest loans from the church, should be an example for other campesinos (Fierro Martínez 66).[13]

Over the next several decades, Old Colony churches in a majority of the colonies in Mexico changed. They began to allow rubber tires on farm tractors; they also allowed cars and trucks and telephones; after NAFTA, almost all colonies connected to the national electricity grid. Jason H. Dormady's "Mennonite Colonization in Mexico and the Pendulum of Modernization, 1920–2013" (2014) even suggests that Mennonite privileges in education and exemption from military service no longer officially exist due to recent secularization laws. This has not yet affected the Mennonites' lives. Dormady also presents significant concerns about the Mennonites as they interact with the government, and for their future, particularly regarding water use (Dormady "Mennonite Colonization" 190).[14] Velia Patricia Barragán Cisneros' *Los mennonitas* [sic] *en la historia del derecho: Un estatuto jurídico particular* [*Mennonites in the History of the Law: A Particular Judicial Status*] (2006) reflects on these more recent changes, and she expresses concern that Mennonites are losing their distinctiveness. She worries that their morals are straying, and is somewhat mollified by her incorrect assumption that Mennonites have their own police force (Barragán Cisneros 167, 170).[15]

These historical accounts relate to the way that Mennonites live in Mexico today. Recently, Liliana Salomán Meraz's *Historia de los menonitas radicados en*

Durango [*History of Mennonites in Durango*] (2010), has presented a more complete portrayal of the community. After several years of working in the Nuevo Ideal colony as a teacher in a school for less traditional Mennonites, she wrote this book. In addition to immense respect for her subjects, she describes the history of Mennonites in Durango by analyzing newspapers from the 1920s to the present and interviewing community leaders. Her work, and that of historian Royden Loewen and sociologist Luann Good Gingrich, provides an idea of typical Mennonite life in Mexico.

Calvin Redekop's *The Old Colony Mennonites: Dilemmas of Ethnic Minority Life* (1969) details some religious practices that continue into the present.[16] These sources and my own experience of visiting Mennonites in Mexico suggests that Old Colony worship services are unique. They begin as early as 8:00 a.m., the men and women sit on opposite sides of the church. These services include prayers, songs, and a sermon. There are several men who, under the authority of their local Bishop, are ordained by the congregation. One will preach on a given Sunday, either his own words or a sermon of another minister. They also have two silent prayers for which the people kneel. The most distinct part of an Old Colony service is the singing. *Vorsinger*, a group of men, lead the church in singing; people bring their own *Gesangbuecher* [hymnbooks] with them. The more conservative Old Colony churches will sing *Langewiese*, or *Auleliese* [a slower melody], called, that some have compared to Gregorian chanting; other Old Colony churches, sing a still slow *Kurzewiese* [short melody]. Old Colony people join the church upon baptism, usually a few weeks before marriage. They will celebrate communion twice a year. Old Colony women typically wear dresses in darker colors that go to mid-calf, with stockings for church. The way a woman wears a kerchief, and the embroidery on it, may indicate the colony she comes from. More traditional men wear homemade overalls and shirts, and the less traditional ones would wear jeans and button-down shirts. To work they wear Mexican or Southwestern style cowboy hats, or baseball caps. Young men who have not yet been baptized might have flashy belts. Most men are clean shaven with short hair.[17]

The other Mennonites in Mexico belong to a variety of churches, which follow the Mennonite beliefs of adult baptism, nonresistance, by avoiding the military draft, and various understandings of separation from society. Some belong to groups like the *Kleine Gemeinde* that have plain dress, an evangelical approach to their religious beliefs, and a less restricted understanding of technology. Children who attend their schools learn how to read and write in German and Spanish. Others belong to churches that partner with Spanish-speaking Mennonites in Mexico, such as the *Conferencia Menonita de México* [Conference Church in Mexico], or the *Conferencia Misionera Evangélica* [Evangelical Missionary Conference]. These groups sponsor schools that follow the government's guidelines and do not follow strict guidelines regarding clothing (Kraybill 232–34).[18] The Mexican government, and Mexican culture, do not distinguish between these groups. They typically assume that all Mennonites are somewhat like members of the Old Colony church. Those who live closer to the Mennonite communities in Chihuahua are somewhat aware of subtle differences between these groups.

Mormonism began several centuries later than the Anabaptism that led to the Mennonites. It began in the United States, during the Second Great Awakening (1790–1840), which was a period of intense religious revival. In 1820, a young man called Joseph Smith received a vision in the woods near his parents' home in Palmyra, New York. He believed that he saw Jesus Christ, who he understood to be the son of God, and learned that Jesus' message was one of atonement for sin. Joseph Smith received a second, more significant revelation in 1823, which showed him what he understood to be additional scriptures, that is, additional writings from God. Thanks to these visions, he began a religious movement that moved from New York to Ohio, Illinois, and Utah. In each state, the early Mormons faced persecution for their unusual beliefs.

Persecution grew more intense once the US public began to suspect that this new religious movement was practicing polygamy. Joseph received two revelations regarding polygamy, specifically, polygyny. First, in 1931, that polygamy was acceptable to God. Then, in 1834 that it was commanded by God (Hales "The Beginnings of Mormon Polygamy"). Then, in 1852, Brigham Young reiterated Joseph's earlier quieter proclamations regarding polygamy. He officially announced it, and in 1862, the United States government criminalized polygamy for the first time. In the 1880s, the federal government increased legislation against polygamy, and many families left the United States for Mexico and Canada. In 1890, an LDS president, or highest level of leadership, proclaimed that plural marriage, which is what the church called polygamy, was no longer commanded. In 1904, another president proclaimed that these marriages are no longer *permitted*. During this time period, in Mexico and the US, many families continue to live as they had been living. Some men sought to continue polygamous lifestyles and performed multiple marriages. Eventually these men organize into a group that continues to believe that Joseph Smith was a prophet, and that polygamy is a way that they can show their religious devotion. Over time, this group divides into multiple other groups. Today, there were more than four hundred groups that call themselves Mormon and believe that they are the Restored Church. In other words, each group believes that they are following Joseph Smith's interpretation of how to return to the message of Jesus as relayed by the New Testament (Hales "Chronology").[19]

In Mexico, as in the United States, the largest and longest-standing of these groups is the LDS church. Members of the LDS church with roots in Utah have reflected on their experience. Some, like Thomas C. Romney's *The Mormons in Mexico* (1938), represent earlier points of view about the relationship between Mormons and Mexican society. He predicted that the Mormon colonies will have a positive influence on the "highly emotional" Mexicans (T. Romney 310). His work forms a background for other scholars, such as F. LaMond Tullis. Tullis' *Mormons in Mexico: The Dynamics of Faith and Culture* (1987) reflects on the Mormons' difficult return to Mexico in the 1920s (Tullis 95).[20] Today, the LDS church believes that Joseph Smith was a prophet who invited them to return to what they understand as Christian tenets, where Jesus Christ is a savior who atones from sins. In the view of the LDS church, the Book of Mormon and Doctrine and Covenants enhance, rather than detract from, the story of Jesus in the Bible. It also includes the Pearl of Great Price, the writings of Joseph Smith, in its holy books. The LDS church places significant emphasis on the family, as for them, families can continue to be bonded to one another after death.[21]

In practice, the LDS church requires that its members commit to their beliefs with significant time, as it has a primarily lay leadership. Each member contributes to their individual congregations; men are priests, bishops, and church leaders. Most members have specific duties in their churches, such as working with children, adolescents, music, or visiting people. Families commit to spending at least one evening each week together in religious devotion and a fun activity. The vast majority of young men, and many young women, also serve the LDS church as missionaries. In addition to this time commitment during the week, the LDS church meets on Sundays, for three hours. The first hour is called sacrament meeting, and is much like other Protestant churches, with hymns, preaching, and a communion, which they call sacrament, of bread and water. The first Sunday of every month, they fast from two meals and share testimonies. During the second hour of church, people attend Sunday School and then for the third hour, older adolescents and adults attend meetings, either of priests, for men, or relief society, for women. Members keep what they term the Word of Wisdom, that is, life without smoking, alcohol, coffee, and, depending on interpretation, caffeinated soft drinks or hot drinks. Children are baptized when they are eight, which the LDS Church understands as the age of accountability. Older members of the LDS church in good standing may also go to temples, buildings that are different from the places where they meet on Sundays. These temples, which are open to the public only before they have been consecrated, are places for church members to meet other spiritual needs, to celebrate religious wedding services, and for other rituals important in their lives.

A few chapters in this book also discuss the lives and perceptions of the LeBaron polygamous group.[22] Social scientists and historians have already compared the LeBarons to Mennonites and to LDS Mormons. Anthropologist Janet Bennion's *Desert Patriarchy: Mormon and Mennonite Communities in the Chihuahua Valley* (2004) compares the three groups. Bennion asserts that the desert fosters patriarchy in each of these religious groups and concludes that this isolated environment allows Mennonites and Mormons to preserve their ways of life. This is useful only in so far as it places the lived experiences of Mennonites, LDS Mormons, and non-LDS Mormons alongside of one another (*Desert Patriarchy* 6–7).[23] Historian Philip R. Stover also mentions these three groups in his work *Religion and Revolution in Mexico's North* (2014). He focuses on the changing influence of the Catholic Church in Mexico and part of this change, he observes, is the result of the influence of minority religious groups (Stover 301–30). Moreover, historian Jason Dormady's *Primitive Revolution: Restorationist Religion and the Idea of the Mexican Revolution, 1940–1968* (2011) places this group alongside of multiple polygamous groups in Mexico. He describes the divisions among Mormons in the US and their influence on Mexico, including polygamous groups that have existed since Mormonism's inception as well as smaller polygamous groups that emerged when some Mormons left Mexico for the US in the 1910s.

The LeBarons are a spiritual descendant of the group of men who believed that polygamy was God's commandment, and who disagreed with LDS church leadership over ending this way of life. The LeBarons, like other polygamists, calls themselves Mormon and believe that the LDS church is not the true church. This group, like other fundamentalist Mormon groups, ties their genealogy and authority to continue polygamous marriages, directly to Joseph Smith (Bennion *Polygamy in Primetime* 60). Its first leader, Alma "Dayer" LeBaron, had grown up in Colonia Dublán, in Mexico and was educated in Colonia Juárez. In 1904, he married Barbara Johnson (Hansen Park "Episode 76: The LeBarons"). At that time, he would have been acquainted with polygamous families but would not have seen new polygamous marriages taking place.[24] He then received a revelation that he should have a second wife. Revelations are important to Mormons, because they understand that Joseph Smith had a personal revelation that led to a new way of understanding.[25] After this revelation, Barbara leaves Alma LeBaron and returns to the US. During the revolution, Alma moved back to Utah, like many Mormons in the early 1900s. There, in 1910, he married Maude McDonald and then in 1923, he married Onie Jones (Hansen Park "Episode 76: The LeBarons"). They returned to Mexico in 1924 and lived briefly in Colonia Juárez, where Alma LeBaron, like many others in the area, had fruit orchards in Colonia Pacheco. The LDS church asked the three, now in a polygamous situation, to leave the LDS church. The LeBarons moved to a nearby municipality, Galeana, and developed an affiliation with other then-preeminent polygamous Mormon leaders of the church in the US (Hales). These ties were furthered when a leader of the "Allred Group," now called the Apostolic United Brethren (AUB), lived with the LeBarons in the 1940s (Hales). In spite of this affiliation with polygamists, two of Alma Dayer LeBaron's sons, Joel and Ervil, served missions with the LDS church (Bennion *Desert Patriarchy* 57). Joel, Ervil, and their brother Ross, continued to receive revelations that they were the true leaders, and so they ended the affiliation with the Allreds in 1955. Joel LeBaron establishes the Church of the Firstborn of the Fulness [sic] of Times in Mexico; another brother, Ross LeBaron, starts a related church in Utah. Eventually, Ervil LeBaron splits from Joel's movement, again regaining authority, establishing the Church of the Lamb of God in 1971. He orchestrates Joel's murder in 1972, and the murder of Rulon Allred, the leader of the Allred group, in 1977. Ervil attempts to have another brother, Verlan, murdered at Rulon Allred's funeral, but this plan fails, and he dies in prison in 1981. That same year, Verlan died in a car crash in what some say were suspicious circumstances (Hales; Bennion *Polygamy in Primetime* 50).

Today, this group, as Bennion explains, shares many practices with other fundamentalist Mormon groups. It is based on a united order, or shared economy, and polygamous families, which they call celestial marriage. The economy largely relies on migrant labor in the United States and small businesses in Mexico. In terms of family structure, it is patriarchal, where women and children defer to the male head of the household (Bennion *Desert Patriarchy* 60; *Polygamy in Primtetime* 49). The LeBarons add what they would call "kingdom building." Unlike some polygamous groups, the LeBarons have a long history of actively proselytizing.[26] This means that in Mexico their community has US and Mexican roots, although those with US roots lead the community. For this reason, they sponsor a bilingual school in the same building as their church, with English as the dominant language. There, children attend school to the equivalent of a fifth or sixth grade. Janet Bennion, who displays a remarkable understanding of their community even though she is an outsider, has not been able to explore their religious services. Former members of this community, such as Anna LeBaron, do not discuss this aspect of their community either (Hansen Park "Episode 121"). Other former members, such as Ruth Wariner, simply explain that there was preaching in church and that they had to memorize scripture at home (134, 319). This group, while sharing some historical contact with the LDS Mormons in Colonias Juárez and Dublán, has a distinct lifestyle. For this reason, I present the groups as distinct from one another.

MENNONITES AND MORMONS IN MEXICAN AND IN US POPULAR CULTURE

Popular culture reflects some of the more unusual aspects of each group; in Mexico, these typically include plain dress and relationship to criminality, either as criminals or innocent victims. This book focuses on the representations in visual and print culture. Visual culture is defined here as those examples of culture meant for visual pleasure, consumption, or meaning. In this case it includes photographs, television shows, webcomics, and film. Print culture refers to the culture surrounding printed or written documents, and, here, refers to legal documents and narrative histories. This vocabulary choice is deliberate as it emphasizes that these cultural artifacts are products of a specific time, from a specific group, for a specific audience. It also, following the work of scholars like Nicholas Mirzoeff, notes that an artifact's cultural significance includes its production, circulation, and reception, and that the consumption of visual culture is central to the postmodern period (1–13). This approach thus highlights the role of interpretation and contextualization. For this reason, the book places the representations of both religious groups in their historical context because it believes that an identity is created, and so should be understood, in its context. From this perspective, then, studying Mennonites and Mormons in visual and print culture sheds light on the Mexican society that produced it.

This approach is well documented in Mexican cultural studies, with the work of Emily Hind, Pedro Ángel Palou, and others. It has also been used to explore religious and cultural minorities. Scholars of education have examined Mormon education in the US to understand broader educational trends in the United States (Esplin et al. 388). Literary and cultural critics who focus on tropes relating to the representation of African-American and Jewish people are also informative for my study. Critic Eugenia DeLamotte, for instance, has drawn parallels between representations of African-Americans in eighteenth- and nineteenth-century British and American literature and emerging scientific discourse around race (17–18). More recently, Sara R. Horowitz deals with the representation of Jews and Judaism in US culture. She observes that representations can oscillate between adoration and hatred. Horowitz states that: "Real and imagined Jewish economic successes in America contribute to the perception of Jews as a privileged rather than oppressed minority, not only 'white' but 'elite' . . . Jews are victimized by their own positive stereotypes" (123). This development or imposition of another identity on a religious and ethnic minority group is similar to the way that Mennonites and Mormons are understood in Mexico.

The book does not aim to provide a comprehensive history of the representation of these groups in Mexico; rather, its chapters are like discrete windows on that interaction. The windows reveal the views of government officials, ejidos, novelists, and television producers toward these groups. They show that Mennonites and Mormons have been viewed in different ways: with hostility, uneasy acceptance, and, on occasion, with admiration. Theirs has never been an entirely comfortable fit within Mexico but they have enjoyed enough support, particularly because of their economic contributions, that they have weathered the crises and survived.

The first of these windows is the "birth" of these groups in Mexico. In other words, examples of culture that deal with the Mennonite arrival in early twentieth-century Mexico and to the Mormons' post-Revolutionary return. The Revolution was a loose coalition, which, by 1940, solidified under the control of a single political party that was beginning to develop the notion of a single mixed race as Mexico's future. The first chapter focuses on how the Mennonites and Mormons are represented in migration documents' (1926–59) photographs and accompanying descriptions in light of the desire for a single race. Following this initial period, the *Partido Revolucionario Institucional* [Institutional Revolutionary Party] (PRI) built society through alliances with other players, including with campesinos invested in reforming landholding patterns in Mexico. The second and third chapters deal with both groups' relationships with one of these revolutionary emphases, landholding patterns, in particular, to *ejido* [land redistributed through agrarian reform] conflicts from 1927 to the present.[27] Economic crises in the 1980s, NAFTA in 1993 changed Mexico, and the US' antidrug campaigns marked Mexico and, given these geopolitical changes and shifting global markets, it became known for drug-trafficking. The fourth chapter explores how the religious minorities fit into this stage of Mexican history. I contrast the representation of the Mennonites' supposed criminality with the Mormons' perfect victimhood. To do, I analyze a webcomic, *MacBurro* [*McDonkey* or *McStupid*] (2013–15), and two television shows, *The Bridge* (2012–13) and *Los héroes del norte* [*The Heroes of the North*] (2010–15) and a narrative history of the kidnapping of a boy from a small polygamous Mormon group. The final chapter reflects on the present, and considers ways to develop mutual understanding, with images of love, technology, and death in the Mennonite community in Eunice Adorno's photography collection *Las mujeres flores* [*The Flower Women*] (2011) and Carlos Reygadas' film, *Stellet Licht* [*Silent Light*] (2007). Mennonites and Mormons are represented as outliers—a closer study shows us that the representation of these minorities follows trends in the understanding of Mexican nationhood.

Liminal Sovereignty also dialogues with critics of the ways both religious minorities have been represented in the United States' visual culture, particularly popular television and books. This is because no scholar has explicitly studied how Mormons or Mennonites are represented in popular culture in any Latin American country.[28] So, I engage with David Weaver-Zercher's

The Amish in the American Imagination (2001), which analyzes how the Amish, a group related to the Mennonites, are represented in music, film, and narrative fiction (5–10).[29] He concludes that this presence suggests that the Amish are integrated in the United States (D. Weaver-Zercher 196). I suggest that the experience and representation of Mormons and Mennonites is similar—they may advocate for separation but are firmly embedded in the surrounding culture. I also ground my work in the circulation and consumption of popular culture. This influences the way I analyze the circulation of legal documents, letters, and memos as well as television shows and films. For this reason, I draw on Valerie Weaver-Zercher's *Thrill of the Chaste: The Allure of Amish Romance Novels* (2013), which surveys Amish-themed romance fiction and situates its immense popularity in commodity theory. She interviews the genre's readers and writers, including Amish people. She suggests that the popularity relates to US nostalgia for the past and for its (often mistaken) belief that life is simpler in that community (V. Weaver-Zercher 179–80). This also lends itself to the Mexican audience's recent interest in Mennonite and Mormon stories on screen and in photography.

This book also engages, in several chapters, with the portrayal of women as criminals, as beautiful corpses, and as members of polygamous Mormons communities. For this reason, I turn to contemporary feminist approaches to the study of Mormonism, particularly those that suggest the representation of Mormons on screen facilitates their integration into the US.[30] Critic Tanya Zuk's "'Proud Mormon Polygamist': Assimilation, Popular Memory, and the Mormon Churches in *Big Love*" (2014), which deals with the ways that different Mormon churches are portrayed on television, argues that the portrayal of suburban polygamists on *Big Love* will encourage their acceptance (94–95). Bennion's *Polygamy in Primetime* also discusses this television show, and uses it to encourage advocacy for better legal recognition of polygamous family arrangements (139–58). She believes that such legal recognition will allow for better prosecution of abuse within the community (Bennion *Polygamy in Primetime* 160–61). Similarly, the narrative history and interviews with Mexican polygamous Mormons, which I analyze in chapter 4, paint an encouraging image of this group. In my view, their reception in the cultural and literary realms as exceptional, then, points to an overall climate of exceptionality.

OVERVIEW OF CHAPTERS

Chapter 1. Mennonites, Mormons, and the Registration of Foreigners in the 1930s and 1940s: A Rare Attempt to Promote Integration

The first chapter examines the migration documents that foreigners used to identify themselves to the Mexican government. It situates these documents in then-current understandings of race and gender, and in relation to the post-Revolutionary government's desire to physically re-create the nation. The chapter argues that during this period, when Mormons returned to their colonies and the Mexican government granted legal exceptions to Mennonites, officials profiled both groups in unexpected ways that would cast some members of both groups as carriers of national ideals and would reject others. It pays special attention to the identification photographs on the documents and the ways that they confirm or challenge the written profiles. The differences between text and image facilitate my reading of the ways some people were represented as outliers. These include women married at young ages without children, women wearing "risqué" clothing, and people with unusual levels of Spanish language proficiency (cf. "Turley Wilson Tenna Augusta" and "Bergen Friesen, Helena"). They disrupt monolithic understandings of both communities. The chapter suggests that these documents portray Mennonites as Mormons as almost part of then-prevailing ideas about Mexico.

Chapter 2. Whose Land Is It: Mormons, Ejidos, and Agrarian Reform

This chapter studies situations where Mormons are understood as foreign, as American, and as invaders, and are only tentatively allowed into understandings of the nation because of their economic prowess. This chapter investigates these varying opinions by reading documents that represent agrarian conflict between Mormon colonies and ejidos [collectively owned land]. It contextualizes these representations within Mexican agrarian reform law, enshrined in the constitution. It focuses on three conflicts between Mormons and the ejido system: the LDS Mormon Colonia Pacheco and the ejido with the same name, which introduces us to legal terminology and archival discrepancies. These are exacerbated in another conflict between the LDS Mormons in Colonia Dublán and Colonia Juárez and the Casas Grandes ejido, which continues in the present day. A third conflict, between the LeBaron colony, who also claim the word Mormon but do not belong to the LDS church, in Galeana, Chihuahua, and the bordering Galeana ejido, was similar, but was resolved in the 1980s.

Chapter 3. Mennonites and Agrarian Reform: Can Mennonites be Mexican?

The next chapter looks at representations of Mennonites as foreigners who benefit the nation's economy and in documents that portray agrarian/related conflicts. This chapter analyzes two conflicts—between La Batea colony and the Niño Artillero ejido and La Honda colony and the J. Santos Bañuelos ejido, all in the state of Zacatecas. *Liminal Sovereignty* focuses on the letters, maps, and population surveys that Mennonites and *ejidatarios* [people living on *ejidos*] submitted to the Land Claims Bureau (cf. Antonio Herrera Bocardo's "Carta a Joel Luevanos Ponce y Arturo Medrano Cabral") and documents that report on dispute resolution and "Acuerdos sobre inafectabilidad agrícola" ["Agreements about Land Ineligible for Agrarian Reform"] in the *Diario Oficial de la Federación* [*Mexican Federal Register*].[31] The representation of Mennonites in these documents shows a heterogeneous group, with divisions along class and gender lines. It also suggests that the government favored the Mennonites because of their economic power, at the expense of the ejidos. This perception allowed the Mennonites to join the nation, albeit conditionally.

Chapter 4. Mennonites and Mormons in Mexico's Drug Wars: Criminals and Victims on Screen and in Literature

This chapter shifts from representations of Mennonites and Mormons in relation to the post-Revolutionary goal of land redistribution to their representation in relation to crime, which has become almost a synonym for Mexico or representations of Mexico in recent years. The chapter focuses on Mennonite mobsters in Tijuana in Giancarlo Ruiz and Charles Glaubitz's webcomic *MacBurro* (2013–15), Mennonite musicians in Gustavo Loza's television series *Los héroes del norte* and Mennonite cartel members in Elwood Reid's television show *The Bridge*. These criminal or deviant Mennonites are now integrated in dominant culture even as they are marked by the Mennonite religion. In contrast, polygamous Mormons are portrayed as victims of senseless crime.

Sixteen-year-old Eric LeBaron Ray was kidnapped in 2009. Javier Ortega Urquidi's *Los güeros del norte* [*The White People of the North*] (2010) describes how Eric was eventually released; then, the cartel retaliated by killing two of Eric's relatives. In response, his older brother Julián became a peace activist. Julián's experience is included in Lolita Bosch's *México: 45 voces contra la barbarie* [*Mexico: 45 Voices Against Barbarity*] (2014). These representations integrate Mennonites and Mormons in networks of violence in Mexico.

Chapter 5. Contact Zones in *Stellet Licht* [*Silent Light*] and in *Las Mujeres Flores/The Flower Women*

This chapter concludes the study of representations of the lives of religious Mennonite and Mormon minorities in Mexico by dealing with the representation of contact zones between Mennonites and the surrounding community, focusing on death, music, and technology. It examines Carlos Reygadas' film *Stellet Licht* [*Silent Light*] (2007) and Eunice Adorno's collection of photographs, *Las mujeres flores* [*The Flower Women*] (2011). It considers several scenes that relate to songs in the film, radio, camera, and telephone use in both works. This chapter, and, indeed, the entirely of *Liminal Sovereignty*, focus on portrayals of the minority religious communities by majority culture. It does so because I believe that the best way to build bridges between the minority communities and majority culture is through mutual understanding grounded in its historical context.

1

Mennonites, Mormons, and the Registration of Foreigners in the 1930s and 1940s

A Rare Attempt to Promote Integration

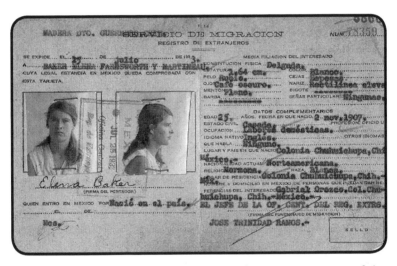

Figure 1 Elena Farnsworth y Martineau Baker. Image courtesy of the Archivo General de la Nación, Fondo "Departamento de Migración, Subserie estadounidenses."

ELENA FARNSWORTH Y MARTINEAU BAKER

This image, representing one of the members of these minority communities, is from an interaction with bureaucrats representing the majority community. It is taken from a 1933 Mexican migration document and portrays Elena Farnsworth y Martineau Baker, a young American woman of the Mormon religion. It consists of her photograph and basic information about her, as recorded by a Mexican official. In the photograph, she stares at the camera in a way that suggests her determination, and her expressionless mouth indicates that she has been photographed before and that she, like most people, is not interested in a bureaucratic photo. The way her long hair is pulled away from her face in a low half-ponytail and the fact that she wears a sleeveless top, with a high V-neck, gives her a somewhat stylish appearance. Her card says that she is twenty-five years old, married, and engaged in domestic labor. The official has described her "physical constitution" as thin, though she looks quite average. The official may describe her this way because that is what he expected for a young woman from the US. Her official reference, Gabriel Orozco, reflects the fact that the Mormons had some contact and interaction with the surrounding community. Indeed, Mormons had some Spanish-speaking people in their churches at that time. In spite of this apparent contact with the outside world, the card says that Elena speaks English and no other languages. This means that she does not speak Spanish, though her name is written in a way that suggests Hispanicization. That she was born in Mexico, in the Mormon colony, but was still required to register implies that legally, she continued to be a foreigner.

This card is one of thousands that the Mexican government required of resident foreigners from 1926 to 1951 (H. Herrera , Informe 1).[1] According to Mexico's *Archivo General de la Nación* [National Archive] approximately 40,000 of these cards are for Americans. Of these, a modest number are for Mormons. About 4,000 cards are for Canadians and most of these are for Mennonites. Others are for people from various places, including the Middle East, Europe, and Asia. When I, while in Mexico's *Archivo General* in 2015 researching other matters, happened to come upon these cards my first thought was, might there be cards for my relatives? Thanks to a kind archivist, I soon found myself looking at the cards of my great-grandmother and several great-uncles and aunts who were part of the small Mennonite migration from Canada to Mexico in 1948, well after the larger migration of the 1920s.

I then wanted to learn more about this registration. Literature on the history of Mormons and Mennonites in Mexico did not deal much with them. Literature on the Mormons did not mention the registration at all and that on the Mennonites had only a few small references to it.[2] Theresa Alfaro-Velcamp in her excellent *So Far From Allah, So Close to Mexico: Middle Eastern Immigrants in Modern Mexico* (2007) refers to the registration a number of times but does not say what its purpose was or how the registration was carried out. My search in the archives was not fruitful on these points either. There is a line on each card acknowledging the right of the registrant to reside in Mexico, but that right is not granted by this card; it already existed. Bruce Wiebe, who had worked with Mennonite Archives in Manitoba, Canada, informed me that in 1989 the archivist in Mexico City, Juan Manuel Herrera H, had written to the Mennonite Heritage Centre in Winnipeg about the Mennonite cards, believing that they might be of interest to Canadian Mennonite researchers. Reportedly, after staff at the Heritage Centre had expressed interest, Mr. Herrera had sent them information about 4,000 such cards made for Mennonites. But he had provided little by way of explanation. As a result, the cards and the registration process remain largely unexamined.

The registration represented a significant encounter between the post-Revolutionary government and the recently arrive Mennonites and the Mormons returning home.[3] The Mennonites and the Mormons, both of whom had had negative experiences with the governments where they had lived before, were apprehensive about this government's intent: was this registration requirement a sign that it would also take steps against their way of life. For its part, the Mexican government had broad policy objectives to which this registration was to contribute. For this reason, they were interested in people's race, color, and appearance. This allowed the officials making the cards to categorize the people from these groups. In some cases, their written descriptions are different from what is obvious in the photographs, and some of the people present themselves in ways quite unusual for their communities at that time. This chapter sheds light on these and related questions.

The registration of foreigners was one element in the post-Revolutionary government's overall intent to promote the integration of the various kinds of people living in its territory. In the first part of this chapter, I explore the integration project, and in the second part I look at a sample of the registration cards in light of that intent and in light of certain cultural aspects, showing both similarities and differences. Close examination of that integrationist intent and of the work of gathering the information, that is, registering the people to yield a fuller understanding of Mexico, and of these groups, in that era.

THE REGISTRATION IN THE CONTEXT OF THE GOVERNMENT'S NATION-BUILDING POLICIES

At a basic level, the post-Revolutionary government wanted to assert control over its territory, given that fighting from 1910 to 1920 had almost "reduced

Mexico to a patchwork of warring factions" (Knight "Racism, Revolution, and *Indigenismo*" 84). They may have worried that these groups would rise up again with the help of resident foreigners. Indeed, there were coup attempts in 1924 and 1927. And from 1926 to 1929, there was the Cristero War in which many Catholics, supported by the church hierarchy, fought against the government because of its anticlerical measures.[4] In addition there was concern about people with close connections to the US and possible incursions they might provoke. Also, in the half century before the revolution, a large number of foreigners from many different countries had moved to Mexico, some with little documentation, given that passports with photographs had not yet become a standard requirement. A registration would at least give the new government some solid information about how many foreigners there were, where they had come from, where they were living in Mexico, and what they were doing there.

Control over the territory was merely one element in the government's agenda of nation-building. That agenda also meant building a common identity and loyalty among the country's disparate groups. In the sixteenth and seventeenth centuries, the Spanish colonizers' locally born descendants, known as *criollos*, attempted to remain separate from the various indigenous groups. Gradually, the number of people who identified as mestizo, or mixed race, grew, though the *criollos* held most of the power.[5] In the mid-nineteenth century there were legal reforms toward an equality of citizenship but the tripartite schema of white, mestizo, and Mexico's indigenous would form the basis of the country's censuses later that century (Stern "Eugenics" 156). In the later years of the nineteenth century, in a push toward development and modernization, the government worked to attract immigrants. It passed the Colonization and Naturalization Act (1883) to encourage foreigners to settle sparsely populated areas (Pegler-Gordon 16, 28). Also, it sought investors, particularly from Europe, to counterbalance those from the US, to help develop mines, build transportation and electricity infrastructure, expand agricultural production, and increase exports (Alfaro-Velcamp 183). These modernizing changes, however, dispossessed many peasants so there was resentment, as is evident in the then-popular saying: "Mexico, mother of foreigners and stepmother of Mexicans" (Alfaro-Velcamp 158).

Despite antiforeigner sentiment, Alfaro-Velcamp observes that Mexican policy makers continued to welcome immigrants, particularly Europeans, "who were perceived to potentially 'better' the nation with skills and capital—and in some cases fair skin" (Alfaro-Velcamp). Justo Sierra, Minister of Public Education and Fine Arts from 1905 to 1911, said: "We need to attract immigrants from Europe so as to obtain a cross with the indigenous race, for only European blood can keep the level of civilization ... from sinking which would mean regression, not evolution" (Knight "Racism, Revolution, and *Indigenismo*" 78).[6] The reference to "a cross with the indigenous race" points to the mestizo idea on which the post-Revolutionary government would try to build a national identity. Already in 1909, before the revolution, Molina Enriquez stated: "all the work that in future will be undertaken for the good of the country must be the continuation of the mestizos as the dominant ethnic element" (qtd. in Knight "Racism, Revolution, and *Indigenismo*" 85).[7] Alfaro-Velcamp adds that the mestizo idea "represented a way ... to create a liberal model of homogenous integration of all ethnic groups. By encouraging individual groups—specifically indigenous peoples—to shed their distinctive characteristics and to become mestizo, they could become part of an evolving Mexican nation" (Alfaro-Velcamp 17). In Europe and the US, it was held that hybrids were "inherently degenerate" but in Mexico the mestizo idea provided "an appealing and invigorating vision of racial amalgamation that resonated well with the ideals of (post) revolutionary nationalism" (Stern "Eugenics" 161). José Vasconcelos, the post-Revolutionary Secretary of Public Education, articulated a vision for the mestizo idea with particular eloquence. In a long 1925 essay called *The Cosmic Race* he compared the Mexican situation to what he called the Anglo-Saxons, claiming:

> It seems as if God Himself guided the steps of the Anglo-Saxon cause, while we kill each other on account of dogma ... They do not ... have ... in their blood the contradictory instincts of a mixture of dissimilar races, but they committed the sin of destroying those races, while we assimilated them, and this gives us new rights and hopes for a mission without precedent in History. ... The advantage of our tradition is that it has a greater facility of sympathy towards strangers. This implies that our civilization, with all defects, may be the chosen one to assimilate and to transform mankind into a new type; that within our civilization, the warp, the multiple and rich plasma of future humanity is thus prepared. This mandate from History is first noticed in that abundance of

love that allowed the Spaniard to create a new race with the Indian and the Black, profusely spreading white ancestry ... Spanish colonization created mixed races, this signals its character, fixes its responsibility, and defines its future. (17)

Thus, the mestizo idea had particular implications for foreigners and for the indigenous people, as if both were to move toward a middle ground. Stern adds that Vasconcelos envisioned the mestizo as a "spiritual beacon of Hispanic civilization," which rejected European scientific doctrines of race, derived from Darwin and Comte, which had the effect of seeing the mestizo as inferior ("Mestizophilia" 191). Alfaro-Velcamp sheds further light on this situation: "the *mestizo* construction aimed to temper the influence of foreigners and the visibility of the indigenous, thereby limiting plurality" (italics in text, 19). This construction of the mestizo idea was helped by the creation, in 1929, of *Partido Mexicano Revolucionario* [Mexican Revolutionary Party] (PRM), which would become the *Partido Revolucionario Institucional* [Institutional Revolutionary Party] (PRI). The PRI then ruled Mexico continuously for the next seventy-one years and it employed Vasconcelos' language as "a type of 'meta-discourse' ... to explain national identity ..." (Alfaro-Velcamp 19). Alfaro-Velcamp continues:

The post-revolutionary construction of the *mestizo* was in large part based on the ideas of intellectuals ... who suggested that the lack of ethnic integration was at the root of many of Mexico's problems. They advocated a type of unity—arguably homogeneity—to integrate the divided Mexico ... [thus] limiting ethnocultural plurality and allowing for hegemonic discourse. (italics in text, 159)

The registration of foreigners was related to this broad effort to build a national identity on the basis of the mestizo idea. The registration would be a way of assessing the foreigners' racial characteristics so as to take them into account in the overall effort to build this new identity. Hence the questions on the cards about race, color, eyes, nose, general appearance, and constitution. The questions about face shape relate to ideas about phrenology, the science of cranial shape. It was believed that certain physical features were more criminal than others; the Mexican government thus sought to avoid criminals whenever possible.[8]

The Mennonites and Mormons remained separate and distinct. This suggests that integration was incomplete. Alfaro-Velcamp concurs, holding that most foreigners did not begin to identify as mestizo, that they retained much of their own heritages while also developing significant roles in Mexican society, and that the Mexican people usually accepted that. Nor, in the first decades of the twentieth century, was there a major movement of indigenous people to become mestizo (Knight 98; Stern "Eugenics" 164). Alfaro-Velcamp concludes: "Despite the intellectuals' attempts to construct a monolithic Mexico, the Mexican populace ... developed into a pluralistic society that allowed many ways of being Mexican" (Alfaro-Velcamp 159). She says that Mexico in fact developed a "rich cultural mosaic" (Alfaro-Velcamp 19).

The overall goals of integration and assimilation may not have been achieved; however, the registration of foreigners was, nevertheless, undertaken as one element in the pursuit of these goals. I look at the broader efforts that the government made to achieve those goals in order to better situate the registration of foreigners as an element in them. To do this, it is helpful to acknowledge the work in Mexico on eugenics, an idea that was supported in many countries in the half-century before World War II, though now universally rejected because of its connection to the racial horrors of the Nazis (Stern "Eugenics" 152). Narrowly understood, eugenics called for the biological improvement of a population, for example, by preventing so-called unfit people from having children (Stern "Eugenics" 165). Thus, for some decades in parts of the US and Canada people with mental illnesses were forcibly sterilized; and for people to get married they first had to pass a medical test; also, in many states in the US, mixed race marriages were outlawed because any children born of such parents were believed to be inherently degenerate (Stern "Eugenics" 160, 171). In the US, the Race Betterment Foundation was set up in 1906 by John Harvey Kellogg. On immigration, wealthier and better-educated Americans, particularly those whose ancestors had come from English-speaking or northern European countries, were concerned about "impoverished hordes of swarthy newcomers from the ostensibly less civilized European countries of Poland, Russia and Italy ... [bringing] a massive influx of defective 'germ plasm' ... [thus] threatening to contaminate and destroy America's superior racial stock" (Stern "Eugenics" 166). One result of this sentiment was the 1924 National Origins Act that restricted the immigration of people from southern and eastern Europe and banned Asians and Arabs completely (Stern "Eugenics" 167).

The idea of eugenics also enjoyed support in Mexico but with substantial differences. Instead of being focused on keeping an existing race pure, the intent in Mexico was on building a new mestizo race, and there was a certain confidence that eventually the various groups would all blend into a mestizo nation (Stern "Eugenics" 159). This implied a firm rejection of the view that children of mixed race parents were degenerate. Further, Mexican intellectuals and policy makers held to the Lamarckian theory about "the inheritance of acquired characteristics" first advocated by Jean Baptiste de Lamarck, a French biologist, in the early 1800s (Stern "Mestizophilia" 190). This theory, which was also accepted in France, Italy, and some other Latin American countries, was different from the Mendelian theory, commonly held in the US and Germany, which claimed that "hereditary material was transmitted ... with absolutely no alteration" (Stern "Mestizophilia" 190). The Lamarckian view "flourished in Mexico because it implied that human actors were capable, albeit gradually, of improving the national 'stock' through environmental intervention and, eventually, of generating a robust populace" (Stern "Mestizophilia" 190). In effect, this meant that race was seen as more than a biological phenomenon, that it could be influenced by social forces. And, if acquired characteristics could be passed on through the process of inheritance, then it was important both to prevent people from acquiring negative characteristics and to help them gain positive ones. This led, among other things, to extensive campaigns against venereal diseases, alcoholism, and tuberculosis, and to the promotion of maternal and infant health (Stern "Mestizophilia" 192).

This also had implications for the government's approach to marriage. Already in the 1920s Mexico required both parties to get a clean bill of health before it would issue them a marriage license. And in 1941 the Mexican Eugenics Society published a "Moral Eugenics Code" that was essentially a Ten Commandments for married couples ("Código de moral eugénica" 10–11). Further, the 1947 Migration Law stated that it: "promoverá las medidas adecuadas para conseguir la asimilación y arraigo de los extranjeros, otorgándoles facilidades cuando contraigan matrimonio con mexicanos por nacimiento o tengan hijos nacido en el país" ["will promote the adequate means to reach the assimilation and support of foreigners, making things easy for them [to become citizens] when they marry Mexicans by birth or have children born in the country"] ("Ley General de Población" *Diario Oficial* 27 Dec. 1947, 4). Clearly, the Mexican government wanted to attract immigrants who would contribute to the race. Indeed, according to historian Moisés González Navarro, immigration was seen as a way of beautifying the race (vol. 2, 71). Beauty was also a reason for the programs against syphilis, tuberculosis, and alcoholism, even poverty, because these conditions made people less attractive (Stern "Responsible Mothers" 378). In spite of this desire, there is no evidence that the government ever pressured the Mennonites or Mormons to marry outside of their communities.

These views on building a national identity also had implications for schooling. According to Knight: "By dint of education, migration, and occupational shifts ... Indians could become mestizos ..." ("Racism, Revolution, and *Indigenismo*" 73).[9] Not surprisingly, the government, in the 1920s and 1930s, worked hard to promote public schools among the various indigenous Indian groups in the hope of bringing them into the national narrative. Knight adds:

> The rural school ... became the center not only of education (neutrally defined) but also of ... political mobilization and nationalist propaganda. The *maestro rural*, [rural teacher] acting ... as the front-line soldier of the secular state, was expected to counter the influence of the church and to stimulate sentiments of patriotism. ("Racism, Revolution, and *Indigenismo*" 82)

Through schooling, indigenous groups would be encouraged to see their customs, music, rituals, symbols, and folklore as belonging to the Mexican nation; also, they would see themselves as citizens, equal to all others.

This new Mexican would fuse together the present and past, and bring the country into modernity. Joshua Lund has written extensively about the hybrid or mixed race. In his view, this new mixed-race person represented the possibilities in western modernity (*Mestizo State* 20). As David Dalton has convincingly shown, this mestizo was more than a hybrid of indigenous and European. It was a way for the State to infuse the indigenous population with modernity, such as public schools and public health programs.[10] Moreover, in spite of this mixed-race rhetoric, Mexico remained problematically slanted toward white people, and, as a result, the descriptions on immigration cards were generous toward the Mennonites and Mormons.

In spite of these favorable descriptions, the Mennonites also had some negative interactions with the Mexican government. Both the minority religious group and the government were deeply invested in the importance of schooling. Thanks to the permission the Mennonites had received in 1921 from President Obregón, they had set up village schools with their traditional six-year German-language curriculum. It emphasized writing, arithmetic, and religious subjects, for which the Bible, the catechism and their church hymnbook were the primary texts. Then, in May 1935, an inspector toured the Mennonite schools in the Chihuahua area and, upon finding that they did not conform to Mexican education laws, ordered that they be closed (Sawatzky *They Sought a Country* 154). The Mennonites were shocked. In June 1936, three leaders from Durango traveled to Mexico City to ask president Lázaro Cárdenas to help them because they were concerned about education, land tenure, and the safety of women and children in their colony. The president eventually granted them an audience and after what I assume was a successful meeting, Cárdenas wrote the governor of the state of Durango, general Severino Ceniceros, to remind him that the Mennonites are:

> un importante factor el desenvolvimiento económico de ese Estado y por estimarlo así de estricta justicia, mereceré a usted que con todo rigor se repriman los actos delictuosos que antes se mencionan y se otorgue a las personas y patrimonio de los propios colonos, la protección a que tienen derecho.

> [an important factor for the economic development of this State and because of my esteem for them, and simply for reasons of justice, I would beg you to suppress the criminal acts that are mentioned here and that you would give the colony's people and heritage the protection to which they are entitled.] (Cárdenas "Carta al Señor General Severino Ceniceros")

The same day, Cárdenas writes to Mennonite leaders John P. Wall and A. A. Martens, temporarily living in a hotel in downtown Mexico City. Cárdenas reiterates that he will uphold Mennonite exceptions in Mexico in the realm of education. He adds that he has already given orders to local and military authorities from their region "para que se les impartan a sus personas, a sus familiares y a sus bienes, la protección a que legalmente tengan derecho" ["to give your people, family members and property the protection to which they have a legal right"] (Cárdenas "Carta a los Señores John P. Wall y A. A. Martens"). Cárdenas highlights to the state governor that these

Mennonites are part of the national project, and that this group also belongs in the nation. Both letters allow for military force in Durango to protect the Mennonites from Mexican citizens. Thus, the president acts against campesinos and ejidatarios in order to protect some foreigners.[11]

Though the President relented in the case of the Mennonite schools, the government's general commitment continued. The 1936 Population Law called for the "fusion of all the nation's ethnic groups" and "the general protection, conservation, and improvement of the species" (Stern "Eugenics" 159). Understandably, this commitment was accompanied by a strong interest in demographic surveys and classifications. They needed precise knowledge of the people in order to promote such improvements. At a 1923 Congress on the Child, a leading Mexican scientist had called for "a serious study of the distribution of the great Mexican family; to determine the characteristics of the Indian, the Creole, and the mestizo and to precisely ascertain the results of their unions in order to finally determine how to exalt the qualities of the Mexican and discard his defects" (Stern "Mestizophilia" 193). Stern reminds us that there were "repeated calls for a state-guided anthropological census of every inhabitant in the republic . . . [so as to] gather data in order to make racial mixing a postrevolutionary mandate efficaciously guided by knowledge experts" (Stern "Mestizophilia" 193). A good number of studies were carried out. School children were measured and tested in terms of how well they conformed to the mestizo vision (Stern "Responsible Mothers" 371, 384). In 1940, the anthropologist Carlos Basauri, published *La población indígena de México* [*The Indigenous Population of Mexico*], a three-volume treatise on the indigenous people in which he measured various physical features including their foreheads, cheekbones, noses, lips, ears, teeth, skin color, using the concept of anthropometrics developed by Alphone Bertillon of France in the 1880s. Others, like Gómez Robleda, did somewhat similar work. In his *Pescadores y Campesinos Tarascos* [*Tarasco Fishermen and other Peasants*], he focuses on vulnerable populations, as, I assume, they would be easier to measure.

The interest in getting detailed information about people's racial traits was not limited to Mexico. It also existed in the US; however, it was driven more by a desire to identify people who were to be kept out, not by a desire to promote people's assimilation (Pegler-Gordon 28, 70). For the US, an early method for doing this was to require prospective immigrants to present photos. Interestingly, when this started in the 1890s, it was required primarily of Chinese people. They were screened most closely. Years later, of course, photographs were required of all immigrant applicants (Pegler-Gordon 13). Photographs were said to show racial features that might otherwise be overlooked (Pegler-Gordon 70, 77). Yet, some officials said that Chinese people all looked the same and that an applicant could bring in a photograph of a different person and claim that it was of themselves and that it was impossible for an official to tell. Eventually the US government began to require two photos of each person, a frontal photo and another in profile. Another issue was that some Chinese immigrant applicants, demonstrating a certain personal agency, would bring in photographs that showed them in western dress and hairstyles and sitting on western chairs so as to appear as similar to US styles as possible. The suspicions of the Chinese were such that eventually almost all people of Chinese descent living in the US were required to carry photograph-bearing immigration documents to prove that they had a right to be there (Pegler-Gordon 41, 63).[12]

Photograph-bearing identification papers also came into use in Mexico, albeit for different reasons. They included passports, *salvo conducto* [safe passage] papers and other identification documents, issued either by the federal government or by state authorities. Some were issued to enable Mexicans to travel to the US, which many did either to visit family or to work and to be readmitted to Mexico. Some were issued to "the head" of a family but then named other family members covered by it.[13] More often they were issued to individuals. All had both a description and a photograph. The descriptions included a lot of detail concerning the person's (1) age, (2) civil or marital status, (3) nationality, (4) occupation, (5) height, (6) color, that is, color of skin, (7) eye color, (8) hair color, (9) beard, (10) moustache, (11) particular signs, (12) traveling companions. Other documents also refer to the person's (13) forehead, (14) eyebrows. (15) eyes, (16) nose, (17) mouth, and (18) chin ("Solicitud de Pasaporte . . . Chaviva Kreiner Gasman"). It is striking that there are so many references to race and appearance. It indicates that in addition to facilitating people's travel, the government sought information for the task of building a race. For our purposes, it is important to note that the interest in such traits is evident also in the registration cards for foreigners.

The suspicions about people and about photographs noted earlier can take different forms. Certainly, the Mormons and Mennonites had suspicions about the government's overall intent and whether the registration would lead to actions against their way of life. The Mormons might even have wondered if the officials taking their photos and writing down the information were among those who, during the revolution, destroyed their farms and homes. Conversely, government officials can be suspicious of the people who come before them, even of their photographs, as we have seen in relation to US officials and Chinese immigration applicants. The idea of suspicion in relation to pictures and photographs is not new. Art historians have used the term "aesthetics of suspicion." Art critic Boris Groys' *Under Suspicion: A Phenomenology of the Media* observes that the idea of suspicion suggests that something is lurking under the surface (19).[14] Our situation, however, includes a positive kind of suspicion. Specifically, when the descriptions that the officials have written down differs from what we see in the photographs, it is usually in the person's favor. This places them closer to Mexico's ideals.

The earlier discussion sheds considerable light on the intent of the post-Revolutionary government to work on the goal of nation-building, particularly as it related to race and immigrants. The government wanted to promote the integration of the country's disparate groups, including the immigrants, and to build up a mestizo race. The emphasis on race was not unique to Mexico. To do this, the government needed extensive detailed information about its people. Various surveys and studies were carried out. The kind of detailed questions that were asked in the registration of foreigners suggest that this registration was one element in the government's broad nation-building goal. The fact that that goal was not fully achieved does not deny that it was pursued.

THE REGISTRATION CARDS IN THE CONTEXT OF POLICY AND CULTURES

We turn now from the government's overall policies to the cards themselves. and to the work of registering the people. My basic claim, as noted earlier, is that the registration of foreigners was a way for the government to gather information to advance the goal of promoting their integration and eventual assimilation. I also indicated that the government did not implement this policy as fully as the initial enthusiasm suggested. That does not deny that the registration was not for that purpose. The officials who did the registering probably focused on their immediate task of getting the photographs of the people and answering the questions on the cards. It was tedious work. The officials had at least some awareness of the government's long-term intent so they looked at the people with that in mind. As they contemplated the possibility of how these people might move toward integration, the officials reflected on where the cultures of these groups differed, where they were similar and how they might interface. In this section I also probe some aspects of what, in some ways, is an intercultural encounter. Two offer an overall perspective; a series of cards of women and men illustrate gender roles as they are prescribed by these cultures. Finally, several cards indicate various levels of familiarity with the people's use of the Spanish language.

An Overall Perspective

KATHARINA BUECKERT EPP Katharina Bueckert Epp, born in Saskatchewan, Canada in 1903, is a thirty-year-old Mennonite woman at the time when this card is made on July 15, 1933. It says that she crossed the border from the US into Mexico at Ciudad Juárez on July 13, 1922 ("Bueckert Epp Katharina"). This means that she was one of the early Mennonite arrivals in Mexico. The written account describes her physical constitution as strong; her hair as dark brown; her eyes as clear brown; her chin as low; her color (skin) as white; her race as white; her eyebrows as open; her nose as straight and high; and that she does not have a beard or a moustache nor any particular features. She is said to be 1.65 meters tall. The questions are remarkably similar to those that Basauri and Gómez Robleda used to classify indigenous people and those that the government used on passports and identification documents, referred to in the preceding section.

The "complementary information" section of the card states that Katharina is single and that her occupation is her home, almost certainly her parental home; further, that her first language is German and that she speaks no other language. Her nationality is Canadian and her religion is Mennonite. Her race, a category in addition to that of color, is white. She is said to live in Campo 5, V[illa] Cuauhtémoc in the Mennonite colony. The Mennonites also had German names for their villages, and Campo 5 was called Grünthal, though the card does not say that (Schmiedehaus 150, insert). Katharina's dress is dark and that it appears not to have a collar is in keeping with what was expected of Old Colony women. Her hair, with a parting in the middle, is combed back and tied in a bun. The way she has written her name, similar to the *Kurrent* [handwritten Gothic German script] that she learned in her traditional village school, is not confident. Her facial expression suggests that she is uninterested in the then-lengthy photography process.

Katharina's card names David Redekop as her reference. His name appears on most of the Mennonite registration cards of this time. He was a Mennonite but not a member of the Old Colony Church. He was from a very small group that had come from Europe to Mexico in 1924, after fleeing the newly formed Soviet Union. Interestingly, when the ancestors of these Old Colony Mennonites now in Mexico moved from Russia to Canada in the 1870s, Redekop's Mennonites stayed in Russia at that time developed a less separatist and more modern stance. Thus the Redekop family, having found refuge in Mexico, learned Spanish, pursued higher education, and engaged with the larger society. Before long David Redekop had built up a very sizeable business on the basis of exchanges between the Old Colony people and Mexican society, while keeping the trust of the more conservative Old Colony people. As a trusted intermediary, he may well have been crucial in persuading the Old Colony Mennonites to participate in this registration.

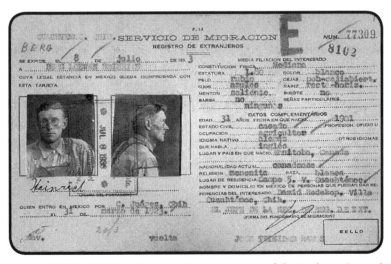

Figure 2 Heinrich Berg Loewen. Image courtesy of the Archivo General de la Nación, Fondo "Departamento de Migración, Subserie canadienses."

HEINRICH BERG LOEWEN The card of Heinrich Berg Loewen was also issued in July 1933. The questions on it are the same as those for Katharina. He comes from Manitoba, Canada, entered Mexico on March 31, 1923, and is thirty-one years old. His photo shows that he is wearing overalls. This would be entirely in keeping with what was expected of Old Colony men ("Berg Loewen Heinrich"). Regarding his appearance, his nose is described as straight and horizontal even though it does not appear that way, in accordance with prevailing stereotypes of white people, who were desirable in Mexico. The card also states that Heinrich is married, a farmer, speaks German as his first language and claims to speak English as well. He was nineteen when he moved to Mexico, and so he had some English schooling in Canada. Of course, we are also told that he is Mennonite, white, and "Canadense" or "Canadan," a common typo.

One curious point is that at the place for his signature he has written only his first name, Heinrich. The name "Berg" is printed on the top left corner, probably by the official. He writes a single surname. which suggests that he was uncertain about which surname to use. The Mennonites' surnames were the same as their father's surname; men's mothers' surnames might be acknowledged with an initial in between the given name and the surname. According to this practice, Heinrich's name would be Heinrich L. Berg. The standard practice in Mexico, however, placed a person's mother's surname last. Thus, his name was written as Heinrich Berg Loewen. This difference in cultural practice has created widespread confusion. If Heinrich had been able to speak Spanish then he could have asked the official which names he should use in his signature.

Women's names involved an additional complication. On official documents, they would have their two birth surnames, that is, their mother's and father's, and in the early twentieth century, there might also be a "de" and then the husband's surname. In the Mormon or Mennonite communities in Mexico, women would generally adopt the surname of their husbands upon getting married. Sometimes officials would then write down all three surnames on the documents and sometimes only one.

Reading these two cards suggests that this registration was a significant encounter. For many of the Mennonites, this was the first time that they, as individuals, came before Mexican government officials. And the officials had not seen Mennonites in such a close-up way before either. In all likelihood, the officials were puzzled that the men wore overalls and the women long dark dresses. This was so different both from Mexican styles and from what they expected of Canadians and Americans. They likely also wondered why these people wanted to live in Mexico but not learn Spanish. The fact that they did not speak Spanish reduced what little power they had in this encounter; it may also have made the officials more inclined to classify the people and write down information about them in accordance with their preconceived notions. If the officials considered these people with the question of their possible integration in mind, they probably saw it as a very long-term prospect.

Gender Perspectives on Women

Three of the cards I examine in this chapter are for Mennonite women and three are for Mormon women. Their cultures are different from that of Mexican society. And some present themselves in ways that deviate from the stereotype of their own cultures, as if to assert a degree of personal agency. Before looking at them, however, we want to briefly explore the role of women in Mexico's culture. There may be some points of similarity, given the influence of the religion and tradition in all of them.

One indication of the role of women in Mexico is that if they were under twenty-five, then they could not immigrate by themselves; they had to be accompanied by a parent or "persona honorable residente en el país" ["an honorable person who is a resident of the country"] ("Ley de Migración" 3). This restriction was likely to protect the virginity of young women and this may relate to the widespread veneration of the Virgin Mary in the Catholic Church and her most famous apparition in Mexico as the Virgin of Guadalupe. In the 1530s, the Virgin Mary appeared to a devout indigenous man, Juan Diego, at Tepeyac, north of Mexico City. This veneration has emphasized that it is very important for women to be virgins until becoming married, after which they should become mothers. If they failed to meet these expectations, they would not be seen in a positive light. But a woman's role, so defined, has implications for her body. According to Dominika Gasiorowski:

> Her role, however revered . . . is incidental—she is passivity personified and life is formed through her, but not of her. This disavowal of women's bodily forms is very problematic, as claims of bodily injury cannot be legitimized if the materiality of the body is put into question. (504)

Understandably, this "immaterial" body had to have a materialized counterpart. In the Mexican context, this was represented by the Malinche who, as a slave girl of Hernán Cortés, the sixteenth-century Spanish conqueror, was also his translator and rape victim, or lover, depending on one's interpretation. Both female images—the Malinche and the Virgin of Guadalupe—have a place in Mexico's culture. Emily Hind's excellent work, Femme*nism and the Mexican Woman Intellectual from Sor Juana to Poniatowska* (2011) explains the dichotomy between them but she holds that these archetypes are malleable, in part because in some ways they duplicate one another. She says: "La Virgen de Guadalupe, despite her darker skin, stands for María (Mary), and [the darker skinned] La Malinche is also variously known as Malinalli, Malintzín, and doña Marina" (Hind Femme*nism* 28).[15] The final name of the Malinche is more European and resembles María. But there is another role, different from the Virgen of Guadalupe and the Malinche. Hind argues, quoting the Mexican essayist Roger Bartra, that in the eyes of many Mexican men the ideal woman is the *Chingadalupe* (Femme*nism* 30), one who is pure but who also enjoys being a sexual partner. This role involves risks, as there could be consequences for women who deviate from the ideal roles.

The culture of the Mennonites and the Mormons also had a strong religiously based emphasis on women being virgins until they got married and on becoming mothers thereafter, though in their cultures this was not related to a figure like the Virgin of Guadalupe. But to be labeled as sexually available outside of marriage in their communities had consequences. Certainly, their cultures are patriarchal, as is Mexico's, and according to historian Temma Kaplan, accepting patriarchal gender norms is a way of accepting the social order. This means that "even deviations as seemingly trivial as haircuts and unique forms of dress elicit the wrath of those seeking social stability" (263). Kaplan continues, noting that in early twentieth-century Mexico, "the violence men direct toward women who violated hair and dress codes had less to do with the women themselves than with the fact that they were outside of the control of men and showed it" (T. Kaplan 266). In spite of these prohibitions, some Mennonite and Mormon women made modest deviations from it. They certainly did not overthrow the patriarchal order but they created some space for themselves within it. The photographs help us to identify these deviations, particularly as they relate to dress and hairstyles. We also see how the bureaucrats' descriptions do not always match what we see in the photographs and consider some possible reasons for that.

HELENA BERGEN FRIESEN   Our first card is of Helena Bergen Friesen, made in 1935. She is nineteen but looks older and she is not married. Regarding her appearance, her hair is freshly combed back and tied into a firm bun; her dress, though in the traditional style, is checkered and relatively light, not dark; her eyebrows are described as sparse but a close look suggests that she might have tweezed them; also, that she might be using some make-up ("Bergen Friesen Helena"). She was allowed to "touch up" her appearance because she was not yet married. Whatever the reason, these characteristics suggest that she wanted to make a positive impression on the officials. She knows no other language than German but she signs her name with the anglicized Helen instead of the German Helena, which was been used in the colony and which is printed near the top of the card. This indicates that Helena cared about how she presented herself and self-articulates her identity with the outside worth. Her careful handwriting is also noteworthy, reminding us that neat writing was emphasized in the traditional Mennonite village schools. Her facial expression, in my opinion, does not suggest fear but a willingness to cooperate. There are, then, a number of subtle indications that Helena was exercising a certain personal agency, that she was not unthinkingly compliant with the norms of her culture, and that she was somewhat open to the outside world.

JUSTINA WIEBE Our next card is of Justina Wiebe, a woman who happens to be my great-aunt. She was in the small group of Mennonites who migrated to Mexico in 1948. The card was issued in 1949. The questions on it have evolved slightly from those of the 1930s. There is now no question about her chin but there is one about her mouth, which is described as regular ("Wiebe Justina"). The card notes that an identifying feature is a scar on her right hand. It also states that she is twenty-two years old, single, and works at home. Regarding her appearance, it is noteworthy that her dress has a collar with an embroidered trim, and it looks like her dress has shoulder pads. She also has short, styled hair. In these ways, she deviated from Old Colony norms. Generally, Old Colony people strictly interpreted the Biblical passage, "but if a woman has long hair, it is her glory? For her hair is given to her for a covering" (1 Cor. 11:15). For them, it mandated that women should not cut their hair. She may have been allowed these deviances because her community was not yet well established so the norms were not strictly enforced and because she was single. All photos of her after she got married show her in very traditional dress, thereby indicating support for the social order. She, like Helena, likely presented herself in these ways because she still understood herself as a young woman from Canada, or she felt that this way the officials would understand her better. The fact that the official describes her nose as straight even though it does not look that way may suggest that the official wanted to describe her favorably.

The references to her language abilities are noteworthy, too. Her first language is said to be Dutch but other cards describing Mennonites refer to German. It is possible that the official asked her, through an interpreter, and that she answered by saying *Dietsch*, which is the Low German word for the Low German language, and that the official understood *Dietsch* as Dutch. Another possible reason is that during World War II, some Mennonites in Canada described themselves as Dutch, rather than German, so as to avoid being associated with the enemy power.[16] In addition to the matter of *Dietsch*, the card says that Justina speaks English. This is because she had completed eight years of public school in Saskatchewan before her family moved to Mexico. Her English language ability may have impressed the officials. This, and her hairstyle, were what they expected from a young Canadian woman. It may have led them to see her as conforming to the archetypes of femininity.

MARGARETHA BANMAN DYCK   Margaretha Banman Dyck was born in Canada on September 24, 1919, and arrived in Mexico on June 6, 1922, when she was not yet three years old. The card was made on June 8, 1936, when she was sixteen. The card states that she is "Canadense" ["Canadan"] by nationality and "mononita" ["Mononite"] by religion. Curiously, her photographs have the rounded edges of a portrait. They appear to have been taken elsewhere, brought to the registration official, and then glued or stapled onto the registration card. Margaretha's dress is dark and without a collar and her hair is freshly combed back and pulled into a braided bun, all of which give her a more conservative appearance than either Justina or Helena. She may be trying, in these ways, to avoid disrupting the social order. That she is married, her civil status is marked as *casada*, even though she was only sixteen is extremely unusual. The sociologist, Calvin Redekop, says that most women got married at twenty-one or twenty-two (188–89). In all likelihood, she had gotten pregnant. To then get married avoided disrupting the social order as would the adoption of conservative dress and hairstyles.

There are a few unusual aspects of this card. The term *casada* is underlined and that there are nine check marks at various points on the card. The official or his superior could have had some doubts, and went over the information a second time to satisfy himself that it was accurate. The card describes her hair as blonde when the photograph suggests that it is quite dark. The description makes her fit with a vision of whiteness so as to save her from appearing as the Malinche archetype or Bartra's stated ideal, the *Chingadalupe.*

I turn now to the cards of three Mormon women. The norms of the Mormon community as they relate to women are different from those of the Mennonites, particularly with regard to dress and hairstyles.[17] Mormon women are allowed more opulent clothing and more modern hairstyles. This may place them closer to what was considered desirable by Mexican authorities.

Ivis Farnsworth Call's document shows a beautiful twenty-two-year-old unmarried woman. She appears relaxed in a modern dress with a V-neck top; her hair is perfectly curled; she wears stylish make-up and her eyebrows, like those of Helena Bergen Friesen, are "sparse" and probably tweezed. It is significant that the official uses the title "la Srta" ["la Señorita" or "Miss"] before her name, which implies respect. This title countered any suspicion of loose morals. He may simply have recorded the way that she introduced herself. Her profile photograph, like Justina's, faces left. Her nationality is said to be North American. Her posture is bent-over, as if she had been hunched over a computer for too long except, of course, there were no computers at that time ("la Srta. Farnswroth Call Ivis").

The card states that her profession is a student. She was not studying in Mexico, because there were no postsecondary academic institutions near her home. The student designation would have been a good cover for missionary work.[18] She needed a legitimate profession, because after the Mexican Revolution, there was such strong anticlerical sentiment in Mexico that official policy prohibited clergy members, including Catholic priests, from wearing any kind of distinctive clothing in public. LDS missionaries in Mexico were not allowed to wear identifying tags until well into the late 1980s.

The card of Jannice Farnsworth Donnal de Beecroft was issued on June 5, 1933, when she, like Ivis Farnsworth Call, was twenty-two years old. And like Ivis, she has presented herself in an attractive way. Her hair is cut in an asymmetrical way, suggesting that she feels a certain inner freedom ("Beecroft Jannice Farnsworth Donnal de"). Her beautiful fur coat, V-neck shirt, and brooch communicate wealth. The fur coat, however, is not clothing for June in northern Mexico. The pictures were taken earlier and brought in later. Her appearance in the photographs likely influenced the officials, who saw her as an example of what they would expect of a young American woman. In the official's opinion, she has a robust physical constitution and a straight horizontal nose even though her hair color looks exactly like Margaretha's. The officials would not have considered her a *Chingadalupe*, because she is married and her work is at her home. And is aligned with the image of purity.

Tenna Augusta Turley Wilson is an eighteen-year-old Mormon woman. She appears modern in her dress and hairstyle. She was born in Mexico and is said to speak both English and Spanish. In her photographs she appears confident, though the photographs themselves are peculiar. Her image in her frontal picture is off-center. It appears to be pasted onto a white background. Her profile photo is cut off toward the bottom ("Turley Wilson Tenna Augusta"). Her pictures expose more skin than I expected, as we can see her collarbone. The description on the card makes Tenna appear whiter, like Margaretha, in that her hair is described as blond even though it looks brown and her eyebrows are described as populated even though they, like Justina's, look tweezed. The card describes her as a student. She was eighteen, so, she could have been finishing high school.[19] One aspect about Tenna that stands out is that she is said to be divorced. This is surprising. In its early history of the LDS church divorce was quite common but once the church officially abandoned polygamy, it became very rare.[20] It is probably not what the officials expected from someone from the Mormon community. In general, Tenna is not seen as complying with the Mexican archetypes for women. Like many of the Mennonite women whose cards we have examined, she was represented as neither entirely pure nor entirely fallen.

The registration cards of these six women reveal significant aspects of their cultures, including their patriarchal structures and gender roles. Though firmly rooted in those cultures, a number of these women were prepared to assert a degree of personal agency; in small ways, they challenged the patriarchal order and created a "cultural space" for themselves. The result stands as a modest challenge to the stereotypes and preconceived notions that are widely held about the place of women in Mennonite and Mormon communities. The way they present themselves suggests that they are not totally closed to the idea of interacting somewhat with Mexican society. That the registration officials, in their written answers, appear to have marked some of the women as having lighter hair and straighter noses than is evident in the photos may reflect a desire to make them appear compatible with Mexico. It is clear, however, that these women do not fit with the Mexican archetypes of the Virgin of Guadalupe and la Malinche, however malleable those archetypes may be.

Gender Perspectives and Ideal Mothers

In Mexican culture the female archetypes also included an ideal mother. According to historian Patience A. Schell, the goal for married Mexican women at that time was to bring up children, care for husbands, and manage homes (115). This was supported by the culture and by the political agenda. They were supposed to repopulate a nation that had become depopulated during the wars of the revolution (Schell 116). They were also to help recraft the nation as mestizo and revolutionary. By bringing children into the world and thus helping to recraft the nation the women would complement the way men did their part with their virility (Stern 370). The ideas of repopulating and recrafting, Stern explains, were particularly important in the northern states of Sonora and Chihuahua where the decade of fighting had caused a major decline in the population. It is in these states, particularly Chihuahua, that most of the Mennonite and Mormon colonies were located in the 1930s and 1940s.[21] Given this commitment to repopulating and recrafting, motherhood and child-rearing had an important place in the vision of the post-Revolutionary state.

In support of this vision, the government took notable steps to assist mothers and to support the work of childrearing. According to historian Ann S. Blum, the presidencies of Lázaro Cárdenas (1934–40) and Ávila Camacho (1940–46) promoted "neighborhood-based programs such as day-care centers and factory crèches, mothers' clubs, and public cafeterias ... [as] important resources supporting single, working mother," (142). In the early 1940s there was a campaign to encourage mothers to register the births of their children and to "legitimize" any who had been born before they were legally married (Blum 127). Also in those years the government organized, "public Mothers' Day rituals on a mass scale [and] distributed labor-saving appliances, including pawned sewing machines, to working-class mothers" (Blum 142). These gifts were rewards for what Stern calls their participation in recrafting the post-Revolutionary nation. Under the next two presidents, Miguel Alemán (1946–52) and Adolfo Ruiz Cortines (1952–58), the maternal role continued to be emphasized. According to historian Sara Luna Elizarrarás, the mother should have a moral superiority, and would be guided by the desire to better those around her, adopting a maternal role in public and in private (152). It can be assumed that the officials who conducted the registration were somewhat aware of these emphases though, as with so much about these cards, the signs of this are subtle.

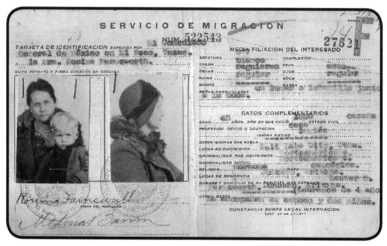

Figure 3 Rosina Farnsworth. Image courtesy of the Archivo General de la Nación, Fondo "Departamento de Migración, subserie estadounidenses."

ROSINA FARNSWORTH The most significant aspect of this card is the most obvious one, namely, the frontal photo is of a mother holding her child.[22] The card says that she has a husband and another child. They are not shown on the card, which implies that women could be seen as devoted mothers apart from their husbands or partners. It is also significant that she is accorded the title "Sra.," meaning Señora or Mrs. She, like Ivis Farnsworth Call, may have introduced herself with a title, or the official accorded her a title of respect. Moreover, she is a visitor in Mexico; her home is said to be in Arizona. This raises questions. It is known that foreigners were not registered if they did not stay in Mexico for at least six months so she must have been there longer, in a second residence in one of the Mormon colonies in Mexico. She may have lived in or visited Colonia García, which the Farnsworth family had helped found It is possible that she had a residence there.[23] There are differences in the photographs. In her profile photo the child is not with her but she is wearing a hat while in the frontal photo she has the child but not her hat. Maybe there were no strict regulations about what kind of photographs were acceptable. Pegler-Gordon who has studied photograph-bearing identification documents extensively, would say that this difference in the two photographs "destabilizes" the relationship between the text and the referent (71).

Aganetha Berg's document also includes, in its frontal photograph, an image of a mother with seven of her children. As with Rosina's photos, there are differences. The frontal photo does not quite fit into the space provided. This suggests that it could have been taken somewhere else and then brought to the registration office. Also, in the frontal photo, the image of Aganetha is so small that it might not be totally reliable for identification purposes. Further, in the profile photo she wears glasses but in the frontal photo she appears not to be wearing them ("Berg, Aganetha"). These variations may reflect the flexibility and improvisation of the presiding officials. Whatever the reason, it creates a destabilizing effect, as noted with Rosina.

Aganetha's card was issued in 1950, and it states that she speaks German and English, that her place of residence is Morris, Manitoba, Canada, and that she is planning to visit her sister in Los Jagüeyes, Chihuahua. Further, her V-neck dress is not what an Old Colony woman would normally wear. Likewise, some of the clothes that her children wear are not in traditional Old Colony styles. These factors illustrate that Aganetha belonged to a group of *Kleine Gemeinde* Mennonites who moved from Manitoba to start a settlement in the Los Jagüeyes area in 1948. Though still conservative, they were not quite like the Old Colony people. Aganetha had grown up in Canada, which explains why she could speak English.

This woman embodied ideals of motherhood. In the moment of contact with the officials, the Mennonite Aganetha, like the Mormon Rosina, represented an incarnation of the archetype of Mexican motherhood. The officials, knowing of the government's efforts to promote motherhood, were sympathetic to them. They were thus flexible about the women's imperfectly matched photographs.

Gender Perspectives of Men

Mexican culture also had archetypes of virile male partners for women. This, too, was emphasized in governmental promotions, especially in the mid-century presidencies of Ávila Camacho, Miguel Alemán, and Ruiz Cortines

(Luna Elizarrarás 86–88). Most of the governmental materials for such promotions, says Luna Elizarrarás, reflect men who are married, have children, and work on their own land or in a small business. Although they might not be able to live up to the archetypal ability to always protect their families, they are mostly perceived as reliable companions for their wives.

The Mexican male archetypes have two opposing images: the philanderer and the emasculated or feminized man. The philanderer does not come up often in the portrayals of Mormon or Mennonite men, but the weakened or feminized man does. The archetype for this role is rooted in Mexico's colonial period when, according to Temma Kaplan, the colonizing Spanish men feminized subordinate indigenous men to enhance their own authority and sense of masculinity. This created a sense that white men were virile but indigenous or mestizo men were more feminized (T. Kaplan 267). The widespread poverty in the Mennonite communities in the 1930s and 1940s caused many men to feel weak and unable to fulfill their responsibilities as providers and could have led to emasculating portrayals. Moreover, their communitarian ethic may have made men hesitant about asserting themselves, and certainly relative to the official's power. Some Mennonite men were emasculated in these cards, and we will examine three of them: Jacob Bueckert Siemens, Peter Braun Thiessen, and Isaac Banman Friesen.

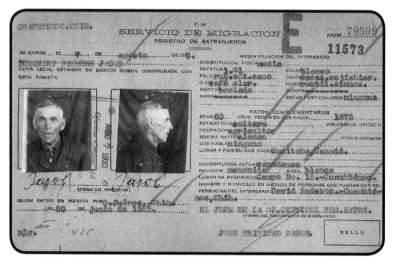

Figure 4 Jacob Bueckert Siemens. Image courtesy of the Archivo General de la Nación, Fondo "Departamento de Migración, subserie canadienses."

JACOB BUECKERT SIEMENS Jacob Bueckert Siemens' card was processed in August 1933. He had entered Mexico in 1923 but was born in 1873 in Manitoba, Canada. He has no accompanying children and is said to be single ("Bueckert Siemens, Jacob"). His eyes and facial expression are unusually empty and hollow, as if he is weak and vulnerable. His signature also indicates that sense of weakness. He has written his first name, Jacob, twice; once under each photograph. He was barely able to write even his first name. The way the letter "b" is formed suggests he is proficient in Gothic script, which he had learned in an Old Colony school. He did not know Spanish so the official may not have been able to advise him.

PETER BRAUN THIESSEN Our next unusual man is Peter Braun Thiessen. He was born on February 26, 1925, came to Mexico on December 2, 1926, and was just fifteen years old when this card is made, though, if anything, he looks even younger ("Peter Braun Thiessen"). The buttons on his shirt are off-center, which gives him a young and disorganized appearance. That he is listed as a student is noteworthy. He had attended the Old Colony village school where it was normal for boys to stop at age thirteen. After that age, he would work alongside his father. The official wrote down that he was a student because he could not think of other credible options, since he was clearly too young to be a farmer.

ISAAC BANMAN FRIESEN Our final unusual man is Isaac Banman Friesen. He was born in Canada on April 12, 1920, and entered Mexico on March 21, 1922. He is twenty-one at the time this card is made so it is not unusual that he would be single though some Mennonite men were married at that age. This means that his family was among the very first Mennonites there. In the photographs, his shirt and coat are impeccable. So, too, is his hair. His posture and facial expression suggest a desire to appear proper and correct. He is said to speak German and no other language. One thing that is unusual is that his occupation is listed as *doméstica*, meaning domestic work in the home. This is the only card where that occupation is listed for a man. This suggests that Isaac was understood as an effeminate man, regardless of how he described himself. These three effeminate men surely would not be charged with repopulating the nation, or with fathering any part of the mestizo race. They are at the edges of the Mexican and Mennonite ideals and likely struggled to be incorporated into either community.

A Perspective Based on the Use of Spanish

Another informative aspect of these registration cards relates to how the officials wrote up the language capabilities of the registrants and what this suggests about how they saw the people. It is generally recognized that in both the Mormon and the Mennonite communities the men know more Spanish than the women. That is because men have typically had more opportunities to interact with Mexican workers, businesspeople, and others, while the lives of the women were more confined. But their schools have been a factor, too. Very few of the Mennonite schools, even in 2017, teach the Spanish language; in contrast, the Mormons have long taught at least some Spanish in their schools. It can be noted, however, that the cards of a number of the Mormon women discussed in the preceding pages indicate that they do not speak Spanish. This holds even for some who were born in Mexico. I begin by looking at two Mormon cards, one of a man and the other of a woman, who is the man's sister, and then proceed to four Mennonite cards, two of men and two of women.

Brigham A. Farnsworth Bingham was born in Mexico, in the Mormon colony of Colonia García, in 1907. His family moved back to the US, as all Mormons did, because of the fighting that eventually led to the revolution was particularly intense in their areas. This means that a large part of Brigham's schooling took place in the US. We do not know when he returned to Mexico and his first registration card is dated January 25, 1927 ("Farnsworth Bingham Brigham A"). The photograph on this card shows him as a young man with blond hair, a casual coat, and shirt. His first language is said to be English but Spanish is said to be his second. Then, for reasons that we do not know, he was issued a second card in 1933 ("Brigham A. Farnsworth"). In the photograph on this document, Brigham's appearance has changed. He looks haggard. His shirt and jacket could be those of a farm laborer. His hair is poorly cut, has jagged edges, and is said to have a lighter color. The description of his features has also changed. He is now said to have a mole by his chin. Further, in 1927 he was an *agricultor propietario* [farmer-landowner] and in 1933 he was an *agricultor* [farmer]. He may have lost property.

The significant change is that in 1933 Spanish is said to be his first language and English his second. Obviously, this is an error; a person cannot acquire a new first language. It is significant is that the officials wrote it down that way. He may have conversed with the officials in Spanish or told the officials that Spanish was his first language. Either way, it strongly suggests that he had become more integrated into Mexico. The bureaucrats who wrote this down acknowledged this and wanted to affirm it.

Brigham's sister, Roien Farnsworth Bingham, born in 1912, five years after Brigham, has only one immigration card; hers was issued one day after his, in December 1933, and by the same official ("Farnsworth Bingham Roien"). According to the photograph her hair as moderately short and styled and she is wearing a button-down shirt with a high neck or scarf, indicating that she conforms to expectations of Mormon modesty. The written description of her features appears to match those we see in her photograph. But the reference to her languages is puzzling. The same official who optimistically wrote that her brother's first language was Spanish, now writes that Roien's first language is "a little Spanish," and that her second language is English. It suggests that she did not know Spanish as well as he did. Yet no one's first language is "a little" of something, still, by describing Spanish as her first language the official is identifying her with Mexico.

For the Mennonites, the language issues are more complex. Their first language was Low German, which is primarily an oral language that they would use in most daily conversations. Their church services, at least in the 1920s, '30s, and '40s, were all been in standard German, as would their printed material including their hymnbooks, Bibles, and any other literature. That is what they learned in their schools and what they used when they wrote letters to friends back in Canada. Some of the people described earlier knew some English from having gone to school in Canada before the migration; others had only ever attended German schools, even as children in Canada. Meanwhile, among those who had lived in Mexico for some years, there were men who could converse in Spanish. Mennonite women, generally, could not. References to these languages appear in different ways on the Mennonite registration cards. The cards indicate that, as with Brigham and Roien, the officials were generous when they described the Mennonites' Spanish-language abilities. The cards' descriptions affirm any sign they could that the people were moving in the direction of becoming integrated into Mexican society.

Johann Loeppky Funk and Bernhard Banman Teichroeb's cards illustrate ways that younger men were partially incorporated into the nation beyond typical markers of whiteness.[24] Johann was born in 1890; he moved to Mexico in 1922 when he was thirty-two ("Loeppky Funk Johann"). He was forty-three when this card was made and he is the only one whose photograph shows him with a smile. He is a farmer, married, and has children so he conforms to the masculine protector role. His card says that he speaks German and "a little" Spanish. Bernhard, whose card was issued in 1940 when he was twenty-five, appears more sedate. Like Johann, he is a farmer and married, and he is said to speak German as his first language and Spanish as his second. In both cases, the written comments about their Spanish abilities are somewhat generous. Johann had come to Mexico as an adult; he had been there for only eleven years when he was registered and it is extremely unlikely that he had taken any formal Spanish studies. Mennonites in those years did not do that. Bernhard had come to Mexico at age nine and had been there for sixteen years when he was registered and it is possible that he had picked up some Spanish. However, on his card the qualifying term "a little" does not appear. These men may have told the official that they could speak some Spanish, even if they were not fluent in it, in order to identify with Mexico, and that the official wrote it down the way he did because he wanted to encourage that kind of identification.

A similar generosity on the part of officials appears in relation to some Mennonite women. Katarina Banman Lepki came to Mexico when she was thirteen. At the time of her registration she was twenty-five and married. She is said to speak German and "a little" Spanish ("Banman Lepki Katarina"). The card of Agatha Banman Thiessen, a twenty-one-year-old married woman who is said to work at home, describes her as speaking German and "Castellano" ("la Sra. Agatha Banman Thiessen"). It is virtually impossible that she could speak Castellano or that she claimed to do so. The designation must have been given by an official who wanted to have Agatha identify with Mexico and its heritage. The reference to Katarina knowing "a little" Spanish reflects a similar motivation.

These documents suggest that the Mennonites and Mormons were allowed to exist at the margins of Mexican society; yet, the officials attempted to include them in small ways, because they understood that they could bring the country closer to its mestizo ideal.

In the post-Revolutionary era, the Mexican government, like that in other countries, attempted to integrate the people living in its territories into a national ideology. These governments attempt to nurture a common identity and loyalty with their flag, their national anthem, the celebration of particular historic events, and having certain narratives taught in schools, and so on. Mexico based its effort to build a common identity on the mestizo race; this used Lamarckian genetic theories, as well as other interpretations of eugenics, from the early twentieth century. The mestizo would stand as a core to which other people, including the foreigners living in Mexico, would be invited to blend in so as to contribute to this new national identity. Its utopian, idealized race was to be created, protected, and strengthened; hence, eugenic efforts aimed to control human reproduction, and enacted race-based restrictions on immigration. The government used a broad range of tools to promote the idea, including education and various social and public health programs. The biological dimension remained important. To advance this dimension it would be necessary to gather a range of detailed information through surveys, assessments, and classifications. The registration of foreigners described in this chapter must be seen as an element in that information-gathering effort.

The government, even though it gathered a lot of information, did not carry through with a broad, long-term program to build the mestizo race. A sizeable number of people who earlier had identified as indigenous did now identify as mestizo. Not many foreigners or immigrants took that step; Mennonites and Mormons were able to continue as fairly separate peoples. This chapter has examined that effort in the context of how the country's leading intellectuals articulated the idea and how the government took steps in working toward it. It has also looked at the mundane work of registering the people and at a number of cultural factors that come into play when their encounter is considered from the perspective of what it might mean if there were steps toward integration.

In this regard, a number of individuals presented themselves in ways that deviated from the stereotypes of their groups and suggested a level of openness toward Mexican society and a respect for the officials; and further, that the officials were eager to affirm such signs, being more generous than a simple reading of the evidence would require.

2

Whose Land Is It
Mormons, Ejidos, and Agrarian Reform

In the first chapter, limited information on foreign residence cards helped us imagine the moment of immigration, complicate the notion of revolutionary mestizaje, and rethink gender norms. This chapter examines how Mormons interact with another group of bureaucrats, who dealt with land, land redistribution, and agrarian reform. This chapter and the one that follows pertains to land redistribution and agriculture refers to land cultivation. I analyze the ways these interactions are represented in the *Diario Oficial de la Federación* [*Mexican Federal Register*] and multiple reports and letters. I show that in these situations, the bureaucrats defined Mormons as part of the Mexican nation based on their economic contributions, even as they exclude the Mormons because they were seen as not quite Mexican enough. They were also seen as foreign invaders, in a rhetoric reminiscent of 1836 Texas independence, the US annexation of Texas in 1845, and the Guadalupe-Hidalgo Treaty in 1848, in which Mexico was forced to cede over half of its territory to the US. These interventions continued into the twentieth century. The Pershing incursion in 1916–17 in pursuit of Francisco "Pancho" Villa, was seen as "an assault on the nation's sovereignty" that "deeply impacted the national conscience" (Will 365). Moreover, throughout the 1920s, the US press often mentioned US business interests in Mexico and the need to have them protected by the American military (Will 366). Some of Mexico's apprehension about its neighbor to the north is reflected in the Constitution, which forbade foreign ownership of land within one hundred kilometers of the US border and elsewhere only if authorized by the secretary of state for foreign relations (Dormady 173, 180).

The Mormon colonies in Chihuahua are seen occasionally as foreign invaders who live close to the Mexico–US border, and who are Mexican but not Mexican enough. This rhetoric is present in the documents that explain agrarian reform in three ejidos, Colonia Pacheco, Casas Grandes and Galeana, and register conflict with Mormon colonies Pacheco, Dublán, Juárez, and LeBaron. An ejido is a name for land granted by the Mexican government to primarily indigenous and always land or title-less peasants. It typically redistributed land from people with significant landholding to people with little or no land. In other cases, it restored land to people who held titles from the colonial era, which was sold without their consent.

I first learned about these conflicts in the summer of 2016, when I stayed with a kind and generous LDS Mormon couple in Colonia Juárez for about five days. During this time, I learned that many Mormon colonies in northern Mexico had been lost through agrarian reform and so there were fewer Mormons with US roots in northern Mexico than there had been before the Revolution. Historians corroborate this population decline. According to a 1985 article in an LDS publication, the *Ensign*, by LaVon B. Whetten, only five colonies were reestablished after the Revolution. She states that "isolation, transportation difficulties, and the lack of schools beyond the primary level caused all but two of them—Colonia Juarez and Colonia Dublan—to be permanently abandoned" (Whetten "Las Colonias"). In 2001, John Wright's "Geographical Note" echoed this perspective: "By the 1920s isolation, poor soils, poverty, and a lack of schools—particularly in the mountains—doomed all but two plateau colonies in Chihuahua: Colonia Dublan and Colonia Juarez" (588). His short article ultimately captures much of my experience: "My initial impressions are many: the kindness of Mormons who seemed hungry for conversation with an outsider, the hands-on stewardship of the land, [and] the division of the races and classes in adults" (Wright 596). This racial division is rooted in conflict around land.

MORMON COLONIZATION IN MEXICO

The Mormons arrived in Mexico between 1883 and 1885, because of adverse conditions in the US, namely antipolygamy laws, and favorable conditions in Mexico. According to the lawyer and legal historian, Gerardo N. González

Navarro, an 1883 Mexican law promoted foreign immigration and internal migration. It was meant for more "civilized" people to colonize supposedly empty land (G. González Navarro 41). As part of their colonization agreements, for an initial fifteen-year period, they were given exemptions from military service and several forms of taxation.[1] They were also given strong economic incentives for populating the area, engaging in agricultural development. In the initial fifteen years of settlement, the government allowed them to create communities with their own form of taxation, which could issue some of their own passports. They were also assured that they would not have to change their family style. The implications of this history have had far-reaching effects, particularly in relation to land claims. These claims have seldom been well-researched, in part because the areas of continued LDS settlement are in fairly remote parts of Chihuahua.

In the twentieth century, only the LeBarons are easily recognized in archival materials while the LDS Mormons are less conspicuous. The LeBarons, one of the four-hundred groups that claims the term Mormon, differ significantly from LDS Mormons. Nevertheless, there is precedent for studying the LeBarons, now divided into several religious groups, alongside of the larger, mainstream, LDS church. Janet Bennion's *Desert Patriarchy* includes the LeBarons in her anthropological study of Mennonites and Mormons in Mexico. Moreover, Jason Dormady and Jared Tamez's edited collection *Just South of Zion* includes Mormons from a range of church affiliations in their work. They appear on legal agreements as "North Americans" or "members of the Mexican Colonization Company." These North Americans sometimes appear in footnotes in the literature on agrarian reform. Daniel Nugent's *Spent Cartridges of Revolution: An Anthropological History of Namiquipa, Chihuahua* (1993) mentions that the agrarian reform commission sold good land to the LeBarons in the 1960s and 1970s, and that there were a number of problematic moments between the Casas Grandes ejido and the Dublán and Juárez colonies (112). Noé G. Palomares Peña's work about US landowners in Mexico also mentions Mormons briefly. He believes that the Mormons did not have problems with the government, and that other US landowners did (Palomares Peña 29).[2] These conflicts are not mentioned in Mormon histories.[3] When they are mentioned, the smaller number of colonies in the contemporary period tends to be attributed to the lack of post-Revolutionary return migration to Mexico rather than to agrarian reform.[4]

A BRIEF HISTORY OF AGRARIAN REFORM

Land and land use were some of the primary reasons for the Mexican Revolution. Even before it officially ended, leaders began making provisions for a better land use system in Mexico. In the era before the Revolution, landlords, including foreigners, gained ownership of Mexico's rural area through *haciendas* [large rural estates]. These *haciendas* maintained conditions that kept peasants in a state of indebtedness and poverty, a situation that was likened to slavery. One of the goals of the Mexican Revolution was to end this situation.

According to González Navarro, in January 1915, the government of then-president Venustiano Carranza began to address this need. It passed a law that rendered any occupation of any type of communal land illegal, even if it had been encouraged by a federal government agency (G. González Navarro 56). In other words, his policy attempted to protect indigenous landholding practices. Then, the Revolutionary government enacted the 1917 Constitution. It continues a commitment to the land, with very different phrasing. Article 27 states: "La propiedad de las tierras y aguas comprendidas dentro de los límites del territorio nacional, corresponde originariamente a la Nación" ["Land and water that are found within national borders, originally belong to the Nation"] ("Constitución" 2). It highlights the nation's inalienable dominion and implies that landowners are subordinate to it. No one was entirely sure how or when this lofty constitutional ideal was to be enacted. According to legal scholar Samuel Baggett, writing in the *Texas Law Review* in 1926, although land use issues were a key cause of the Revolution, nine years after it ended, the laws had not been put into place (1). He uses examples from Maya and Aztec cultures and argues that the legal goal of the ejido would allow some parts of Mexico to revert to precontact legal systems (Baggett 1). Yet, as González Navarro correctly points out almost a century later, the ejidos were not a precontact system of communal landholding. He reminds us that Maya culture understood that land could be private or common. The Aztecs also categorized land, and for them, where some was reserved for religion, some for ordinary people, and some was available as private land. This was *calpulli*, which was then part of a collective *caputlalli* (G. González Navarro 23–26). The term ejido dates to 1573, and comes from the Latin word *exitus*. That year, Spanish king Felipe II made a law regarding the small towns and settlements for indigenous people called *reducciones*. Felipe II argued that they have water, land, and trees. They should also have obvious entrances, exits, and places to work. In this context, the ejido was related to the reducción—it was the size of a square league and was where indigenous people could raise their cattle without mixing with that of the Spanish. So, the ejido was a type of common land in the colonial period (González Navarro 29). The ejido was then more of a connection to the colonial rather than the precontact period.

This historical precedent shows us that the ejido was used in the colonial period to manage Indigenous populations. The first post-Revolutionary version of the federal agrarian code, enacted after being printed in the *Diario Oficial* on July 3, 1934, kept this utopian ideal in mind. It named the new bureaucratic groups that would organize agrarian reform: the *Secretaría de la Reforma Agraria* [Secretariat of Agrarian Reform] (SRA) would operate on a federal level with state representatives (Fabila 482). The *Cuerpo Consultivo Agrario* [Agrarian Consultation Body], a five-member decision making body, under the executive or presidential power, would make final decisions. In addition to creating these decision-making bodies, the code adds that land that cannot be cultivated is not eligible for redistribution (Fabila 482). The only land available for redistribution was if a landowner had in excess of 50 hectares (Fabila 488, 491). The law was modified in December 1934 and December 1936 to reassure private property owners that they could own up to one hundred and fifty hectares of land, if it required irrigation, or three hundred hectares if it did not (Fabila 547). So, in the first two decades after the Mexican Revolution, agrarian reform moved from an ideal to a relatively clear code.

A closer examination of these laws and processes demonstrates significant problems. These laws also gave the president extraordinary powers. Nugent explains that agrarian reform was a way for the state to control people. In the ejido system, *ejidatarios* [ejido members] would be forced to maintain a relationship with the state (Nugent 88–89). Anthropologist Claudio Lomnitz adds that ejidatarios did not legally own the land and so they depended more on the government than they would have as private property owners (*Deep Mexico* 75).

The state made these problems worse by irregularly implementing agrarian reform laws. Susan Walsh Sanderson's *Land Reform in Mexico: 1910–1980* (1984), explains that while land reform was a politically viable and popular decision, it was never done well (2). She establishes that ejidos in areas active in the Revolution could expect better land (Walsh Sanderson 47). The bureaucrats and ejido leaders were also notoriously corrupt (Kelly 554). The ejidos, then, appeased some in Mexico and reinforced state control over others. Moreover, as historian Martina E. Will has argued, not all leaders were committed to this program. They wanted to dismantle the large estates and promote small-scale farming but they also believed that private property and medium-sized farms would be better for the important goal of increasing agricultural productivity (362). Lazaro Cárdenas (1934–40) supported the ejidos with roads, irrigation works and credit. During his six-year administration seventeen million hectares were distributed among 800,000 people and agricultural productivity increased. (Otero 284). Overall, from the 1920s to the 1980s, they sporadically redistributed land, and when they did so, it was of varying quality. By 1988, more than three million households lived in more than 28,000 ejidos (Kelly 544).

The conflicts in this chapter and the next intensified in the decades after Cárdenas' initial redistribution. Cárdenas' immediate successor, Manuel Ávila Camacho (1940–46) was also committed to the land-reform program but Miguel Alemán (1946–52) was less so. Alemán gave more aid to the private sector, and under his tenure private farmers began to illegally rent land from individual ejidatarios and build up large scale agricultural operations. The result became known as *neolatifundismo*. Presidents Adolfo Ruiz Cortines (1952–58), Adolfo López Mateos (1958–64) and Gustavo Díaz Ordaz (1964–70) did not make land reform a priority either. Luis Echeverría, who came to power in 1970, began to emphasize ejidos because his party was losing support in rural areas. He became: "determined to show that the promises of the Mexican Revolution—land, education, labor rights—were still very much alive ..." (Soto Laveaga 116). Echeverría fashioned himself after Cárdenas and used passionate speeches to convince those who had been excluded or thought they had been excluded from the postwar economic gains to continue to support him and his party (Soto Laveaga 180). Despite his rhetoric, Echeverría also supported the private agricultural sector, which, by this time, was quite strong. In 1991, President Salinas de Gortari amended article 27 of the constitution and allowed ejidatarios to sell their parcels of land or to use them as collateral for making loans; he also protected private holdings from future redistribution claims, thus effectively ending the land reform agenda.[5]

This irregular implementation of laws, and changing laws throughout the twentieth century, created conflicts between the state, ejidos, and private landowners. Three conflicts with Mormon landowners exemplify this triangulation and give evidence that the perception of Mormons oscillated between valued contributors to Mexican economy and US invaders—echoing the movement for Texan independence between 1820 and 1936, which establishes a precedent for concerns about US presence in Mexico. This perception was heightened after the Mexico–US War ended with the treaty of Guadalupe–Hidalgo in 1848 and Mexico losing much of its territory. The first conflict this chapter explores is Colonia Pacheco, which is the name of the ejido and the Mormon colony; the second is the Casas Grandes ejido, and its conflict with Mormons in Colonias Dublán and Juárez and the final conflict is between the Galeana ejido and the LeBaron polygamous group.

COLONIA PACHECO

The conflict that began in the early 1950s shows shifting understandings of who belonged in Mexico and who did not in the 1950s. In 1953, a group of *vecinos* [neighbors] petitioned to have an ejido created in this area. Their petition was based on their economic need, which they stated would only be met if they had land that that they could farm. The land the *vecinos* sought to farm belonged to several landowners, including some Mormons. The ejido's petitions and subsequent appeals suggest that in their view, the Mormons had acquired this land in dishonest ways. The documents imply that the American Mormon landowners do not belong in Mexico. They also pejoratively describe some Mexicans as dishonest for living in the US, or for not joining the ejido.

The ejido, as per the process outlined in the agrarian code, petitioned the state representatives of the SRA in 1953, and were denied. Then, in 1956, the *Diario Oficial* declared that the federal SRA had reiterated the state-level decision because there was no available land. The Colonia Pacheco ejido had lost its petition to exist ("Resolución . . . dotación Colonia Pacheco" 13). Between 1956 and 1959, the ejido successfully lobbied its state representatives for its creation. Because the land they were afforded was not extensive, in 1959, the ejido petitioned to expand. The state denied this petition in 1961, but the federal SRA overruled it in 1965 ("Resolución . . . ampliación Colonia Pacheco" 9).

These rejections and resolutions show lengthy time lags between the various government actions. In the first time lapse, between the initial rejection and second petition, ejido leaders and Mormons collect information about each other. Between 1953 and 1956, none of the Mormons living in Colonia

Pacheco owned "too much" land. Yet, who exactly owned land, who lived there, and who farmed there was a matter of contention. The local *Comité Ejecutivo Agrario* [Executive Agrarian Committee], which organized the petitions, surveyed the situation. Their list aligns the Mormon religion with US citizenship and casts converts to Mormonism in a negative light. Manuel Cruz Gutierrez and Aurelio Lopez Quezada, the president and secretary the Executive Committee, compile a list of twenty men in Colonia Pacheco. These ejido leaders send this list to Carlos Mata Provencio, a bureaucrat with the SRA, on March 26, 1956. They list twenty men with their nationality and place of residence. Eight men, Melvin Turley, Lee K. Martinau [Martineau], Julian Lant [Lunt], Guillermo Anderson, Melvin Anderson, Guillermo Jarviz [Jarvis], Gayle Bluth, and Alma Lebaron [LeBaron], are listed as "Americano (Mormon)." Most of these men live in Colonia Juárez ; Julian Lunt, Guillermo Anderson, and Melvin Anderson lived in Colonia Pacheco, and Gayle Bluth lived in Colonia Dublán. The final Mormon, Alma LeBaron, lived in Galeana (Cruz Gutierrez and Lopez Quezada). Another man, Arnulfo Vargas, is listed as being "Mexicano (Mormon)." The other eleven men were simply listed as Mexican. Ten live in Colonia Pacheco—Luis Dominguez, Albino Montes, Rodolfo Trevizo, Rafael Martinez, Pascual Avila, Lazaro Villa M., Francisco Villa, Jose Ma. Artalejo, Albino Artalejo, and Eusebio Mendoza (Cruz Gutierrez and Lopez Quezada). This list provides few details about the lives of these men. We have the impression that the men of US background are wealthier and less Mexican than the others. As a result, they would be more justifiable candidates for land redistribution than the eleven non-Mormon Mexican men.

The following day a Colonia Pacheco leader provided his version of this list. Its subtle differences from the previous list show the influence of a more careful bureaucrat, who wrote down the men's birth names rather than Hispanizing them. For instance, it lists the men with their English names; Guillermo Anderson becomes William Anderson, and Guillermo Jarviz becomes William Jarvis (Turley 27 Mar. 1956). Lee K. Martineau is given his full name, Leland, and Julian Lant is listed by his first name, Alma, and his surname is spelled Lunt (Turley). Arnulfo Vargas, remains the same and Trinidad Artalejo becomes Manuel Artalejo. Then, Turley adds other landowners: Evaristo Arreola, Genovevo Cerna, Alejandro Cerna, Heber M. Cluff, Higinio Cruz, Anacleto Guillén, Reynaldo Hernandez, Blas Mendoza, Sixto H. Johnson [Johnson], Mariano L. Wilson, and Manuel Arras (Turley). On this list, Genovevo and

Alejandro Cerna join the ejido. Cluff, Johnson, and Wilson are Mormon land-owners living in other colonies. Because Turley was more knowledgeable of the area, he knew about men who lived elsewhere and kept their land in Colonia Pacheco. Cruz Gutierrez and Lopez Quezada also made assumptions about land in Pacheco based on the best information available to them.

The next day, Cruz Gutierrez and Lopez Quezada produce another list. This report, written together with bureaucrat Carlos Matas Provencio, sheds light on individual Mormon landowners. It states that Alma (Julian) Lunt rents out most of the land in Colonia Pacheco; this implies that he is a wealthy farmer who can afford not to work the land himself. It adds that Heber M. Cluff is from Colonia García and thus implies that he may also rent out his and. Two other men with English-sounding surnames, Sixto H. Johnson and Mariano L. Wilson, reside in the US. Cruz Gutierrez, Lopez Quezada, and Mata Provencio state that in 1942, Mariano L. Wilson "vendio [sic] su propiedad a Melvin Turley y se fue a los Estados Unidos, regresando en el año de 1954" ["sold his property to Melvin Turley and went to the United States, returning in 1954"] (Cruz Gutierrez, Lopez Quezada, and Matas Provencio). So, there are fewer Mormon colonizers than Turley suggested, and those who remain own more land than they may like to admit. The ejido leaders then elaborate on Alma LeBaron: "Si es colono, pero no vive en la colonia, sino en la Angostura, cerca de Galeana y tiene rentado su terreno a Rafael Espinoza, Ejidatario de Col. Hernandez" ["Yes he is a colonizer, but he does not live in the colony. Rather, he lives in la Angostura, near Galeana, and rents his land to Rafael Espinoza, who is part of the Colonia Hernandez ejido"] (Cruz Gutierrez, Lopez Quezada and Matas Provencio). There are other complicating factors. Some ejidatarios have enough money to rent additional land, including from these nearby Mormons. Evarista Arreola, for instance, whose name appears on the list from March 27, has apparently never cultivated any land but works as a trucker for Leland K. Martineau. Similarly, Manuel Arras is not a "colono," but had previously been part of the Zaragoza Ejido. In 1956, he was a "vaquero del mormon Adrian Wheet, quien le tiene rentado un potrero muy grande al colono Alma (Julian) Lunt" ["cowboy or cattle man for the Mormon Adrian Wheet [Whetten], who has rented his large cattle ranch to the colonizer Alma (Julian) Lunt"] (Cruz Gutierrez, Lopez Quezada, and Matas Provencio). Genovevo and Alejandro Cerna do not have land titles, and so are part of the ejido petition. Others, like Higinio Cruz, do not have titles to their land, but have lived there for a long time.[6] The shifts between these documents show that the ejido does not have an airtight case. Rather, the people in the ejido have been affected by poverty and landlessness and worked for other men, or migrated to the US to seek work. The comparatively wealthy Mormons have shifted into their Mexican roles and have taken advantage of the situation by buying or renting large sections of land. The bureaucrat Matas Provencio summarizes the situation and ignores the ejidatarios' tensions and economic difficulties:

> La realidad, es, que en la Colonia Pacheco, existen actualmente 22 (venti dos) colonos, de los cuales 9 son extranjeros (americanos) pertenecientes a la Secta Mormona y el resto o sea 13, son mexicanos, dos de los cuales, a pesar de estar cultivando terrenos de la Colonia, figuran en el grupo solicitante de la misma [ejido].

> [The reality is that in Colonia Pacheco there are currently 22 (twenty-two) colonizers, of which 9 are foreign (American) belonging to the Mormon Sect. The rest, or 13, are Mexican, two of whom, in spite of cultivating land belonging to the Colony, are part of the group applying for the same [ejido].] (Matas Provencio 10)[7]

In this logic, Mexicans are applying to create an ejido that will redistribute land owned by people with an unusual religion who are from the US. This shows significant suspicion of the Mormons, and the belief that they should never have been allowed to purchase the land. It follows that this situation could be rectified by allowing people who are already living and farming the land to hold title to it.

COLONIA DUBLÁN, COLONIA JUÁREZ, AND THE CASAS GRANDES EJIDO

This sense of the primarily indigenous ejido's superior morality and the Mormons' foreignness is exacerbated in the case of the Casas Grandes ejido.[8] Each stage of this conflict emphasizes that the Mormons are American, not Mexican. The Casas Grandes ejido began in 1778, when a *caballero* [knight or cavalier] called Teodor de Croix recognized that a group of people cultivated the land: "He resuelto y así lo declare, se creen y funden cinco poblaciones en los parajes siguientes . . ." [It is resolved that five villages be created in the following locations]. One of them was in eight leagues in every direction from a church near what is today Casas Grandes (Osuna Reyes 1). The Spanish Crown validated this declaration in 1782, recognizing actions on the American continent. The declaration then moved through various levels of Spanish colonial government to become law. This land possession was reapproved by the Mexican government in 1889, well after Mexico became independent from Spain in 1810 and implemented new laws upon becoming an officially secular country in 1857.

The Mormons took advantage of this gap and purchased land in 1883, and began to establish colonies in 1885. A wealthy landowner of the Hacienda may also have seen the writing on the wall and decided that he could make it someone else's problem by selling it. Then, in 1893, the Mormons reached a special legal agreement with the government that allowed them to create colonies in the north. The ejido offers its interpretation of these events in 1980. The ejido's lawyer, Héctor Manuel Osuna Reyes, wrote a letter to the Director of Landholding in Mexico, Lic. Gonzalo Gómez Flores. Osuna Reyes claimed that three men had sold the land in the Casas Grandes area to the Mormons. In 1882, "Ignacio Gómez del Campo, Luis Garcia Tenuel y Ramón Guerrero, [dieron] concesiones éstas que aparentemente dieron origen a las Colonias Juárez y Dublán, que en la actualidad [están] fincadas dentro de los linderos del propio Ejido ..." ["Ignacio Gómez del Campo, Luis Garcia Tenuel and Ramón Guerrero [gave] concessions which were those that apparently gave rise to the Juárez and Dublán colonies, which are today within the borders of the Ejido ..."] (Osuna Reyes). In his view, these men had no right to sell it even though the presidential decree confirming the ejido's right to the land would only come about seven years later.

This in-between period was particularly contentious. In 1963, the *Cuerpo Consultivo Agrario* commissioned Francisco Mariscal Moreno, from the *Departamento de Asuntos Agrarios y Colonización* [Department of Agrarian and Colonization Matters], to decide whether the Mormons had bought the land illegally. He reports that:

La COLONIA DUBLAN y a la COLONIA JUAREZ, establecidas desde 1893 ... las cuales están en su mayoría en poder de los mormones establecidos en esa zona ... la Compañía [de colonización] quedó autorizada para establecer Colonias agrícolas, ganaderas e industriales, en terrenos de propiedad nacional. ...

[The DUBLAN COLONY and the JUAREZ COLONY, established since 1893 ... are, for the most part, in the hands of the Mormons who have established themselves in this zone ... The [Colonization] Company has been authorized to establish agrarian, ranching and industrial Colonies, in territory that is national property] (Mariscal Moreno, Memorandum to the Delegate, 2).

Mariscal Moreno claims that the Mormons have controlled the land since 1893, when they signed an agreement with the government on what should have remained national property. This subsumes ejidos into the nation, ignores their interests, and pits the Mormons against national interest.

This tension between the Mormons, the ejido, and the nation grew in subsequent years. In 1921, the population of the Casas Grandes ejido asks for their land to be restored to them. The *Diario Oficial* confirmed the positive resolution in 1927. The ejido claims that about 6,000 people have been living on these eight-by-eight leagues since time immemorial and it establishes the validity of the 1778 declaration by Teodoro de Croix ("Secretaría de Agricultura y Fomento" 1). The claim returns to Croix's language and defines the boundaries of the ejido with the church at the center and eight leagues in each direction from the church. This would, it acknowledges, mean that some landowners who do not have title to their land would lose their land ("Secretaría de Agricultura y Fomento" 6). This land agreement would also impact:

pretendidos derechos de extraños; y nuestras leyes constitucionales en vigor no han hecho más que reconocer los principios de equidad y justicia social que aquellas leyes consagraran en beneficio de los indígenas ... no puede producir prescripción que invalide los derechos de este mismo pueblo. . . .

["purported rights of foreigners; our current constitutional laws have not done more than recognize the rights for equality and social justice that these laws consecrate for the benefit of indigenous people. . . . cannot produce any prescription that would invalidate the rights of these people" ("Secretaría de Agricultura y Fomento" 7).

The petition thus highlights the role of indigenous people in Mexico and emphasizes that the Constitution should protect them rather than foreigners. It also, curiously, upholds colonial laws.

MURDER IN DUBLÁN: MORMONS KILLING OFF OPPONENTS IN THE 1930S

Documents from various parts of the federal government suggest, on a rhetorical level, that opposition between the Mormons, the indigenous ejidatarios and the nation. Nevertheless, the federal government remained largely uninterested in events in remote parts of the state of Chihuahua and it was content with the balance of power in that region. One strange case, the unsolved murder of an otherwise unremarkable man, Victorio Ponce, in Nuevo Casas Grandes, Chihuahua, in 1935, eight years after the ejido was restored, illustrate some of these tensions. He was involved in the ejido but never wrote letters or acted as a leader for local ejido or campesino organizations. Victorio Ponce was perhaps related to some prominent members of the Ponce family in Nuevo Casas Grandes, who were very involved in the Revolution, and, consequently, in actions against the Mormons (Morgan 230). Joseph Barnard Romney's account of the Mormons during the Mexican Revolution also mentions members of a Ponce family who had asked the Mormons for assistance, which the Mormons did not provide (34–35).

Campesinos were upset that Ponce's murder was unsolved. Leaders of several ejido and affiliated organizations decided to complain. They wrote letters to then-president Cárdenas because they believed that he could help them; after all, Cárdenas' administration had begun agrarian reform efforts in earnest. The letters aimed to provoke the president, as they strongly implied that influential Mormons were responsible for Ponce's murder. Mexico's reputation for impunity is long-standing, and it is very common that cases are not prosecuted. It is less common, however, for people to complain to the president about these oversights. Two leaders from the *Liga Campesina* [Campesino League], Pedro Acosta Chavez and Porfirio Rivas, even argued that Mormon power in the region was so great that it rendered local authorities useless. In other words, they find a convenient scapegoat in a group that is different from the surroundings and they effectively use anti-US rhetoric. In spite of these efforts, the authorities in Mexico City do not appear to have responded and so the campesinos in the north were dissatisfied. As a result, people kept sending letters, many of which allude to Mormon involvement. No letter, however, explains why the campesinos were suspicious of the Mormons. A week later, on April 25, Manuel Corres, then the federal work inspector in Colonia Dublán, wrote a letter to the President.[9] He echoed Acosta Chavez and Rivas and implores the president to intervene. Corres similarly encourages federal authorities to act against this murder: "de la manera más vhemente [sic] ruego a usted [Sr. Presidente que] se digne ordenar se investigue el asesinato que según presunciones de todo el pueblo lo asesinaron un individual llamado [Pablo] Vega y un Mormón que es minustro [sic] del culto y se apellida Brown" ["in the most vehement manner (Mr. President) I implore you that you might investigate the assassination that, according to the village's suspicions, was committed by an individual named Pablo Vega and a Mormon minister whose surname is Brown"] (Corres).[10] Corres offers more details: "Debo decir a esa digna autoridad que estos individuos no es la primera víctima [que hacen], y por eso queremos que se haga justicia" ["I must tell this dignified authority that these individuals this is not their first victim, and for this reason we want justice to be served"] (Corres). In Corres' view, Mormon leadership has developed sufficient influence to commit murder with impunity. This letter does not go into detail and so I conclude that was based on resentment to the ejido conflict that found Mormons a convenient scapegoat.

The federal government eventually responds. On May 18, 1935, Francisco Ramírez Villarreal, the undersecretary of state, writes a letter to the governor of the State of Chihuahua.[11] He summarized the previous telegram as a: "denuncia ante el C. Presidente de la República el asesinato de Victorio Ponce, ocurrido en la Colonia Dublán, según dice por elementos mormones" ["report to the President of the Republic regarding the murder of Victorio Ponce, which occurred in Colonia Dublán, which people say was committed by Mormon elements"] (Ramírez Villarreal 18 May). He does not reproduce the names of either accused assailant but he still sheds negative light on Mormons. An unsigned letter dated two days later repeats much of the same information: "De la Colonia Dublán, de ese Estado, se recibió en la Presidencia de la República un escrito en el que se denuncia el asesinato de Victorio Ponce, según se afirma, por elementos mormones" ["From Colonia Dublán, in this State, the President of the Republic has received a written account that reports on the murder of Victorio Ponce, which affirms that it was committed by Mormon elements"] (Ramírez Villareal 20 May). He wants to remove himself from the situation and give it to the governor, so that the governor might pursue action. Ultimately, no Mormon was officially implicated and the matter was unresolved or resolved in an unofficial manner.

Some parts of the federal government did not care much about campesino problems in the North, and sought to preserve the status quo rather than investigate whether, how, or by whom Victorio Ponce had been murdered.

1950S: LAND IS INELIGIBLE FOR SALE

Two decades later, the Casas Grandes ejido cultivates most of the land from the 1927 restitution agreement. They are not, however, cultivating land owned by the Mormons. So, they petition for a complete restoration of land. The Mormons also lobby the state and federal governments. In 1950, the federal government gave the Mormons five certificates of *inafectabilidad ganadera* [ineligibility for agrarian reform due to cattle ranching]: "La concesión de inafectabilidad ganadera es . . . la sustracción de unas tierras a la afectabilidad agraria y no el cercenamiento de la facultad de venderlas que tenga el dueño de ellas con base en su derecho de propiedad" ["The concession for ineligibility for agrarian reform for cattle ranching is . . . subtracting some land from land that is eligible for agrarian reform, and not the curtailment of the owner's ability to sell his land, which he would have based on private property rights"] (Villalón Valencia). These certificates mean that land cannot be redistributed through agrarian reform.

The Mexican government agency gave certificates to Charles Whetten, Roy J. Adams, Claudius Bowman, Irvin B. and Gordon M. Romney, and Samuel J. Robinson on March 28, 1959, and they, like the reports on the murder of Víctor Ponce, show a strong bias in favor of the Mormons. The first section of each agreement, or "resolutions," state the man's name and background. In Whetten's case, he is a Mexican national and he showed his land title in the Agrarian Department ("Acuerdo sobre inafectabilidad . . . El Alamito" 4). The *Diario Oficial* adds that the land does not relate to the Casas Grandes ejido petition for expansion. This is because:

> el repetido predio no fué afectado al restituirse a dicho poblado su ejido, por lo que estimó que está libre de afectaciones agrarias, además de que el citado núcleo de población tiene satisfechas sus necesidades a ese respecto, con las tierras de su ejido; que en el caso, la finca constituye una pequeña propiedad ganadera cuya capacidad forrajera está totalmente cubierta.

[The property in question was not part of what was to be restored to the people of the ejido, so it is considered to be free from agrarian redistribution; in addition, the aforementioned population group has had its needs met in this regard, with its land already; and so in this case, the *finca* constitutes a small property for ranching whose capacity for cattle fodder has been totally covered.] ("Acuerdo sobre inafectabilidad . . . El Alamito" 4)

The declaration continues, stating that the land owned by Charles Whetten cannot be redistributed through agrarian reform, either to expand an ejido, or to create a new one ("Acuerdo sobre inafectabilidad . . . El Alamito" 4). In response, the beneficiary of this certificate will be required to increase his cattle herd, improve pastures and water supply. Bowman's elaborates on the ejido conflict: "La Delegación Agraria correspondiente manifestó en su informe de 13 de noviembre de 1947, en relación con . . . el trámite [del] expediente de ampliación de ejidos del poblado Casas Grandes . . . ambos expedientes deben resolverse en forma simultánea" ["The Agrarian Delegation that has dealt with this matter stated in its report from November 13, 1947 that the Casas Grandes ejido' expansion petition, which is currently in process . . . should be resolved simultaneously [with the ineligibility certificate]"] ("Acuerdo . . . Claudius Bowman" 6). The other certificates point to similar tendencies. The Mormons are being given special treatment because they can bring money into the region even though this is directly against the constitutional mandate to protect indigenous people, the mandate to protect land as a national good, and the 1927 restitution agreement with the Casas Grandes ejido.

TENSION BETWEEN PROGRESS AND RIGHTS IN THE 1960S

The ejido makes further petitions in the 1960s. We observe rising tension between the ejido's legal right to the land and the Mormons' technical skill in farming. The first report from this time period highlights the Mormons' legal purchase and contribution to progress. In 1961, Mariscal Moreno, then an engineer in the Secretary of Agrarian Reform, writes a report on the Mormons. He states that they began farming in 1893; and that by the mid-twentieth-century, they used the land for agriculture and farming (Mariscal Moreno "Memorandum sobre la Restitución" 2). Mariscal Moreno explains that the Mormons, who received the certificates in the 1950s, acquired this contested land. He states that each acquired his land through legal means (Mariscal Moreno "Memorandum sobre la Restitución" 4–5). In addition to these purchases, Mariscal Moreno observes that the: "hectáreas en poder de mormones ... están dedicadas exclusivamente a la producción agrícola y ganadera y en particular a la explotación frutícola de manzana, ciruelo, durazno, etc., y últimamente en agricultura a la producción algodonera" ["hectares owned by Mormons ... are dedicated exclusively to agricultural production and cattle ranching and in particular to growing apples, plums, peaches, etc., and most recently to producing cotton"] (Mariscal Moreno "Memorandum sobre la Restitución" 5). Thus, in this bureaucrat's view, the Mormons used the appropriate channels to foster a level of economic productivity that had contributed to the region. He concludes his report by stating that the Mormons are always seeking to better their communities, lauding them for their economic contribution and legal sale.

Other reports also favor Mormons. In 1964, engineer Luis G. Alcerreca reports to the *Cuerpo Consultivo Agrario*. He observes that the land the ejido seeks will not be granted to them. In his view, "Como se ve por el documento anterior, la aclaración no puede ser más precisa, pues se define que ... hectáreas pertenecían entonces a diversos dueños, colonias, cauces de ríos, zonas de protección del ferrocarril, zona urbana y otros ejidos ... no fueron material de la restitución" ["As can be seen in the previous document, the clarification could not be more precise, because it is defined by ... hectares which at that time belonged to various owners, colonies, river channels, railway zones, urban zones, and other ejidos ... which were not part of the restitution" (Alcerreca 13 June 1964, 17). He argues that various productive zones, such as the railway, and water supply, were not to be restored to the ejido. By extension, the *Cuerpo Consultivo Agrario* should not move to restore the land—occupied by Mormons—to the ejido.

The *Cuerpo Consultivo Agrario*'s decision-making body responds in an undated report. It states that:

el ejido que nos ocupa, siempre ha estado invadido, parcialmente hasta 1927, por haciendas o compañías que se han dedicado a la explotación ganadera en su mayor parte, pertenecientes la mayoría de estas a personas extranjeras venidas del país del Norte, Estados Unidos de Norte América; otras grandes superficies también son explotadas y poseídas ilegalmente por individuaos de la misma nacionalidad, quienes también les dedican a la ganadería . . .

[The ejido in question has always been invaded, at least partially, since 1927, by haciendas or companies who have dedicated themselves to cattle ranching; the majority of these people are foreigners who come from the North, the United States of North America; other large areas of land are also exploited and owned illegally by individuals of the same nationality, who are also dedicated to ranching]. (Cuerpo Consultivo Agrario 2–3)

The report alludes to the Mormons in its discussion of North American citizens. It equates them to the landowners who had long exploited farm laborers in the region. The report also implies that the Mormons are less deserving of living on this land. It states that the colonies were originally sold to North American citizens or their children, who were also Mormon. They have built their colonies "en terrenos despojados al ejido como consecuencia de esas nulas e ilegales escrituras de compraventa . . ." ["on land that was stripped away from the ejido as a consequence of illegal land sales, which should be rendered null"] (Cuerpo Consultivo Agrario 35–36). In the report's view, then, the colony is foreign; even though, by the 1960s, the majority of the people who live in the colony would have been eligible for Mexican citizenship by birth or naturalization (Cuerpo Consultivo Agrario 12). They should not be allowed to live there.

The sense that these Mormons are foreign, in terms of their un-Mexican religion and US nationality, increases the sense that the ejido has been wronged. The report adds:

el ejido de referencia hasta la actualidad no disfruta de la total superficie que le corresponde por encontrarse nuevamente invadido, invasiones que han sido sostenidas como consecuencia de una serie de interpretaciones que se han vertido . . . tanto por la Dirección Jurídica de este Departamento como por diversos funcionarios que nos precedieron en la Consultoría a mi cargo.

[the ejido in question has not been able to use the entire area that corresponds to it, as it finds itself newly invaded, invasions that have been sustained as a consequence of a series of (legal) interpretations that have come from the Judicial Directors of this Department as well as various bureaucrats who preceded me in the Decision-Making body, of which I am in charge.] (Cuerpo Consultivo Agrario 10)

These invasions are blamed on previous legal interpretations by the decision-making body that granted certificates of ineligibility.

The report sides with the ejido and is highly skeptical of the Mormons. It states that the certificates that render some land ineligible for redistribution, "violando flagrantemente los derechos de los ejidatarios" ["flagrantly violating the ejidatarios' rights"] (Cuerpo Consultivo Agrario 15). Later, it states that these certificates should all be considered invalid (Cuerpo Consultivo Agrario 36). The report also criticizes Luis G. Alcérreca: "dicho funcionario, sin hacer el análisis ni el estudio jurídico sobre la situación que guardan los terrenos que tienen las Colonias Mormonas Dublán y Juárez, que pertenecen legalmente al ejido de Casas Grandes" ["this bureaucrat, without having done the necessary analysis about the Mormon Colonies Dublán and Juárez and their judicial situation, which belong legally to the Casas Grandes ejido"], made a decision in favor of the Mormon Colonies (Cuerpo Consultivo Agrario 26). The land titles, as well as the later certificates, then, are illegal, and mean that the Mormons are invaders; yet, the Mormons are helping the area "progress." Part of this progress could have been made by unofficially paying the aforementioned bureaucrat.

EXPANSION COMMITTEE IN THE 1970S

Actions in the 1970s increase in light of the reports from the 1960s. They continue to focus on the fact that the Mormon invaders are from the US, and discount events, such as land sales, which had taken place during the Porfirian period. In the 1970s, a committee within the ejido begins petitioning for land. Their correspondence shows that they believe their land has been invaded, and that if the federal leaders would uphold colonial laws, they would agree with the ejido. On February 15, 1970, the leaders of the ejido's expansion committee, David and Fausto Flores Vizcarra write a letter to then-president Gustavo Díaz Ordaz (1964–70). They tell the president that their land has been illegally invaded. A year later, Samuel Valenzuela, from the Comité Pro-Tierras La Laguna, the ejido's expansion committee, sends a two-page memo to Augusto Gómez Villanueva, the head of the Department of Agrarian Matters and Colonization. Valenzuela reiterates that any agreement made under the government General Porfirio Díaz is illegal (Valenzuela 2). This would include the agreement with the Mormons in 1893. At the same time, the colonial law remains valid. The government does not respond.

In light of this faulty communication, on October 10, 1972, José de la Luz Rodríguez writes a letter to the Director of Land and Water, in the Department of Agrarian Matters and Colonization.[12] He explains that:

> Somos 35 Jefes de familia que estamos solicitando una pequeña superficie que colinda con el Fundo Legal del poblado de N. Casas Grandes, Chih. Para establecer en el [sic], la pequeña Granja Familiar ... estamos solicitando únicamente cien hectáreas del Predio que detenta Don. Martin Jeffers a nombre de un señor que solo lo conocemos de apellido 'Zamora' desconocido por completo para nosotros. ...

> [We are 35 Heads of household and we are asking for a small area that borders on the Legal Edge of Nuevo Casas Grandes, Chihuahua. In order to establish in it a small Family Farm. ... We are only asking for one hundred hectares of property that Mr. Martin Jeffers is holding for someone who we do not know except that his surname is "Zamora."] (J. Rodríguez 1)

They would like to farm land that is owned by someone who shares a surname with the head of the expansion committee, and they are no longer petitioning for restitution. José de la Luz Rodríguez continues:

> Es completamente necesario que este Depto. de Asuntos Agrarios y Colonizacion [sic] nombre una Comisión para que se haga una investigación exhaustiva de régimen de la propiedad en lo que respecta a las tierras Ejidales que están totalmente invadidas por Mormones y Mexicanos que han obtenido dentro de la superficie Ejidal propiedades en forma por dem_as [sic] sospechosa.

> [It is completely necessary that this Dept. of Agrarian Matters and Colonization name a Commission to conduct an exhaustive investigation of the chain of property ownership because the Ejido's lands are totally invaded by Mormons and Mexicans who have obtained property in the ejido in suspicious ways.] (1)

Rodríguez trusts the department and believes that it can uncover how the invaders had acquired the land. He is also exasperated, because, as he notes, the department has already wasted ten or twelve years on paperwork (J. Rodríguez 1). The letter highlights the inefficiency within the department and alludes to its corruption. His direct tone implies a lack of political skill and his failure to use bureaucratic languages suggests that he was written the letter himself.

One year later, the ejido and another peasant group tried to negotiate directly with the president. José Álvarez Zapata, the ejido's leader, and José Parra Barajas, the National Representative for the *Central Campesina Independiente* [Independent Peasant Organization] (CCI), write a letter to president Echeverría in December 1971.[13] They remind the president of the order to create the ejido. Álvarez Zapata and Parra Barajas state: "porque una resolución presidencial en ningun [sic] tiempo puede ser atropellada ni menos cabada [sic] mucho menos con extranjeros que son los que esta n [sic] invadiendo las tierras, pedimos a usted Señor Presidente su valiosa intervención" ["because a presidential decree cannot be stalled or ended, much less if it pertains to foreigners, who are those who are invading the land, [so] we ask you Mr. President for your intervention"] (Álvarez Zapata and Parra Barajas). They echo earlier documents by stating that foreigners have no right to have invaded this land. They also emphasize that the president could intervene. Little changed in the ejido and the Mormon colony in spite of these letters.

BUREAUCRATIC INACTION, 1979–81

The next series of actions take place under the Mexican president, José López Portillo (1976–82) and refer to similar historical events. The Mormon identity of the invaders fade further into the background, but the question of invasion remains ongoing.

In January 1980, a representative from the expansion committee, Velia Muñoz Salcido, writes a letter to the Minister for Agrarian Reform, Antonio Toledo Corro. Muñoz Salcido, the first woman's name in this slew of reports, has inherited Samuel Valenzuela and the Flores Vizcaino brothers' work. She states that there are "cinco-certificados dentro de este Ejido que ocupan norte-americanos invasores, y alcanzan una superficie de 53, 359 -00–00 Has.

Sin faltar uno que otro malinchista mexicano" ["five certificates in this Ejido occupied by North-American invaders, which reach an area of 53,359 hectares. Not to mention a few Mexican race-traitors"]. She is more pointed than other letters as she interprets the five certificates:

> Desde lainicacion [sic] de este grupo, el certificado de Samuel J. Robinson, es en el que estamos pidiendo ACOMODO. Al fallecer Samuel J. Robinson, la hoy Vda. de Robinson traspaso a los Hnos. Jones y estos Señores están fraccionando el terreno . . .

> [since the group has begun, the certificate for Samuel J. Robinson is the one we would like ADJUSTED. When Samuel J. Robinson died, the widowed Mrs. Robinson sold her land to the Jones Brothers and these men are dividing up the land . . .]. (Muñoz Salcido)

In Muñoz Salcido's view this group of Mormons has been causing problems since it arrived in Mexico and she seeks action to restore the eighteenth-century. She begins this attempt to press uninterested bureaucrats into communication after Robinson's death because it was likely easier to pursue action against a widow. It yielded few results and these petitions and resulting bureaucratic inaction.

2012–14: THE CASAS GRANDES EJIDO'S MORAL WEIGHT AND LEGAL PRECEDENT

In recent years the ejido has created a website. It presents itself as a peaceful, legal, and generous landowner. The home page greets us with the green words "Ejido Casas Grandes" on a slightly darker green background. Underneath the words of welcome are three images: a cow, a sheep, and a farmer.[14] The website's first section gives the history of the ejido and highlights the ejido's generosity and moral right to the land.[15] Other sections, "Documents from the Casas Grandes Ejido," and "Documents Related to the Casas Grandes Ejido," include moments when the ejido has allowed some land to be expropriated for municipal needs and has donated some land to the Universidad Autónoma Ciudad Juárez.

The section called "History of the Casas Grandes Ejido" cements the ejido as the land's moral and legal landowner. It states that the ejido was founded in 1778, like the Janos, Galeana, Namiquipa, and Cruces ejidos. It has been:

"sujeto continuamente a invasiones y pretensiones de privatizar sus tierras. Desde esos años, se han decretado diferentes leyes de desamortización que han pretendido privatizar la tierra social" [subject to continual invasions and attempts to privatize its land."] ("Historia del Ejido Casas Grandes"). The Casas Grandes ejido is not unique. This section then adds that the ejido is part of the historical events that led up to the Revolution, when a governor of Chihuahua in the early twentieth century deprived the ejidos of their land. In the website's view, this was the straw that broke the camel's back ("Historia del Ejido Casas Grandes"). Consequently, the ejidatarios are the true heirs of the Revolution, and thus have further moral rights to their land. This rhetorically offers the rights to their land. The website's final section, the "Últimos Acontecimientos en el Ejido Casas Grandes," ["Recent Events in the Casas Grandes Ejido"] adds to this moral weight. It states that the ejido's lawyer, and fellow ejidatario, Noé García Enríquez, was kidnapped on January 22 [2014] and that they will not negotiate further until he has returned ("Últimos Acontecimientos").

There has now been almost a century of action in this case. Several facts stand out. First, that Mexico, an independent country, sometimes upholds colonial laws. Even though its system of government has changed quite dramatically, Mexico does see value in some parts of the past. Second, that Mormonism is strongly connected to the US in the popular imagination in northern Mexico. Third, that there are negative portrayals of immigrants. The Mormons would like to believe that they are exceptionally talented private property owners. Yet, the belief that Mormons bring economic value to a community overshadows their portrayal as invaders. The presidential declaration, the certificates and later reports and petitions, oscillate between these two ideas. Finally, indigenous rights are important and those rights, especially when constitutionally guaranteed—supersede whatever economic gains can be taken from the land. The ejidatarios also have an important legal and moral right; however, in this case, economics will take precedence.

LEBARON COLONY

The final case that I examine in this chapter is between the Galeana ejido and the LeBaron colony in Galeana, Chihuahua. The documents about this ejido and its conflict emphasize that the Mormons are foreign, and, in many ways, echo the Casas Grandes ejido's case. They also point out that a variety of campesino groups intervened extensively on the ejido's behalf in order to stay what was perceived as a foreign invasion.

This ejido, like the Casas Grandes ejido, was recognized by Teodoro de Croix in 1778. It was to be eight leagues in every direction from the church of San Juan Nepomuceno ("Resolución ... restitución ... Galeana" 1). This land, like in the Casas Grandes ejido, was used by the ejido until the mid-nineteeth-century reform laws. Then the people in the area petitioned to have it returned to them in 1921 and it was approved. This was recognized on a federal level in April 1927. Then, in 1939, the federal SRA granted the ejido more land ("Resolución ... dotación ... Galeana" 10).

The ejido was in conflict with the LeBaron colony. The conflict centered on the family of the man listed as Alma LeBaron in archival documents, called Alma "Dayer" LeBaron in his community.[16] The LeBarons, we might remember, return to Mexico in 1924. They first live in Colonia Juárez, and have an orchard on their land in the Mormon Colonia Pacheco. After they are asked to leave Colonia Juarez, they begin their own farm, and, eventually their own religious group under Alma LeBaron's authority, in the Galeana area. This farm was part of the land Teodoro de Croix had recognized in the late eighteenth century, and that the SRA recognized as part of the Galeana ejido in 1927. By the 1950s, Alma "Dayer" LeBaron still owned some land in Colonia Pacheco but his family established in the Galeana area. Land conflict began around 1970, at the same time as religious struggle within the colony. In March 1970, Luis G. Alcerreca, who had also intervened in the Casas Grandes case, wrote a letter to the General Secretary of Agrarian Matters, Sadot Garces de León. Alcerreca mentions agrarian conflict: the LeBarons are complaining about the destruction of their livestock, wells, and fences. He states that in February he received a letter from three LeBaron leaders, Floren Le-Barón, Gamaliel Ríos M., and José Butchereit [Butchreit]. Alcerreca explains that the Mormons Le-Barón, Ríos, and Butchereit accused the Ejido Commission of having:

> destruido sus alambradas, lo que ha dado lugar a que el ganado entre a sus parcelas destruyendo sus sembradíos. Que así mismo se les niega el uso de los agostaderos a quienes tienen derecho, por lo que piden las garantías necesarias.

> [destroyed their fences. In this way, cattle have come into their fields, which has destroyed their crops. In the same way, those who have the

right to land for cattle grazing have been denied its use, so they ask for the necessary guarantees.] (Alcerreca 2 Mar. 1970)

These men complained that the Ejido Commission had destroyed their property but the ejido may not have seen the land as the LeBarons had. Alcerreca is sympathetic to the LeBarons' needs.

Later, an undated letter from the "Vieja guardia agrarista de Chihuahua Ing. Víctor Manuel Bueno G." ["Old Agrarian Guard from Chihuahua, named after Engineer Víctor Manuel Bueno G."] to Lic. Javier García Paniagua" confirms this.[17] It implies that the government is helping these non-Mexicans stay on ejido land. It also shows us that not everyone agrees with ejido leadership—regardless of whether it has been destroying fences. The *Vieja Guardia* is very disturbed because it sees corruption in the ejido and perceives that the government is favoring the LeBarons. It appeals to bureaucrats to try and resolve the situation. It explains that in its view, "El comisario ejidal . . . ha constituido en cacique de la región" ["The Ejido leader . . . has become a cacique in the region"] (Bueno G.). In other words, he has become like a traditional leader, PRI party member, or a typical bureaucrat. This also suggests that there is internal conflict in the Galeana ejido, and its members appeal to various bureaucrats as they seek resolution. The *Vieja Guardia* explains that it sees that the ejido commission has come to "favorecer a un grupo de MORMONES EXTRANJEROS de la Colonia 'LEVARON' enclavada dentro del ejido" ["favor a group of FOREIGN MORMONS from the 'LEVARON' colony (which was occupying land) inside of the ejido limits"] (Bueno G.) The *Vieja Guardia* adds that:

desde hace años les ha venido ampliando con exceso sus posesiones en terrenos de riego de dicho Ejido y les sigue concediendo más tierras, ahora en la porción de terrenos de los hijos de ejidatarios del lugar y vecinos, tienen elegido para su acomodo; todo para obstaculizar el acomodo de los solicitantes, que tienen mejores derechos para que se les conceda terrenos ejidales.

[for many years they have increased the amount of land that they owned that does not need to be irrigated. (This is the land) they own within the Ejido, and they continue to be conceded more land. Now, they can choose what they want from the children of ejidatarios and its neighbors; this is all to make things difficult for the applicants (from the ejido), who have more rights to live on ejido land] (Bueno G.)

It is unclear whether the LeBarons held a legitimate title to the land; the *Vieja Guardia* certainly believes the land sale and continued occupation were illegal.

The letters were somewhat effective. In 1980, Donaciano Martínez García and Antonio García Ramos, from the Northern Rural Credit Bank, wrote to Mauricio Moreno at the *Secretaría de la Reforma Agraria*. They refer to 1978 actions and their letter describes a *Sociedad Colectiva Ganadera* [livestock cooperative] the LeBaron colony owned. Martínez García and García Ramos, the cooperative's creditors, inform the cooperative's members that Alma LeBaron Melchor has dissolved the cooperative that he had held with Eusebio Moncada Ponce and Leopoldo Almerás Delgado. Martínez García and García Ramos add that on April 25, 1978, the local judge and notary Gilberto Zúñiga Flores had listed the cooperative for sale. The LeBarons thus lessened their territorial claim by selling their livestock and preparing for agrarian action; yet no letter addressed ejido corruption.

A final letter, from Víctor Manuel Serrano Palomino to Efrén González Mendoza on May 22, 1980, reiterates that the bureaucrats did not care about the ejido. Serrano Palomino, a state representative for the *Secretaría de Desarrollo Agrario, Territorial y Urbano* [Secretary of Agrarian Development, Land and Urban Development]. He explains why the ejidatarios seek expansion. He states that there is some land supposedly owned by Joel LeBaron and his brothers: "propiedades que les que en caso dado, de no comprobarse por su propietarios que se encuentran fuera de los terrenos del ejido también serían aprovechables como terreno susceptible de cultivo debido a su excelente calidad" ["properties in this case, cannot be proven to be outside of the ejido land claims, and they (these properties) should be cultivated because they are of excellent quality"] (Serrano Palomino 5). The LeBarons, then, have only a tentative claim on their excellent land.

The LeBarons have had a conflict with the ejido for several decades, and they have some claim to the land based on a legal but not moral ownership. Several letters are also that allude to their relative wealth, which contrast echoes the Casas Grandes conflict. Even if the LeBarons had a title to their land and it had been on uncontested territory it is unlikely they were perceived as rightful owners. The ejidatarios and the LeBarons were pawns in a broader corrupt bureaucracy. The state does not kill anyone. But, its negligence allows the LeBarons to buy land even though it had already been granted on a state level to the ejido. This leads to the bureaucrats that take the LeBarons' side. The ejido leader, also recognized in Mexican law, and likely tied to the ruling party, is also said to be corrupt. This is further violence on the ejido. The LeBarons buy land questionably in the 1920s, which is state-sanctioned violence. They make a very small concession in the 1980s. The ejidatarios, for their part, abandon the ejido in large numbers. Those who remain, or the dwindling numbers, are said to destroy LeBaron property. This is a violence that is clearly the last recourse of the desperate. They form their own independent organizations to advocate for themselves when official channels fail, and reach a very modest success with the LeBarons dissolving a livestock cooperative. More recently, cartels have kidnapped and killed some members of the LeBaron colony, and another LeBaron has become an important member of the PRI on a federal level.

Correspondence from these three cases shows that bureaucrats and ejidatarios viewed LDS Mormons and the LeBaron group with suspicion. In the popular imagination, both groups were connected with the United States and thus, with invading Mexico. Indigenous ejidatarios go further and malign Mormons, even going so far as to accuse them of murder. The bureaucrats echo this suspicion, sometimes favoring the ejidos. At other times, they align with the LDS Mormon colonies or with the LeBarons, because the bureaucrats believe that their US roots will bring economic value to the region. Carefully examining archival material and the many gaps or imperfections in the archive illustrates a complex situation that has ongoing ramifications.

3

Mennonites and Agrarian Reform

Can Mennonites be Mexican?

This chapter deals with land conflicts between Mennonites and Mexico's agrarian reform program. In particular, it studies two conflicts in the 1960s and 1970s, including communication from lawyers, bureaucrats, Mennonite leaders, and ejido leaders. I examine two case studies, conflicts between ejidos and Mennonite colonies in the state of Zacatecas. These show us ways that Mennonites have and have not been perceived as belonging to Mexico.

In 1921, Mennonites from Canada bought two large blocks of land in Chihuahua, which totaled 225,000 acres (91,054 hectares).[1] They were aware that Mexican campesinos were already living on this land (Sawatzky *They Sought a Country* 45). For this reason, the Zuloaga family, who sold them part of the Hacienda Bustillos, promised that these people would be removed from the land (Sawatzky *They Sought a Country* 67). These people, however, counting on promises of land made during the Revolution, filed to have this land granted to them through the ejido program (Will 360). Indeed, according to historian Martina E. Will's "The Mennonite Colonization of Chihuahua: Reflections of Competing Visions," in September 1921 the Governor of Chihuahua, Ignacio Enriquez, had awarded provisional possession of 7,323 hectares of Zuloagas' land to those who had made the petition (Will 360).

The Zuloaga family and the Chihuahuan government attempted to resolve the situation. The Zuloagas offered other land; however, the campesinos, who had already established themselves and their lives in that area, did not want to move (Will 360). By 1923, as more Mennonites from Canada came and began to occupy more of the land, tensions increased. Sawatzky says there were "angry confrontations," and that free-ranging Mexican cattle repeatedly destroyed Mennonite crops; and that when the Mennonites built a stout fence in the area to keep these animals out, it was cut time and again (*They Sought a Country* 68). In June 1923, the governor of Chihuahua expropriated 7,344 hectares, including 5,000 from land the Mennonites had bought but not yet occupied (Will 361). The Zuloagas absorbed the loss by subtracting the value of that land from the amount that the Mennonites still owed to them (Sawatzky *They Sought a Country* 69n2). Then, in the fall of 1923, the federal government sent a commission to study the issue. It identified the Zuloaga family and the campesinos forming the ejido as the key parties to this conflict. In spite of this report, local officials "looked the other way" (Will 361). This situation led some Mennonites to wire those in Canada who were still planning to come to stay there until the matter was resolved (Will 360). In 1924, the government expropriated more land from the Zuloagas and ordered them to provide money for relocation costs and to build a dam and reservoir so that the new agrarian communities would have water (Will 361; Sawatzky *They Sought a Country* 70). Alongside this initiative, the government sent troops to protect the Mennonites (Will 368).

That response eased conflicts; however, in late 1924, there were rumors that the full set of privileges promised to the Mennonites would be reviewed (Rempel and Rempel 299). This represented a serious crisis for the Mennonites. They asked a local businessman, Walter Schmiedehaus, to go to Mexico City to intercede for them. Schmiedehaus was a well-educated man from Germany who had immigrated to Mexico to start a business, and, for a time, was the German consular representative in Mexico. Upon receiving the Mennonite request, Schmiedehaus went to the capital. Schmiedehaus emphasized that the Mennonites were peaceful, hardworking, and productive people, motivated by their particular faith, that they were innocent victims in this dispute, and that the primary parties to the conflict were the Zuloaga family and the campesinos. He argued that the government should insist that the Zuloagas provide other land for them. In the end, Schmiedehaus received assurances that the land conflict would be resolved and that the privileges given in 1921 by President Obregón would be honored (Rempel and Rempel 299). Schmiedehaus was also told that the new President, Plutarco Elías Calles (1924–28), was interested in visiting Chihuahua and seeing the Mennonite colonies. According to Sawatzky, "by mid-1925 the last of the *agraristas* [campesinos petitioning for ejidos] had left the Mennonite colonies" (70).[2]

In November 1925, Calles visited the Mennonites in Chihuahua. They were harvesting an exceptionally good crop and the President was amazed at "the rapid transformation that the region had undergone" and "pronounced himself greatly impressed with the colonists'... enterprise" (Will 357n8; Sawatzky 130). He also, according to Mennonites, purportedly wished that Mexican *ejidatorios* could come and learn from the Mennonites (Rempel and Rempel 304). Nevertheless, conflict continued. Martina E. Will states: "Throughout the 1930s Mennonites and campesinos registered their complaints with successive officials, and federal troops were again called in to protect Mennonite lives and property rights" (362). Some of this protection may have been needed, because of conflict related to the Mexican Revolution. There was lingering tension, and the Mennonites, their farms, horses, and machinery, were easy targets (Dormady "Mennonite Colonization" 183).

In reflecting on these problems, Mennonites from the Chihuahua area, Gerhard Rempel and Franz Rempel, have observed that neither side understood much about the other. The Mennonites knew little about campesinos and their long struggle for land or about the new legal provisions to make land available for them (Rempel and Rempel 299). The Mennonites were understood as foreigners. Sawatzky adds that:

> The actions of the Mexican country people must be regarded as stemming from dislike not so much of the Mennonites per se as of foreigners generally. They had been peons under the Spanish *hacendados* (hacienda owners) and, more recently, the *mineros* in the foreign-owned mines... near the... Mennonite colonies. (68)

The perception of the Mennonites as foreigners may also have been a factor in the June 1923 decision of the Chihuahua governor, Ignacio Enriquez, to retake the 5,000 hectares of Mennonite land. Will states: "It appears that he was not consulted on the colonization of the Mennonites in his state, and he was ambivalent... in his dealings with them." Will quotes a 1922 newspaper reference to the governor, which stated:

> [S]o long as the lands are not given to the residents of the pueblos, he considers it unjust that preference be given to foreigners... and that Mexicans have to see themselves deprived in their own land of rights which are so easily obtained by citizens of other countries. (362)

This echoes anti-US sentiment we saw in land conflict with Mormons, in spite of the fact that just two years earlier, Álvaro Obregón has spoken of welcoming "all men of capital and enterprise, nationals and foreigners" (Dormady "Mennonite Colonization" 173).

The Mennonites in Chihuahua served these governmental objectives for several reasons. Chihuahua was vulnerable to American interests, especially because revolutionary fighting, followed by an influenza epidemic, had decimated the area's population. The state's agricultural production had fallen by three-fourths and the number of cattle by ninety percent (Dormady "Mennonite Colonization" 172). The government wanted to rebuild Chihuahua both for the economy of the country and as a way of reducing the chances of future US incursions (Will 366). The Mennonite colonists contributed to these purposes; by protecting them, the government was able to showcase Mexico as a place where foreigners and their investments were safe (Will 363–67).

Mennonites also settled in Durango, in what was first called the Hague colony and what is now commonly called Nuevo Ideal. It began in the 1920s with 35,000 acres (14,164 hectares of land) (Epp 119).[3] At the same time, other people petitioned to have the land redistributed to them, and the Mennonites protested (Dormady "Mennonite Colonization" 181; Sawatzky *They Sought a Country* 194). In 1936, President Cárdenas ordered them off the land the Mennonites had purchased (Dormady "Mennonite Colonization" 182).

During the 1930s, Mennonites in Chihuahua and Durango were vulnerable to violence, and in response, the government deployed troops to protect the Mennonites. In 1936, the Mennonites in Durango sent a delegation to meet with President Cárdenas. His response, in June 1936 was a request to the governor of Durango stating:

> By virtue of respecting that said colonists constitute an important factor for the economic development of that State and to respect that fact with strict justice, it behooves you, to reprimand the aforementioned crimes with all rigor, and to mete out to the people and patrimony of the colonists the protection to which they have a right. (Dormady "Mennonite Colonization" 183)

The following year, there was more conflict. This is due in part to the Mennonite practice of holding the legal ownership of all their land in the names of only a few colony leaders. This created the appearance that those leaders had huge holdings. In 1937, the mayor of what is now Nuevo Ideal, Durango, advised the Mennonites that the colony's land would be expropriated (Sawatzky *They Sought a Country* 195). A similar situation occurred in 1941 and in 1962 (Sawatzky *They Sought a Country* 196).

In these situations, the Mennonites were seen as not belonging because they were foreigners. Their separate way of life was not always seen as a good fit in Mexico. Landowners, however, were interested in selling their land to the Mennonites rather than having it expropriated and so Mennonite communities were often caught up in existing conflicts. Moreover, the Mennonite economic contribution was recognized as important, and contributed to the government's interventions on their behalf.

MEXICAN SCHOLARS AND JOURNALISTS' IDEAS ABOUT MENNONITES

One of the implicit messages from the land conflicts in the original colonies was that the Mennonites were seen as foreigners and, in some ways, they did not belong. Some Mexican scholars and journalists reiterate this message. In 1948, Martha Chávez Quezada wrote an economics thesis about the Mennonites in Chihuahua for a group of professors at the *Universidad Nacional Autónoma de México* [National Autonomous University of Mexico] (UNAM). She and her professors were interested in Mexico's economic growth and in what the Mennonites had to offer to this projected growth. She noted, among other things, that 96 percent of all the oats produced in Mexico came from the Mennonite colonies, which provided better fodder for cattle and could contribute to a more balanced diet. She added that Mennonite cheese was being marketed all over Mexico and that Mennonites were also supplying slaughter houses in Monterey with hogs for export to the US (Dormady "Mennonite Colonization" 177). Even though she noted these and other economic contributions, Chávez Quezada was critical of the Mennonites for how they related to Mexican society and the nation, stating that the:

> aspecto (de) social . . . esta colonización ha sido un fracaso, sobre todo si se toma en cuenta que el objetivo trazado por los distintos gobiernos . . . fué [sic] el de aumentar la población nacional, tanto en calidad como en cantidad. La experiencia de los menonitas ha tenido esta limitación en cuanto a la asimilación del grupo a la nacionalidad mexicana.

[social aspect (of) . . . this colonization has been a failure, especially if
we take into account that several governments' main goal . . . has been
to increase the national population, both in quality and in quantity. The
Mennonite experience has been limited in terms of the way this group
has been assimilated to the Mexican nation.] (91)

The Mennonites' large families contributed to the population quantity and
the reference to population quality has racial overtones. Chávez Quezada also
felt that the Mennonites treated other Mexicans in a respectful manner but
she believed they should learn Spanish, as well as some geography and history
(Chávez Quezada 91). Following her line of thinking, this would allow for a
more appealing increase in the population.

Eight years later, in 1956, Rodolfo Sotero-Galindo wrote a thesis for his
law degree. He indicated a similar duality of commending the economic
contribution of the Mennonites while raising questions about their role in
Mexican society. Sotero-Galindo drew heavily on the work of Chávez Quezada,
without citing it, and he, too, focused on Mennonites in Chihuahua. Also,
like Chávez Quezada, he wrote for an educated audience in Mexico City. He
discussed the exemptions that had been granted to Mennonites in relation to
military service, schooling, and landholding patterns. Then he asked whether
these exemptions should continue, given the failure of the Mennonites to integrate and that these exemptions contradicted the ideals of the Revolution. He
expressed particular concern about the tendency of the Mennonites to marry
within their sect and race, saying that this goes against the Revolutionary goal
of mestizaje (Sotero-Galindo 70–71). He also pointed to the failure of the
Mennonites to teach the Spanish language in their rudimentary schools (71).
He concluded: "el aspecto social de estas colonias ha sido un fracaso" ["the colonies' social aspect has been a failure"] (Sotero-Galindo 82). Sotero-Galindo,
who likely worked as a lawyer or bureaucrat, believed that the Mennonites
should help Mexico achieve its Revolutionary goals of racial amalgamation
and education.

In subsequent years, some journalists published articles with similar critiques for audiences in Mexico City. H. Leonard Sawatzky claims that these
views were common near the Mennonite colonies as well. He says that when
the Mennonites first came they were seen as, "superiors, culturally and in terms

of economic wealth" (*They Sought a Country* 323). This changed, he argued, with the spread of public education and the modernization of some Mexican farms. As a result, he believed that people resented the Mennonites' special status and privileges. Sawatzky argues that:

> Political activists [in Mexico] . . . eagerly foster and exploit resentment and antagonism against [the Mennonites], stressing the point that they are Canadian or Russian or whatever, *not* Mexican, and making political capital out of the implied injustice and affront to the Mexican people inherent in the existence of the *Privilegium* [the legal exemptions granted to Mennonites]. (*They Sought a Country* 324)

Carlos Denegri would be one. In 1957, he wrote a series of articles called, "29 estados de ánimo" ["29 states of mind"] in the national newspaper *Excelsior*, which referred to 29 different groups in Mexico. The third article deals with the Mennonites' economic power. He called to Ciudad Cuauhtémoc as the "ciudad capital del imperio menonita" ["capital city of the Mennonite empire"] and was incensed that the Mennonites have privileges that other Mexicans do not (Denegri 10). Further, he contrasts the Mennonites with the Rarámauri [Tarahumara] people. In his view, indigenous people should have more rights to the land than the Mennonite settlers. Then he warns, ominously: "desde la alta sierra, millares de ojos indígenas contemplan con aparente indiferencia, pero con el misterio innato de su raza, el inusitado espectáculo de una colonia de extranjeros posesionadas de las antiguas tierras de sus antecedentes" ["from the mountains, thousands of indigenous eyes contemplate, with apparent indifference, but with the innate mystery of their race, the unusual spectacle of a colony of foreigners who possess the ancient lands of their people"] (Denegri 10). He is concerned about the Mennonites' lack of integration, which he perceives as more performative than authentic, and that they are keeping their economic gains for themselves.

In 1965, the national illustrated newspaper, *Nosotros* [*Us*], carried a three-part series of articles that was negative about the Mennonites. This tabloid-style newspaper seems designed to incite strong reactions. The writer, Mario Anguiano Hernández, focuses on the Mennonites in Chihuahua; indeed, he seems unaware of other Mennonite settlements—in Durango, which started in the 1920s, in Tamaulipas, which started in the 1950s, or recent land purchases in Zacatecas. This lack of awareness points out his lack of careful research. In his first installment, Anguiano Hernández reprinted the Mennonite privileges that were given by President Obregón in 1921. He then argued that they contradicted several Revolutionary goals (Anguiano Hernández "La república menonita de Chihuahua" 20–21). In his second installment, he stated that the Mennonites occupied land that was granted to an ejido through agrarian reform and that this contravened the Revolutionary goal of giving land to landless Mexicans enshrined in the constitution (Anguiano Hernández "Las autoridades cómplices" 21). Anguiano Hernández continues in this vein, casting Mennonites as an anti-Revolutionary group:

> El problema menonita es una espina en la marcha de un México con clara visión de su futuro; un contraste abierto con nuestro carácter de pueblo libre y una situación a la que nuestras autoridades—las más altas del país—tendrían que enfrentarse.

> [The Mennonite problem is a thorn in Mexico's path to a better future; it contrasts directly with our character as a free people. It is a situation that our authorities—the highest in the country—will have to confront.] (Anguiano Hernández "Feudalismo menonita" 29)

He was likely angry because he, like other Mexicans, had only recently become aware of the Mennonites' privileges. According to Will, the letter that granted these privileges was not published in the *Diario Oficial de la Federación* [*Mexican Federal Register*] or the *Periódico Oficial del Estado de Chihuahua* [*Official Register of the State of Chihuahua*] "for reasons of public order . . . so as not to awake jealousy in the Mexican campesinos" (Will 357n7). Will adds that the daily papers in Chihuahua had said very little about the Mennonites throughout the 1930s. They stated only that the government had given them permission to settle there, without mentioning any details. Obregón, in an interview in May 1922 with an American journalist, was vague and evasive about the commitments he had made (Will 358).[4]

This shows that the Mennonites were not understood as belonging. Their economic contribution was welcomed but their social stance was critiqued. Some more recent writers, however, have been more accepting. In 1989 the economist, Santiago Fierro Martínez, wrote an article about the Mennonites in Durango that reflects an awareness of both positive and negative aspects of that community. He considers whether it would be possible to apply the Mennonite colony structure to a group of Mexican villages, believing that it would be economical and result in various improvements in the lives of many rural Mexicans. However, he doubts that it could be so applied because, he says, so much of the success of the Mennonites is due to their rigorous religious system (Fierro Martínez 65). Fierro Martínez argues that the Mennonite way of life is in fact fulfilling Revolutionary goals because of their particular social structure, not in spite of it (66). This then enables him to conclude that the Mennonites do belong to Mexico.[5]

In 2006, Liliana Salomán Meraz echoed this perspective in her short book, *Historia de los menonitas radicados en Durango* [*A History of Mennonites in Durango*]. She wrote for a popular but educated audience and her book was published thanks to the support of several cultural programs in Durango. Based on interviews, archival research, and personal experience, her book sold well in grocery stores in Nuevo Ideal, the town closest to the colony, as well as in stores in the colony itself. She captures both the beauty and the hardship of the Mennonite people and takes it upon herself to challenge false statements, such as the belief that Mennonites are happy when people die (Salomán Meraz 93). She notes that the community has problems, such as alcoholism, and explains how the community strives to deal with them (Salomán Meraz 98). Her balanced approach is rare; it does not oscillate between fascination and rejection. It shows that the Mennonites have some unusual ways but it accepts them as fellow human beings and as belonging to Mexico.

LAND CONFLICTS IN ZACATECAS

Land conflicts later in the twentieth century develop in the context of these perceptions. Communications between bureaucrats, lawyers, and Mennonite and ejido leaders reveal various perceptions of the Mennonites. Peter T. Bergen's commemorative books of these colonies, *La Honda: 50 Jahre* [*La Honda: 50 Years*] was published in 2014; and *La Batea: 55 Jahre* [*La Batea: 55 Years*], in 2017. These German books are primarily meant for Mennonites, and they consist mainly of pictures and brief historical accounts based on interviews with colony residents.

La Batea

People from Durango needed more land, and so they began looking for large blocks that they could purchase. Colony leader Isaac Bueckert went to Zacatecas to see La Batea land and to talk to its owner, Angel Mier. Bueckert also wanted to inquire with the Agrarian Reform office about any claims, or plans, for this land. Mier did not want him to do that, and so Bueckert had backed away from the venture completely (Bergen *La Batea* 3, 5, 6). Sometime later, a different leader from Durango, Diedrich Braun, took up the matter and proceeded to make the purchase. H. Leonard Sawatzky says that the owner, Angel Mier, "was anxious to sell" because he feared his land might be expropriated for an ejido (Sawatzky *They Sought a Country* 182n36). Sawatzky also notes that the Old Colony Church in Durango, in an unusual move, took no responsibility for the financial commitments and that it endorsed the venture only after the deal was completed (Sawatzky *They Sought a Country* 180). Moreover, Braun, who negotiated the deal, never moved to La Batea. This points to potential problems. In fact, there was so much conflict that the colony was nicknamed "La Batalla" [The Battle], which sounds similar to La Batea in Spanish.

Seventy-five Mennonites from Durango, and five from colonies in Chihuahua, moved to La Batea in 1961. The actual purchase did not take place until 1962, because Mier was willing to let the Mennonites try out the land for one year (Bergen *La Batea* 73). The Mennonites then bought 3,000 hectares of cultivated land (Sawatzky *They Sought a Country* 180). The archival documents refer to other developments around this time, specifically, that on October 11, 1962, there was a presidential decree that created the ejido, Niño Artillero, for campesinos in the area, that is, the Sombrerete municipality. According to the official announcement in *Diario Oficial*, the government would acquire this land from Bertha Murillo Pichardo, who Bergen explains is Angel Mier's wife ("Resolución sobre el nuevo centro de población . . . Niño Artillero" 14–15; Bergen *La Batea* 5). Soon thereafter, Bertha Murillo sold some of that same land to the Mennonites for the initial 3,000-hectare purchase.

The ejidatarios and Mennonites challenge one another. According to Sawatzky, the Mennonites reported that there were other people living near the land that had been promised to them, who destroyed the water pipes that they had installed for their cattle. Soldiers were brought in to force these people to leave (*They Sought a Country* 196). According to Bergen, these people soon returned to land the Mennonites had purchased. Bergen's account suggests that the Mennonites worked with the authorities over a long period of time to try to get this land back and failed. Bergen concludes: "dieses Land haben die Mennoniten hier schließlich ganz verloren. Den Agraristen war diesen Land schon versprochen bevor die Mennoniten herzogen" ["In the end, the Mennonites lost this land. The agraristas (ejidatarios) had been promised this land before the Mennonites moved there" [Bergen *La Batea* 4]. Franz Wiebe, a Mennonite who lived there at that time says that he lost 20 hectares of land. He added that the Mennonites were soon able to rent this land from the ejido.

The Mennonites in La Batea then purchased an additional 1,500 hectares in 1963 to start a fourth village. People who lived there at that time say that this soon became very contentious. Susan Driedger and Katharina Redekop explain that they settled just a few hundred meters from the Mennonite farm yards. Mennonite leaders appealed to the authorities; so did the ejidatarios because both groups believed that the land was rightfully theirs. In 1971, the ejidatarios listed twenty-four Mennonites who were living on their ejido and they argued that they had never been given access to the full ejido designated for them. They petitioned for "la sub-división de 4 fracciones numeradas del 62 al 65, y comprendidas dentro de las 72 pequeñas propiedades que señala la resolución presidencial del NCPE [Nuevo Centro de Población Ejidal] El Niño Artillero, Mpio. de Sombrerete, Estado de Zacatecas" ["sub-division of 4 lots, numbers 62 to 65, within the 72 small properties that the presidential decree provides for the NCPE [New Ejido Population Center] El Niño Artillero, Sombrerete Municipality, State of Zacatecas"] ("Resolución sobre el nuevo centro de población . . . Niño artillero" 15).

The colony leader Isaak Dyck Thiessen, responded. He retained a notary, Rodolfo Soriano Duarte, to act on behalf of the colony. Soriano Duarte does not challenge the claim that the land had been designated as an ejido. Instead, he places the Mennonites within the goals of Mexico's land-reform program. He points out that each Mennonite family possesses a modest amount of land that does not exceed the amount allowed by the land reform program. To support this claim, Soriano Duarte submits a list of Mennonite owners. His list has three more names than the list submitted by the ejidos (Soriano Duarte 1–2). This is because, according to his list, some of the pieces have been subdivided. Two of these three new owners are women. Their names may have been used to create the appearance of more owners, supporting the claim that each owner had only a small amount. Soriano Duarte's spelling of some names is different than the list furnished by the ejido. As we saw in the land claims disputes with Mormons, the notary rejects Hispanization and casts doubt on the ejido claim.

Two years later, there were attacks on Mennonite crops and animals, as well as threats against Mennonite people. Bergen states:

> Dann im Jahre 1973 kamen mehr Agraristen und siedelten in der Gegend an wo Niño Artillero heute ist. Am ersten waren sie auf der *Arenas Fence*. Da bauten sie Kleine Häuser aus Pappe. Zum Schauder der Mennoniten fingen diese Mexikaner an, die Felder der Mennoniten zu bearbeiten. Jakob K. Giesbrecht und Toño Herrera nahmen diese Sache zur Hand und arbeiten sehr damit ...

> [Then in 1973 more ejidatarios came and settled where Nino Artillero is today. At first, they were on the *Arenas Fence*. There they built small houses made of cardboard. To the horror of the Mennonites, the Mexicans then started to work on their fields. Jakob K. Giesbrecht and Toño Herrera [Antonio Herrera Bocardo] took this matter in hand and worked very hard to resolve it ...] (Bergen, *La Batea* 4)

Colony leader, Isaak Dyck sent a telegram to officials in the Department of Agrarian Affairs in Mexico City. It reached the desk of Víctor Manuel Torres, then the General Secretary for Agrarian Affairs, on April 11, 1973:

> Estamos quieta pacífica posesión terrenos forma colonias menonitas que representó a título dueños según documentos ... negligencia absoluta autoridades estatales ... tuvieron pleno conocimiento hechos situación tornase angustiosa ... ataques a familias, cosechas y semovientes amenazas de muerte. ... invasores dicen recibir ordenes central campesina independiente ... [Somos] pequeños propietarios ofendidos inmensa mayoría nacidos territorio nacional.

> [(We are) peaceful own land form Mennonite colonies documents show that we are owners ... state authorities have completely neglected us ... they had full knowledge facts situation became awful ... attacks on families, harvests, livestock and death threats ... invaders claim to receive orders from the Independent Campesino Organization ... we are small landowners offended the majority are born in national territory."] (Telegram)

Dyck's telegram reveals that Mennonites presented themselves as Mexicans. Dyck, like Soriano Duarte, does not address the question of the ejido. He indicates that the Mennonites are peaceful victims that have legal ownership of the land. He reminds the official that they are small landowners and that the amounts of land that their individuals hold are within the legal limits. He explains that if they are allowed to farm their land in peace they will continue to contribute to Mexico's economic growth. Moreover, most of the Mennonite landowners were born in Mexico and are Mexican. It concludes with a veiled threat that the invaders are taking orders from a campesino organization unaffiliated with the governing political party, the PRI, and one that was increasingly active in the state of Zacatecas. This portrayal of the Mennonites as belonging to Mexico implies an identification with Mexico that goes beyond being valuable solely because of their economic contributions.

Alfredo Polanco Hernández, Torres' secretary, prepared a sympathetic summary of Dyck's telegram for Torres. Polanco Hernández states:

El C. Isaac Dick, quien manifiesta ser apoderado de las Colonias Menonitas La Batea, Sombrerete, Zac., en telegrama que dirige al C. Titular de esta Dependencia, solicita se intervenga en el problema de invasión que confrontan dichas Colonias, por campesinos pertenecientes al Nuevo Centro de Población Ejidal, y de otros lugares.

[Isaac Dick, who claims to be the head of the Mennonite colonies in La Batea, Sombrerete, Zacatecas, has written a telegram to the head of this office, asking that we intervene in the problem that the colony is experiencing, an invasion from peasants from the New Ejido Population Center and other places.]

Ultimately, the ejidatarios who came in 1973 ended up staying their community in Niño Artillero.

In 1980, the *Diario Oficial de la Federación* published a number of resolutions to these land claims. Their first sections give the name of the Mennonite property owner, the amount of land they own, and the names of those who own land immediately around it. Then there are several "considerations" which state that the *Cuerpo Consultivo Agrario* [Agrarian Consultation Body] deemed this to be legitimate private property. The concluding sections explain whether this property can be deemed eligible or ineligible for agrarian reform. There are also several references to Mennonites as a small-scale collective. These agreements suggest that the collective belongs in Mexico. To illustrate, the agreements of February and March 1980 state: "Que de las constancias que obran en el expediente se desprende que el solicitante forma parte de un grupo étnico que, proveniente del extranjero (Holanda)" ["the proof in the file is that we should get rid of the idea that the applicants come from an ethnic group that, coming from abroad (Holland)"] ("Acuerdo . . . lote 4" 51). Later agreements replace Holland with Canada. This shows that Mennonite history before coming to Mexico is irrelevant. One agreement of June 1980 states that this ethnic group:

> desde hace varios años se asentó en el medio rural mexicano, integrando una Colonia, cuyos actuales descendientes son mexicanos por nacimiento que se dedican a la agricultura, contribuyendo con su esfuerzo y su trabajo colectivo a la producción de alimentos básicos para la población;

> [for many years, has settled in rural Mexico, creating a Colony, whose descendants today are Mexican by birth and who work in agriculture, contributing with their effort and collective work to the production of basic foodstuffs for the Mexican population;] ("Acuerdo . . . lote 12" 22)

The Mennonites now have joined rural Mexico and to have become Mexican; their collective work successfully feeds other Mexicans. Another declaration adds a further dimension, stating:

> asimismo, de las constancias aparece que han quedado debidamente satisfechos los requisitos que establecen . . . la Ley Federal de Reforma Agraria, así como los Artículos . . . relativos del Reglamento de Inafectabilidad Agrícola y Ganadera; de conformidad con lo dispuesto por los Artículos 27 Fracción XV de la Constitución Política de la República . . .

> [in the same way, from the evidence we can see that they have complied with the requirements established by the Federal Law of Agrarian Reform and the Articles that relate to the Regulations about Ineligibility for Agrarian or Ranching Reform; they also conform to that which Article 27, part XV of the Political Constitution of the Republic puts forth . . .] ("Acuerdo . . . lote 11" 2)

The resolutions state that the Mennonites abide by all parts of the law, from the Constitution that allowed for land redistribution, to specific laws about land reform that regulate how much property one can own, and that they fulfill all the requirements for seeking the certificates of ineligibility for their land, meaning that it is not eligible for further redistribution. Here then Mennonites are seen as Mexican, as being in compliance with Mexico's laws, and as a small collective fitting into Mexico's larger collective. The Mennonites are connected to the nation, by their productive farming, by complying with the all relevant laws, and by being born there.

La Honda

The Mennonites' other colony in Zacatecas also experienced land conflict with nearby ejidos. Mennonites from Durango planned to buy land from Roberto Elorduy, a friend of one of their leaders. Elorduy had often talked about a large piece of land that he would like to sell to them and when the Mennonites indicated interest, Elorduy insisted that they not go and look at the land until the deal was finalized with the Agrarian Reform office (Bergen *La Honda* 7). The Mennonites had a serious land shortage in Durango and reports indicated that this was good land. So, they began to work with a lawyer to purchase Elorduy's property. They bought around 16,000 hectares of Elorduy's 29,152 hectares in 1964. It was divided into 183 lots, and so each Mennonite family would have just under 100 hectares (Bergen *La Honda* 7).[6] The Mennonite leader who made the purchase, Jakob K. Guenther, worried because of land conflict in La Batea, asked Elorduy about these problems. Elorduy had responded by saying, "life is full of struggles" (Bergen *La Honda* 9).

Conflict began in December 1975. According to Bergen, people had come and settled on fields very close to a Mennonite village. Initially, there were four or five wagons, and people, and the numbers grew. These campesinos built homes and a school and cared for their farm animals. They said that they intended to live there permanently, and explained that they had had plans to acquire this land before the Mennonites had bought it. One Mennonite asked them about their actions and they said that the Mennonites were foreigners who could move back to their home countries and leave this land for them. This particular Mennonite had then pulled out his birth certificate showing that he was born in Mexico.

The local *presidente municipal* [similar to a mayor] Antonio Herrera Bocardo, urged the Mennonites to be patient. He suggested that the Mennonites protest. When several bureaucrats visited the colony, and a large number of Mennonite women and children blocked the main road. This made an impression and the state governor decided to act in their favor. On May 19, 1976, the Mennonites were told to stay indoors and pray. A convoy of trucks made its way into the colony. According to Bergen:

> Der General unter den Soldaten sprach über Lautsprecher. Die Stimme war sehr klar und eindringlich, so dass die Mennoniten es weit und breit auch in den Häusern hören konnten. Er gebot diesen Menschen zu verlassen und die Mennoniten hier jetzt weiter in Ruhe zu lassen. Überdem gab der Sprecher bekannt, dass er von 30 anfange wurde hinunter zu zahlen. Schließlich 3, 2, und dann 1! Und dann rief er: „*Pero ya! Ríndense!*" (Jetzt, übergebt euch!) Dann ertönte eine Trompete sehr laut.

> [The General spoke through loudspeakers. His voice was very clear and emphatic, so that the Mennonites far and wide could hear him in their homes. He commanded the agraristas to leave these Mennonite people alone and to let them live here [in La Honda] in peace. Over the loudspeaker he announced he would count down from 30. Finally, 3, 2, and then 1! And then he called: "¡Pero ya! ¡Ríndense!" [Now, surrender!] Then a trumpet sounded very loudly.] (Bergen, *La Honda* 21)

The ejidatarios had to surrender. The officials loaded them and their goods and took them away. The next day, soldiers were stationed in the place where the ejidatarios had been living. One Mennonite family, who had given the soldiers some water, remembers them saying that they:

> hatten gemeint, dass sie sich auf etwas Furchtbares bereit gemacht hatten und dann hatten sie gesagt, dass dies noch nichts gewesen war. Die Mennoniten aber waren dankbar, alles so friedlich verlief. Denn sie gönnten ihnen nicht Böses.

> [had prepared themselves for something terrible and they said that this was nothing. The Mennonites were grateful that everything went so peacefully because they did not wish any ill on the Mexicans.] (Bergen *La Honda* 21–22)

The Mennonites also note that these people, likely afraid of further military action, never returned.

Archival documents relate similar events. Leaders from the J. Santos Bañuelos ejido, which bordered on the Mennonites' land in La Honda, petitioned for more land in 1976. This letter explains that there is available land in several areas, including the "Ex-hacienda de la Honda, Municipio de Miguel Auza, Zac., que ocupan ilegalmente grupos de Menonitas y grupos del Estado de Durango" ["Former hacienda la Honda in Miguel Auza, Zacatecas, which Mennonites and groups from the state of Durango are illegally occupying"] (Moreno G, Márquez E. and Saucedo). Approximately thirty men signed the letter or affirmed it with their fingerprints.

This petition, close to the time that the ejidatarios began settling in land that the Mennonites perceived as theirs, is significant. It states that the Mennonites illegally occupy the land without explaining the reasoning behind this. It may have been because the land was officially listed in the names of one or two colony leaders, who then appeared to own more land than allowed according to agrarian reform laws. They also note that these people came from another state, Durango. For these people from Zacatecas, which experienced significant poverty, newcomers were a threat. Nevertheless, this claim of illegality vanishes with a notarized copy of the petition and the printed version in the *Periódico Oficial de Zacatecas* (Ibarra Chávez; "Copia de la Solicitud").

Discussions continue between the bureaucrats. Antonio Herrera Bocardo, the *president municipal* who was sympathetic to Mennonites, writes a letter on April 24, 1979, to Joel Luevanos Ponce and Arturo Medrano Cabral, two officials from the *Comisión Agraria Mixta* [Mixed Agrarian Commission] in their defense. The letter situates the Mennonites as belonging to Mexico by describing them as taxpayers who contribute to the nation's economy. He explained that the Mennonites own the "fierros de herrar registrados . . . vigentes y al corriente en el pago de sus refrendos, asi [sic] como las figuras que corresponden a cada uno de ellos" ["their horse shoes are registered and up to date, they are up to date in paying their registrations, as well as the figures that correspond to them individually"] (Herrera Bocardo "Carta" 24 April 1979, 1). A week later, Herrera Bocardo writes another letter to the same bureaucrats, furthering the idea that Mennonites belong to the nation. This letter explains that Pedro M. Klassen had purchased land for 183 people who were heads of households on May 23, 1964, and that several certificates of ineligibility for agrarian reform were issued in January 1979 (Herrera Bocardo "Carta" 2 May 1979, 2). He annexes a number of documents to prove that the original Mennonite land purchase was legal. Herrera Bocardo also argues that the Mennonites are not contravening the Revolutionary goal of agrarian reform and, indeed, that they are helping the now post-Revolutionary nation by farming and producing foodstuffs, which was an especially important contribution since the decades of industrial development (1940–68) had ended.[7] The letter also points out that Mennonites ceded land to the ejido "Manantial la Honda," in 1966. Thus, the Mennonites have already gone out of their way to help ejidatarios. Herrera Bocardo implies that, surely, the ejidatarios do not need more land. He also includes documents to show that the land has been continually culti-vated by Mennonites since 1966 (Herrera Bocardo "Carta" 2 May 1979, 2). The letter concludes by telling the leaders at the agrarian commission that it will be impossible to:

> conceder esta ampliación sobre estos predios [menonitas], tomando como base su total aprovechamiento que queda de manifiesto con la información anterior, y [se pide que] se permita a los habitantes de esta Comunidad trabajar pacíficamente sin entorpecer su desarrollo e impor-tante producción de alimentos, en beneficio de sus mismas familias, y en beneficio de la Nación.

> [concede this ejido expansion onto these [Mennonite] properties, because they are completely used. The previous information demon-strates this, and we ask you to allow the inhabitants of this Community to work peacefully. We would like their development and production of important foodstuffs to increase, in order to further benefit their families and the Nation.] (Herrera Bocardo "Carta" 2 May 1979, 3)

In Herrera Bocardo's view, then, the Mennonites are the legal landowners who fulfill Revolutionary ideals. His reasoning is not far from Echeverría's rhetoric about the nation as a collective project.

Other documents portray ejidatarios more favorably. In August 1979, Arturo Medrano Cabral, an investigator from the *Comisión Agraria Mixta*, reported on a recent visit to La Honda to the Commission's president, Lic. Arturo J. Real Martínez. Merdrano Cabral elaborates on each geographical area affected by an expansion of the ejido, including the Mennonite colony.

The report discusses their extensive economic contribution Mennonites and asserts that they and other people from Durango illegally occupy the ex-hacienda la Honda (Medrano Cabral 3). The Mennonites are seen as valuable for their economic contribution in spite of this illegality.

Fernando Ruiz Castro writes a report for the *Comisión Agraria Mixta* in 1979 and echoes Herrera Bocardo. He portrays the Mennonites in La Honda as belonging in the Mexican nation and as fulfilling Revolutionary goals, not in spite of their social practices but because of them. His uncritically positive perception of this plain religious group seems influenced by a dissatisfaction with the larger culture, somewhat as Amish fiction in the US has become increasingly popular as many Americans feel that their own social fabric has unraveled (V. Weaver-Zercher 25, 54). In Ruiz Castro's view, the Mennonites, who represent an alternative way of life, serve a social good because of their traditional gender roles and because of their communal lifestyle. Ruiz Castro begins by restating the Mennonites' legal claim to the land, based on purchases recorded in the public record, and then emphasizes their economic contribution. He says that the Mennonites' main activities are with livestock, dairy production, and industrialized agriculture (Ruiz Castro 2–3). This echoes the explanations given by other bureaucrats but unlike others, Ruiz Castro aligns Mennonites with the Revolutionary goals of health, hygiene, and education. His report even praises their education system, stating that the Mennonites in La Honda have 17 private schools with 792 students, and that the children learn basic reading and math (Ruiz Castro 4). The report neglects to mention that these village schools are entirely in German. In addition to praising their schools, his report shows how well the Mennonites use the foodstuffs that they produce, explaining: "La alimentación de los habitantes de los campos Menonitas se considera completa ya que consumen los 4 grupos de alimentos desde el punto de vista nutricional" ["The inhabitants of the Mennonite villages have a complete diet, since they consume food from the four food groups, from a nutritional perspective"] (Ruiz Castro 3). From Ruiz Castro's perspective, Mennonites are not merely occupying the land. They also prepare for hard times, which he appreciates: "Cada familia cuenta con una despensa de productos industrializados por ellos tales como mantequilla, salchicha, jamón, étc [sic]" ["Each family has a pantry of products that they have made such as butter, sausage, ham, etc"] (Ruiz Castro 3). Later, Ruiz Castro states that:

La higiene de la Comunidad es magnífica ya que no hay basureros ni estercoleros, las calles se ven limpias. La casa-habitación esta aseada para la higiene personal, cuentan con tres baños de regadera en todos los campos, y el resto de los habitantes practican el baño de tina, sus ropas se ven limpias.

El agua que toman no está hervida, la preparación de los alimentos es higiénico.

[The Community's hygiene is magnificent. Since there are neither garbage cans nor dumps, the streets appear clean. The house-home is cleaned for personal hygiene, and there are three bathrooms with showers in all of the villages. The rest of the inhabitants bathe in tubs, and their clothes are clean.

The water that they drink is not boiled; the way that they prepare their food is hygienic.] (4)

Thus, the report argues that in several important areas, Mennonites are living in an appropriate way that will help the country overall and could serve as an example for others in their region. Their commercial connections are also significant. Ruiz Castro alludes to this as he offers some details about Mennonite clothing:

De acuerdo a sus costumbres el vestuario es adecuado, las prendas femeninas y de casa son hechas a cada época del año por ellas mismas. La ropa masculina la compran hecha en las tiendas que tienen en los campos, y éstas se abastecen en Torreón y de San Luis Potosí.

[According to their customs, their wardrobe is adequate; women's clothing and home furnishings are made for each season by the women themselves. They buy men's clothing in the stores that are in the villages, which are stocked with goods from Torreón and San Luis Potosí.] (Ruiz Castro 4)

Ruiz Castro thus ties together a rosy picture of the Mennonites' social fabric, based on a gendered division of labor. He argues that Mennonite people live fairly well with relatively well-distributed resources (Ruiz Castro 50–51, 64). As for unusual characteristics, Ruiz Castro notes, similar to what Fierro Martinez had already noted, that: "Los menonitas pueden poseer casi todos los bienes que cualquier mortal pueda desear, sin embargo tienen algunas excepciones" ["The Mennonites can own almost all of the goods that any mortal could wish, with a few exceptions"] (Fierro Martínez 51–52). He also points out that Mennonites in La Honda save their money in local banks in the towns of Rio Grande or Miguel Auza and that the colony pays federal and state taxes. He also notes that only one hundred residents of the colony were born outside of the country, and that the rest were born in the states of Chihuahua, Durango, and Zacatecas. He adds that "Debido a los reglamentos tan estrictos de su religión, no causan nunca problemas o conflictos a las Autoridades, y cuando las hay generalmente las resuelven en forma interna y pacíficamente" ["Given their strict religious rules, they never cause problems or conflicts with the authorities, and that when there are problems, they resolve them internally and peacefully"] (Ruiz Castro 5). This matter-of-fact report covers every aspect of their lives, from their garbage to their bathing habits. As it describes them, there is no question that they belong to Mexico. He believes that Mennonites in Mexico as a people group are ready and able to fulfill a range of Revolutionary goals.

Clearly, La Honda land conflict led to extensive discussion among various bureuacrats. On October 1, 1979, there was a resolution in an "Acuerdo sobre Inafectabilidad Agrícola, relativo al conjunto de predios rústicos denominado Fraccionamiento La Honda, ubicado en el Municipio de Miguel Auza, Zac." These agreements follow the format we saw with the Mormon landowners; this case was much more extensive. It granted 172 families permanent exemption from land reform, as it officially recognized that they did not own too much land. As with the agreements in La Batea, in this case the federal bureaucrats recognize that the Mennonites comply with all agrarian reform laws then in force. It reiterates that they are an ethnic group from Holland, who:

desde hace varios lustros se asentó en el medio rural mexicano, inte-grando una Colonia, cuyos actuales descendientes son mexicanos por nacimiento que se dedican a la agricultura, contribuyendo con su esfuerzo y su trabajo colectivo a la producción de alimentos básicos para la población

[for many five-year periods, has settled in rural Mexico, creating a Colony, whose descendants today are Mexican by birth and who work in agricul-ture, contributing with their effort and collective work to the production of basic foodstuffs for the Mexican population] ("Acuerdo . . . La Honda" 2)

In 1979 and 1984, the government also removed the rights of multiple ejidatarios because they were no longer farming this land ("Resolución sobre privación" 3 Oct. 1979, 16; "Resolución sobre privación" 6 Jan. 1985). The bureaucrats were dedicated to the Mennonite community to such an extent that they would use military or police force, the resulting Mennonite exemptions from land combined with a reduced number of ejidatarios in J. Santos Bañuelos, and brought the La Honda land conflict to a conclusion.

This chapter began with the question of whether the Mennonites are understood as belonging to Mexico. Popular forces committed to socialism in land reform, public education, or racial amalgamation had less room for the Mennonites and their way of life, and those groups that believed in the role of the private sector and in foreigners portray the Mennonites more favorably. In spite of these qualifications, Cárdenas, strongly committed to socialism, was ready to overrule other government representatives in defending the Mennonites in very significant ways because of their economic contribution to the country.

In spite of this economic contribution, which has been recognized by bureaucrats and politicians at many levels of government, the Mennonites are still sometimes seen as foreigners. Indeed, they live in separate colonies, speak more German than Spanish and usually wear different clothes. The fact that today most Mennonites in Mexico were born there has softened this critique. When the Mennonites bought their land in Zacatecas, however, landowners were ready to sell in suspicious circumstances in part because they thought that the Mennonites would not grasp the intricacies of agrarian reform law. The Mennonite leaders then found sympathetic bureaucrats who could use what the Mennonites understood as soldiers to ensure that the law was settled in a way that was favorable to them. In the decades after this conflict, popular culture began to tie Mennonites to this extrajudicial force, stereotyping them as criminals.

4

Mennonites and Mormons in Mexico's Drug Wars

Criminals and Victims on Screen and in Literature

Mexico's so-called drug wars have become the subject of literature, film, and other expressions of popular culture and it may be surprising that some of it features Mennonites and Mormons. They do not appear often and usually not in central roles; however, that they appear at all implies that they are seen, at least in certain ways, as belonging to Mexico. In this chapter I look at five works of popular culture that relate to the drug wars in which Mennonites and Mormons, in this case, polygamous members of the non-LDS LeBaron group, are featured. I explore how these works portray these minorities and connect them to Mexico and what this may suggest about ways of being Mexican. It can be noted at the outset that the three works that include Mennonites show them either as criminals or deviants while those on Mormons portray them as innocent victims. Also, those with the Mennonites are fictionalized for popular entertainment while those on Mormons aim to be realistic portrayals of actual events, namely a kidnapping and two related murders. Because the two works on Mormons deal with the same events, I discuss them together.

The Bridge is an English-language television series produced in the US that includes so much Spanish that being bilingual or enjoying subtitles is almost a requirement for watching it. The show ran for two seasons of thirteen episodes in 2013 and 2014. It features two police officers: season one focuses on Sonya Cross based in El Paso, Texas, and Marco Ruiz from Ciudad Juárez, Chihuahua. Cross and Ruiz are forced to cooperate and solve a string of murders after meeting over a murdered body on the Bridge of the Americas that connects El Paso and Ciudad Juárez. In the second season, the two stars return, this time they try to stop the Galván drug cartel by focusing on apprehending its accountant, a Mennonite woman called Eleanor Nacht. The series shows the violence, ugliness, and widespread corruption that comes with the drug trade.

Los héroes del norte is an entirely different television series. It is a comedy that was produced by the Mexican television giant, Televisa. It ran from 2010 to 2014 and featured the adventures of a musical group that included two Mennonites. The group crosses the border with and without documents and makes fun of drug-related violence by mixing up characters' bodies, minds, and voices. When the voice of Friedrich, one of the Mennonites, comes out of the body of a different band member, it suggests Mennonite integration with Mexican society. This series may have served to distract people from drug-related violence, and its relationship with the state. At one point it mixes up the bodies, minds, and voices of the characters. For instance, when the voice of one of the Mennonite characters comes out of the body of another Mexican band member, I would argue that it suggests integration.

The third example of popular culture is MacBurro, a webcomic with two installments. The term MacBurro can be translated as McDonkey or McStupid and has been used to refer to politicians deemed stupid or violent. It features three Mennonite men, three members of the yakuza [Japanese organized crime] led by their obayun [leader], and two Russian security guards. It has a lot of violence and blood and shows the interconnectedness of organized crime, the state, and ties between different minority groups. The setting is a bar called Babel, probably referring to the Biblical story of humanity building a high tower to try to defy God and God thwarting the effort by causing the people to speak in different languages and becoming thoroughly confused.[1] Given that it is set in a port city, and that Giancarlo Ruiz and Charles Glaubitz, the writer and illustrator, are from the Tijuana–San Diego area, it is likely that the comic also reflects Tijuana.

The Mormons are portrayed as a somewhat different part of drug-related violence but those who do are typically portrayed as innocent victims. LDS Mormons do not figure in these representations in a significant way. Indeed, Los güeros del norte [The Northern White People] is a 2010 book by Javier Ortega Urquidi about the 2009 kidnapping of Eric LeBaron, by a drug cartel. It is also about the efforts of his family, and his group of Mormons, the LeBarons, to lobby the government to secure his release, thereby reflecting a rare faith in the government.[2] Eventually, Eric is released but his older brother, Benjamin LeBaron, and his brother-in-law, Luis Carlos Widmar, are murdered. These killings are understood as a consequence of Eric's release and lead the rest of his family to pressure the government to act against this violence. These experiences lead the Mormons to a more critical view of the government. Also, they become active in Mexico's peace movement.

One of these family member's experience is included in *México: 45 voces contra la barbarie* [*Mexico: 45 Voices against Barbarity*], a 2015 collection of forty-five interviews by the journalist Lolita Bosch with Mexican peace activists, experts on violence, and families of victims. My analysis focuses only on one interview, with Eric LeBaron's older brother, Julián. In this interview, as in Ortega Urquidi's book, the LeBarons are seen as innocent victims and as cognizant of the corruption of Mexico's political structures. They are also seen as energetic participants in Mexican peace movements, thus indicating a certain integration into Mexican society.

In my analysis of these works I note how the Mennonite and Mormon experience of violence alludes to that experienced by Mexicans generally, thus implying a significant common ground. I also note, more specifically, how the blood in *Macburro* and that in *The Bridge*, mirror the bodily fluid in *Los héroes del norte*. I contend that this blood and fluid, in turn, mimic that blood shed by the kidnapped Eric LeBaron and his dead brother and brother-in-law, which appear in Ortega Urquidi's portrayals of the events. This blood and fluid can be seen as a life force that relates to the belief in grace as a life force that we see in *The Bridge* and this, in turn, relates to the LeBarons' belief that the Mexican government will enforce its laws that we see in Ortega Urquidi's work.

These conclusions are possible only through the work of the imagination. To develop these ideas, refer to Scott McCloud's *Understanding Comics: The Invisible Art* (1993). He points out that the panels in a comic strip leave a lot unsaid, or unillustrated, that it is why the space between the panels—a space he calls the gutter—is significant because that is where viewers use their imagination to make connections and complete the story. I submit that these beliefs mentioned earlier are potent elements in the gutters and that they, in a sense, complement the all-too-visible blood. Thus the blood and the fluids, and these accompanying beliefs, connect disparate examples of popular culture. As we explore them further, we see how they suggest relationships between different spheres of influence, such as those among journalists, the judicial system and the police, and allow us to imagine and explore how Mennonites and Mormons fit into the early twenty-first-century Mexican context.

Also to be noted are various scholarly perspectives on the interconnected nature of the legal and illegal realms, which can also be terms as law enforcement, and government, versus cartels. Anthropologist Wil G. Pansters says that there are many kinds of violence in contemporary Mexico: political-institutional violence; parastate violence; violence resulting from electoral conflicts; violence for economic gain; and violence for social and interpersonal domination (Pansters 20–21). In other words, the term violence connects these disparate realities. John Bailey and Roy Godson explain how this violence takes root in the Mexico-US border. They observe that this region has widespread corruption, due to ineffective federal and state supervision on both sides of the border (Bailey and Godson 21). They add that this affects "police, border control, judiciary and local government of field office" (Bailey and Godson 21). Similarly, M. Florencia Nelli, a scholar of classics and theater, observes connections between authorities and cartels as she describes kidnappings. In her view, kidnapping in Mexico has become a permanent condition, and is rarely prosecuted. Even when it is prosecuted, she goes on to explain, it rarely leads to a conviction because the authorities are often linked to those who orchestrate the kidnappings (Nelli 56).[3] The historian, Robert Cribb, uses the term, parapolitics, adapted from the more common term paramilitary, to explain this extensive relationship. He believes that security and intelligence agencies and criminal networks have more power than the three branches of government, and that they have close ties with criminal networks (Cribb 8). Similarly, anthropologist Carolyn Nordstrom holds that there are no boundaries between the legal and the illegal, that the illegal, informal, and illicit *are* the economy (Nordstrom 24). That is, buying and selling anything under the table, including sex from sex workers and food from unlicensed vendors, are as much a part of the economy as buying toothpaste, and should be recognized as equivalent and interdependent parts of it. For political scientist Nafeez Mosaddeq Ahmed, power and money circulate through these networks and that relationships between legal and illegal. He claims that in the present period, "the locus of agency (read: power) does not reside inherently in the regular state hierarchy, but rather subsists in a heterogeneous network of interlocking military-industrial-corporate interests with strong institutional connections to elements of the state" (Ahmed 41). This is the reality in the US as well as in Mexico. A journalist character, Daniel, in *The Bridge*, explains it in the following way to Buckley, a CIA agent. Daniel charges Buckley with funneling drug money back into the United States and calling the war on drugs "a bullshit game" that no one can win ("Jubilex" *The Bridge*). Buckley responds: "That's not bad. This isn't a game, it's a business, and we have investments in that" ("Jubilex" *The Bridge*). This television show affirms our worst suspicions about the CIA and adds that the officials in charge do not even care.

THE DEVELOPMENT OF THE DRUG VIOLENCE
AND RELATED POPULAR CULTURE

Drug violence did not suddenly appear in its present form out of nowhere. It developed in an historical context in response to various factors. So, too, did the popular culture that arose in relation to it. As César Jesús Burgos Dávila explains, drug trafficking programs across the Mexico–US border begins in earnest around the 1920s, in response to temperance and prohibition in the United States. Drug production, particularly of opiates, grows in the 1940s, especially in Mexico's northern and eastern states, which have high levels of unemployment (Burgos Dávila 164). Mexico exports marijuana in addition to opiates in the 1950s and 1960s. As the US begins antidrug campaigns, Mexico continues to supply the US with drugs, thanks to collusion with governments on both sides of the border (Burgos Dávila 166). During this time Mexico also became the primary port of entry for drugs cultivated elsewhere and then brought into the US. Over the course of these decades, at the same time the *Partido Revolucionario Institucional* [Institutional Revolutionary Party] (PRI) developed a far-reaching political machine. This enabled the government to control most groups in society, including labor unions, peasant groups, intellectuals, the media, teacher associations, and that the drug trade also depended on this tacit collusion.

The Mexican government initiated several antidrug operations financed by the US. Then, in 1975, the military became actively involved in antidrug trafficking. As Burgos Dávila explains, "Las autoridades sometían a campesinos con abusos y maltratos que llegaban a la tortura física o mental, al arresto y muerte de personas inocentes" ["The authorities mistreated peasants with abuse that reached physical and mental torture, and the arrest and death of innocent people"] (168). The campesinos fled the countryside and went to the cities. It was now easier for drug traffickers to intimidate campesinos that remained and to use larger portions of rural areas for drug cultivation.

During the 1970s and 1980s, Colombia dominated the market as a US supplier, and then by the 1990s, Mexico supplied about three-quarters of the US market (Knight "Narco-Violence" 126). By 2007, according to the US State Department, "90% of the cocaine in the US came from or through Mexico" (US Department of State). And, according to the US Congress, $19–$29 billion flowed into Mexico annually from illicit drug trade. Other sources use even higher numbers (Laurell 252). It is estimated that the drug business has provided 8 percent to 15 percent of Mexico's GDP.

This system of control broke down in the early 1980s because of Mexico's debt crisis and the response of the International Monetary Fund (IMF). In the 1970s, the government increased spending substantially but when international oil prices dropped and interest rates rose, the IMF imposed a major structural adjustment program that required a drastic slimming down of the state. Thus, most public companies were privatized, wages and salaries of state workers, or state-related workers, such as teachers, were reduced by 30 percent to 40 percent, and the budgets for education and social programs were cut back, as were those supporting small farmers (Laurell 250). As a result, political leaders no longer had the largesse with which to retain the loyalty and support of various groups in society. The North American Free Trade Agreement (NAFTA), signed in 1992, further restricted the role of the government. In significant ways it served to "denationalize" the economy. International corporations now set up factories and assembly plants along the border that provided jobs but they also undermined local industries, while the influx of cheap food and agricultural products from the still-subsidized US agribusinesses, undermining local farming operations, resulting in a what Asa Cristina Laurell calls social dislocation, that is, that large numbers of people were forced to move. She states that 500,000 economic migrants made their way to the US annually, while some of those who remained became more open to the idea of using their land to grow opium poppies and marijuana (Laurell 251–52).

These drastic changes also gave rise to protests and opposition. The dominant political party, the PRI, which had ruled under several monikers since 1929, could no longer contain the political debate.[4] There were splits and defections, most notably with the *Partido Revolucionario Democrático* [Democratic Revolutionary Party] (PRD) in 1989, and continued animosity between the PRI and the right-wing *Partido de Acción Nacional* [National Action Party]

(PAN). In this context, aspiring politicians had to compete against each other. This required financial backing, which may have come from drug cartels. In 2000, the PRI lost the presidency to the PAN, but it maintained some power on the state level. Some PRI-affiliated governors had close ties with large and powerful drug interests (Knight "Narco-Violence" 129). As sociologist Fernando Escalante Gonzalbo explains, the selective implementation of the law is subject to constant negotiation in Mexico ("Homicidios"). When this breaks down, trouble starts.

In 2006 the newly elected PAN-affiliated president, Felipe Calderón, sought to redefine this negotiation, to detract from what some consider a questionable legitimacy of electoral victory. He sent 6,500 soldiers to the coastal state of Michoacán to end what he believed was the drug violence there. As this president was more willing to work with the US on issues of security, crime, and drugs than his predecessors, his administration created the Mérida Initiative. The US Congress allocated several billion dollars to this venture, which brought the US Drug Enforcement Agency (DEA) and the Central Intelligence Agency (CIA) to the Mexico–US border and to Mexico itself. Within a few years, 45,000 Mexican soldiers were deployed in the so-called War on Drugs, in addition to increases in Mexican state and federal police forces. It has proliferated the arms trade and in pitting various police forces against one another. Escalante Gonzalbo, analyzing recent homicide data in Mexico, observes that between 2000 and 2006, homicide numbers declined on a national level, although there was violence in states that experienced cartel turf wars ("Homicidios"). In 2007, there was a slight increase, and then the rates increased by 50 percent in 2008, and by a further 50 percent in 2009 (Escalante Gonzalbo "Homicidios"). This violence is concentrated in cities, especially those along the border, where there is competition for territory between cartels. Yet, he claims that this is not the whole story. Violence dramatically increased when Calderón allowed for massive military intervention. This violence exists in tandem with the negotiations around the law in Mexico. Some police and military personnel have joined the cartels, thwart official efforts to pursue cartel leaders, and alert these leaders before a government strike takes place. Further, police rob and kidnap people and hold them for ransom while blaming it on the cartels and that in some areas the police openly cede control to the cartels such that they control large parts of Mexican territory and have significant influence in electoral politics. President Enrique Peña Nieto (2012–18) was expected to change strategies, and return to previous pacts between his party, the PRI, and cartels. This has not happened.

This outline of cartel relationships with the Mexican government contextualizes the cultural artifacts that have arisen in relation to it, which are described as narcoculture. One example is the *narcocorrido*. A *corrido* is a song or ballad telling a story, which, as a form of cultural expression, has long been common in the border region. In recent decades, some drug bosses have commissioned the writing of such pieces in order to build a positive image of themselves as Robin Hood–style bandits who distribute their largesse in patrimonial fashion and sponsor public works such as roofing at a high school, street lighting, a bandstand in a park, community fiestas, and even pay for medical treatment for the poor. These *narcocorridos* emphasize virtues of bravery and resourcefulness in being able to elude both Mexican and US authorities. As Burgos Dávila explains, this musical genre became popular in the state of Sinaloa 1970s, which was experiencing high levels of violence. It told the stories of corruption, government inability to confront drug trafficking. They were popularized in other parts of Mexico as campesinos left Sinaloa in search of better futures. Critic Rafael Acosta Morales describes them as a "genre of epic poetry [that] often serves as a political form of resistance and a source of unity for the less privileged sectors in a state that barely takes them into consideration" (181). A 2016 story by the Associated Press reports that a young cartel gunman, when asked about his aspirations, had answered "to have a *narco-corrido* song written about me" (Peña and Stevenson). Indeed, as Acosta Morales argues, "[i]t is not surprising that communities that are massively criminalized, such as undocumented immigrants or the young men of northern Mexico, who are readily assumed to be criminals if they die in violent circumstances, do not feel part of society" and hope to die as heroes (182).[5] In *The Bridge*, the cartel leader, Fausto Galván, has a similar desire. He appears—uninvited—to a quinceañera party and demands that the musicians play specific music that will reflect his prowess as he dances with a very frightened young woman.

There are also a number of other examples of *narcocultura*, or cultural expression related to the drug trade. However, according to critic Oswaldo Zavala, most do not consider the drug violence in a systemic and critical way; instead they sensationalize the violence of the cartels and their kingpins and "depict a fictitious and glorifying image of powerful drug criminals and their clandestine 'culture' of inhuman excess" and turn "the drug trade and its actors into commercially successful myths" (343). Zavala says most cultural expressions fail to look critically at the ways that governmental policies have contributed to the growth of the cartels, and he argues that they present the cartels as "readily distinguishable from the state structures," as "exterior" to it. In other words, they portray the state as good, even if it is imperfect, and that the cartels as evil, and that the Mexican government and the people must stand united against them. In this way, says Zavala, much of the *narcocultura* provides a justification for the massive deployment of military and police forces, for the prioritizing security over most other considerations, and for suspending human rights and other aspects of the rule of law (Zavala 355).

Few Mexican writers critically analyze the collusion of various arms of the state with the cartels. This critical writing often comes from journalists living and working in the US, because writers are safer there, though even in the US it is not common.[6] The problem is well articulated by journalist, Charles Bowden, who has referred to two Mexicos:

> There is the one reported by the U.S. press, a place where the Mexican president is fighting a valiant war against the evil forces of the drug world and using the incorruptible Mexican army as his warriors. This Mexico has newspapers, courts, and laws and is seen by the U.S. government as a sister republic.
>
> It does not exist.
>
> There is a second Mexico, where the war is *for* drugs . . . where the police and the military fight for their share, where the press is restrained by the murder of reporters and feasts on a steady diet of bribes, and where the line between government and the drug world has never existed. (18)

Bowden's second Mexico echoes the observations by scholars Nelli, Cribb, Knight, Nordstrom, and Ahmed. His distinction between the two understandings of Mexico also helps us to ask questions about the works of popular culture I examine in this chapter: do they imply that the drug trade is an exterior evil and that the state, though imperfect, is essentially good. Are they advancing the idea that it is committed to establishing a reasonably fair social order? Or, do they imply that substantial aspects of the state have become integrated into the drug business to the point where police officers may be most loyal to a cartel? The answers are not immediately obvious but we can note Zavala's observation that "recurrent violence operates ... [as] a spectacle of iconography representing unmediated, excessive human suffering" (Zavala 344). In his view, such portrayals support the view that illegal drugs are solely to blame, ignoring the claim that the cartels act as part of a network that includes acts of violence sanctioned by the Mexican and US governments. Indeed, that the cartels are as much a part of a broader state by the late twentieth- and early twenty-first century as any official state-related organization.

WORKS OF POPULAR CULTURE THAT FEATURE MENNONITES AND MORMONS

The Bridge

The television series, *The Bridge*, which ran for two seasons in 2013 and 2014, was developed by Elwood Reid and Meredith Stiehm, and produced in the US by the Fox subsidiary, FX. It is an adaptation from the Swedish/ Danish show *Broen/Bron* [*The Bridge*], which referred to a bridge between the two Scandinavian countries. The FX adaptation refers to "The Bridge of the Americas" between El Paso and Ciudad Juárez. It, and the surrounding area, are the scene of various crimes that the police officers, Sonya Cross from El Paso, and Marcos Ruiz from Juárez, work to resolve. The series drew a large audience and received critical acclaim. Tim Goodman at *The Hollywood Reporter* called the series, "mandatory viewing for drama lovers" and Maureen Ryan, for *The Huffington Post*, commented: "Mismatched cops forced to work together is one of the oldest TV tropes in the book but *The Bridge* builds such a realistic, detailed world around the detectives here that the dynamic is often fresh."

The two detectives, Cross, played by Diane Kruger, and Ruiz, by Demián Bichir, have central roles, but they interact with a range of other people. One is Charlotte Millwright, a wealthy widow who learns that her husband used their land to smuggle people into the US but soon she, herself, becomes active in the drug trade. Others include bankers who finance the Red Ridge housing development, businesspeople, news reporters, state prosecutors, various police officers, and representatives from the DEA and the CIA. Most of the characters are shown to be corrupt and in collusion with the cartels. The interactions move quickly, even abruptly and, in many cases, involve double-dealing and blood.

On the whole the series suggests an ugly reality where it is often impossible to distinguish between good and evil.

The Mennonite character, Eleanor Nacht, on whom I focus, appears only in the second season. This is the first instance in which I examine a US cultural product rather than one from Mexico. This television show capitalizes on the horror of drug violence through gritty, hyperrealistic portrayals of Mexico. This Mennonite is an important part of this negative portrayal, because it is jarring to have someone from a stereotypically pure group perform nefarious acts.[7] She is the capable accountant of the cartel kingpin, Fausto Galván, who is being sought by the two detectives. Eleanor is almost totally loyal to Galván because he had rescued her from her abusive father who had raped her over the course of her childhood. When Galván found Eleanor, he castrated her father and put him into a cage. Soon Eleanor is a vital player in the work of the cartel, which means that on screen, she interacts with many other people. But often she appears cruel, inhumane, and unkempt, with only a few redemptive qualities. Moreover, she takes some of the cartel's profits for herself, which further places her in a dishonest light. In an interview with Alan Sepinwall, director Reid claimed that the show is based on Carlos Reygadas' *Silent Light*, which, he said, is based on a novel by Miriam Toews about Mennonites in Mexico (Sepinwall). Reid is wrong about the sequence: it was only after Miriam Toews' experience as an actor in *Stellet Licht/Silent Light* (2007), that she wrote her novel, *Irma Voth* (2011). But Reid is right in noting a similarity between his character, Eleanor, and the main character in Toews' novel. Among other things, both involve women who suffer a deep personal betrayal in the Mennonite community. Thus, both works can be seen as studies of the tension between good and evil.

Eleanor's Personal Story

Eleanor Nacht's backstory contextualizes her interactions with two adolescent boys and with a man with some disabilities, interactions that take place in the context of her role in the cartel. Eleanor Nacht's name itself is significant, as is that of her boss, Fausto Galván. Her last name, Nacht, is German for night, thus alluding to darkness. Her first name reminds us of two famous Eleanors: Eleanor Roosevelt (1884–1962), the humanitarian First Lady of US President

Franklin Roosevelt; and Eleanor of Aquitaine (c. 1122–1204), a leader in the Second Crusade who married the French King, Louis VII, and then, upon obtaining an annulment, proceeded to marry the English King, Henry II, thus indicating a remarkable ability to negotiate power within a restrictive system. The images of both Eleanors are evident in Eleanor Nacht who, in unexpected moments, is kind to some characters but is also ready to betray and kill because of her loyalty to Galván. Galván's first name alludes to Faust or Faustus who, according to German legend, was successful but dissatisfied, so he made a pact with the devil, exchanging his soul for knowledge and pleasure. The television series does not say that Fausto Galván made a pact with the devil but it certainly portrays him as an evil person. His last name, Galván, sounds a lot like the last name of El Chapo Guzmán who is a famous cartel leader in real life.[8]

Eleanor Nacht does not dress in a way that would befit either of these other two Eleanors or even a typical Mennonite woman. She always wears ugly clothes, such as shirts with high necks and long skirts. Long skirts, of course, are typical for Mennonite women in Mexico but most would take better care of their clothes; most would also have long hair while Eleanor's is short and jagged. Sonya, the El Paso detective, characterizes her as "churchy" and "down-right devout" ("Sorrowsworn" *The Bridge*). The style of dress plays on false preconceptions about the conservative or ascetic dress of members of religious communities, and acts as a marker of social and cultural difference from others in Mexico and from cartel members. The German actress Franka Potente, who plays Eleanor, speaks English with an accent, to further remind the audience of her Mennonite-ness and otherness. Underneath this German accent and long skirts, Eleanor is covered with tattoos. This juxtaposition mirrors her inner turmoil, and suggests that in this television series, nothing is like it seems. In episode three, "Sorrowsworn," Sonya asks Joe Mackenzie, a DEA agent: "why don't you tell us how she fits into the cartel . . . she's not a girlfriend." This implies that she does not fit the typical model of women in drug cartels. Joe explains that Eleanor is a shunned Mennonite, adding that her name is Eleanor Nacht, and that finding her might lead them to the cartel leader, Fausto Galván.

Eleanor finally discloses some personal information in episode seven, called "Lamia." The episode's title refers to a beautiful queen who, in ancient Greek mythology, became a child-eating demon. In "Lamia," César, a long-time employee of Charlotte, the widow who has become a drug pusher, drives Eleanor to a diner. There, Eleanor is to meet César's boss Charlotte, Charlotte's lover Ray, and the fixer Monte, who makes arrangements for cartel-related people to travel easily with their money or drugs. In the car we see Eleanor's jagged haircut and the turtleneck underneath her sweater. César and Eleanor arrive at the diner and Eleanor sits down at a table. Then Ray, Charlotte, and Monte enter and Ray and Charlotte join Eleanor at her table. Monte's cowboy hat anchors the scene and, interestingly, places Eleanor half in the shadow and half in the light. She then tells her story from this perspective and in the third person, describing a girl from a village in the desert, which probably means Chihuahua. Then, in steady but graphic terms, she refers to the girl's father and her community:

> one day he took her to the barn. The man lay on top of her. His weight crushed her. This went on for many years. Later when this was discovered, the girl was cast out. She lost everything. Darkness was tempting. She met her demons. They took her grace and drank. ("Lamia," *The Bridge*)

The words in this quotation that she was "cast out" refer to her being shunned by the Mennonite community as already mentioned by Joe MacKenzie. The Amish and conservative Mennonites are known for the practice of shunning, as are other conservative Christian groups. If a member violates the church's teachings, for example in the use of technology or in dress styles, then they can be officially excommunicated, after which they are not allowed to participate in the community's activities and other members are to avoid them. Groups that use this practice do so only with individuals who have become members of their churches, meaning that they have been baptized as adults. It is not sure that Eleanor ever was an official church member. It could be that Eleanor was shunned without being officially excommunicated. Eleanor, an innocent victim, was shunned because the Mennonite community unable to acknowledge that her father had committed this horrendous evil and, as a consequence of this inability, there was a lingering assumption in the community that somehow Eleanor must be partly responsible. Similarly, the community likely considered what she had suffered as so shameful that, even if she might be innocent, she could not be welcomed back. Her unkempt appearance was a sign that she had internalized the message, that in a sense she was shunning herself.

The last phrase in this quotation, "They took her grace and drank," is also significant. It has a religious connotation. Grace, as a gift from God, is a basic Christian concept though it is understood in different ways. The producer, Reid, has said that he became aware of the concept through the music of Judee Sill, a woman from a fundamentalist background who became a bank robber, and later had rejected those parts of her past and now sang about searching for grace (Sepinwall). In her case, the search may have meant a search for a sense of being forgiven and accepted and gaining a new perspective and new energy for her life. This idea of grace would reflect general Christian beliefs though there are situations, such as having survived abuse, where individuals believe that they will be denied grace, forever. Catholic Christians might say that they receive God's grace by going to mass where they eat and drink bread and wine that become the real presence of the body and blood of Christ. Other Christians would understand the bread and wine more symbolically, and would similarly understand the meal as one that reflects God's grace. One aspect of this belief in grace relates to life after death, made possible, it is said, by the atonement of Christ shedding his blood on the cross. Historically, Catholic teaching held that before going to heaven one is sent to purgatory in order to be purified but that the amount of time one spends in purgatory can be shortened by buying indulgences.[9] In the Medieval era, these ideas about atonement and purgatory affected popular culture and gave rise to strange beliefs about how the blood of innocent people could reduce a person's time in purgatory, and about witches and soul suckers, also called succubi, who were devils personified as women who would seduce a man and collect his semen and thus drain him of his life force. These bizarre beliefs are from various ancient legends and mythologies. And, as we see, Eleanor would seduce men, at least boys, and trade in the blood of innocent people. This may have atoned for her own perceived sin and reducing her time in purgatory, and Reid and Stiehm used these ideas to show the drug trade's most negative effects, and the interconnected nature of all types of violence.

We return now to Eleanor sitting in the diner with Ray and Charlotte. She tells her story in the third person and describes the next steps in the girl's life:

> When Mr Galván found her, he asked her what she wanted most in the world. She asked for vengeance. So [Mr Galván] went back to her village. He shot the man's wife. She had turned a blind eye to the plight of the child. . . . He took the man back to the city where a starved dog was locked in a cage. He took the dog, put the man in, castrated the man and fed the dog. He taught the man to be a pet. He's still a pet. ("Lamia" *The Bridge*)

Eleanor emphasizes that Mr. Galván is a dangerous man who has powerful ways of obtaining loyalty. In response Ray asks: "is this some kind of parable?" ("Lamia" *The Bridge*). Eleanor replies: "I want you to understand the kind of man we work for . . . do you want to be a pet?" Ray answers: "it's not on the to-do list" ("Lamia" *The Bridge*). Ray now understands that Galván can exercise force on others if they upset Eleanor. And, given the relationship between the cartels and law enforcement, it is unlikely that Galván would ever be prosecuted. The scene ends with Charlotte asking Eleanor: "what happened to the girl?" Eleanor replies: "she survived" ("Lamia" *The Bridge*).

Eleanor gets her revenge in the series' final episode called, "Jubilex." This title alludes to a faceless demon lord in the Dungeons and Dragons role-playing game who oozes monsters, poison, and sloth. This demon lord may refer to Eleanor's father, who until the series' final moments, we only see as disembodied fingernails and hair in a cage. It also echoes the demons present in Eleanor's tattoos, which almost ooze out of her skin. In this episode, Sebastián, a businessman affiliated with Grupo Clio, which had financed the Red Ridge housing development, drives Eleanor and her caged father along a highway. They head toward the acorn tree where Eleanor's father raped her so often in earlier years. When they arrive, Eleanor says to Sebastián: "I want the demon to see my face" ("Jubilex" *The Bridge*). *The Bridge* then shows her father's entire body for the first time. He wears glasses and what looks like a crude diaper; his hair is long and unruly. When Sebastián, Eleanor, and her father get to the tree, she tells him: "you touched me. You took my grace, after that there was only blackness, the feeling of acorns on my back. I want you to feel them" ("Jubilex" *The Bridge*). Clearly, she wants her father to see the consequences of the way he abused her, and that this abuse made her who she is. It took away her life force. She then became a soul sucker, which we see in other episodes, particularly as she relates to young men.

Eleanor and Two Adolescent Boys

Eleanor's relationship with two adolescent boys, Dex and Kyle, emphasizes that she is a soul-sucking demon. Her interactions with them begin in *The Bridge*'s episode, "Ghost of a Flea," a name taken from a small painting done around 1820 by William Blake who, reportedly, claimed to have been told by a spirit that fleas were inhabited by the souls of bloodthirsty men. The painting itself shows a man with animalistic features holding a cup of blood and appearing eager to drink it. The episode in the television series starts with Eleanor crouching in the middle of a garage wearing only her underwear. When two boys, who may be twelve or thirteen, drive by on their bikes, she calls to them: "Please, I need help, I'm cold." One of the boys then asks, what happened to your clothes. She replies that there is "man blood on them" ("Ghost of a Flea" *The Bridge*). The boy suggests calling the police and Eleanor asks him not to. Survivors of abuse are often reticent to disclose abuse to the police but in this situation she exploits this tendency to camouflage the fact that her reticence is because she has just killed a man. She also takes advantage of the boys' desire to please. Eventually, she persuades one of them, Kyle, to take her to his home. He gives her some of his mother's clothes. In return, she says that he can touch her.

The characters' subsequent actions highlight the way Eleanor takes advantage of young men. Later in the same episode Eleanor and Kyle appear in the shadows in the hallway, near a number 99, in what appears to be a storage facility. Eleanor says to Kyle: "what's shared in private should be kept private, do you agree?" Kyle responds, "yeah, I guess" ("Ghost of a Flea" *The Bridge*). She then asks, "have you been with a woman before?" When he answers in the negative she unzips her shirt, steps toward him, and asks, "would you like to touch?" He was perplexed and complains: "I can't see anything." She reassures him, saying, "the light will come. It will paused [pulsed] for you" ("Ghost of a Flea" *The Bridge*). The light will allow the boy to see her; it will also take away his innocence. In this way, *The Bridge* takes the storage locker, a trope of crime television series, and inserts it into a new context. If we are at all familiar with that genre we know that this scene foreshadows Kyle's death.

The next episode, titled "Sorrowsworn," refers to a demon who, according to legend, appears most often after death or after a battle and is able to induce deep feelings of sorrow and despair. This title suggests that Kyle may already be dead. The episode opens in an El Paso police office where the Juárez detective, Marco, tells Sonya that a kid has come with his mom. They go to an interview room where they meet the teenaged boy, Dex. Dex tells Sonya and Marco that he and Kyle met a woman who had tattoos and was scary and that now his friend is missing. Because it is a white boy from the US who has gone missing, probably at the hands of a female Mexican cartel member, the police are at least open to launching an investigation. Marco and Sonya then go to Kyle's house where Sonya interviews Kyle's dad. He says that his van is missing and that some of his wife's clothes are gone, too. While Sonya talks with Kyle's father, Marco plays with Kyle's younger brother. Marco almost blends in with the background because he wears black in a room filled with shadows. This may make him more approachable and trustworthy to the younger brother. Marco then asks the boy a question, "just between you and me," whether anything is missing. The boy responds "Someone took my metamorphosis card" ("Sorrowsworn" *The Bridge*). The metamorphosis card, which comes from the Yu-Gi-Oh! Game, is a card that one plays to sacrifice a monster; in return, one will gain special powers ("Card Tips: Metamorphosis"). The version on television, which had an image of a butterfly on the front, reminds us of change, of leaving one kind of body and flying away; it also refers to a nearby butterfly sanctuary that Sonya had mentioned earlier. Marco believes that Eleanor has used Kyle to obtain his father's car and his mother's clothes. In fact, Sonya suspects that Eleanor and Kyle are still together somewhere. In fact, Kyle's body is already decaying in the desert sun. The light of grace and the temptation of sex that Eleanor offered have had devastating consequences for Kyle.

In a related scene, Eleanor appears in Dex's bed. In this scene, the light and the potential for sex bring them together in a disturbing way. Eleanor tells Dex to be a good boy or she will kill his mother. After she threatens him she leaves, telling him, "Your friend, he's with the butterflies," ("Sorrowsworn" *The Bridge*). This intimates that she has killed Kyle. What we see then is that Eleanor, being a victim of horrendous abuse, has become an abuser and a killer. Later, when Dex describes these events to the police, they go to the butterfly sanctuary; as we suspect, they find Kyle's body. It is in a barrel behind a pallet. The "grace," or life force, that is tied to Eleanor's expulsion from her home community, led to this distorted relationship with teenage boys.

Eleanor and Jaime

Eleanor takes advantage of another marginal character, a day laborer called Jaime. I argue that their relationship—and the blood shed as Jaime works for Eleanor—shows how violence against vulnerable people relates to the precariousness of the informal economy and its connection to the cartels and the police. Eleanor meets Jaime is in the episode "Sorrowsworn," the same episode where it becomes clear that she has killed Kyle. After doing so she goes shopping at a Goodwill store. In the store's change room, she pricks herself until she bleeds. She then puts on her new clothes, leaves the store, and goes to her car. A group of men in a corner of the parking lot start calling out "señora" and swarm her car. But one man, sitting in the corner of the lot, does not join them. He has his head down and wears an old beanie, jeans, and a sweater. The others explain that "he had an accident, he's not right." Eleanor shows immediate interest. She asks him: "¿Cómo te llamas?" ["What is your name?"] He responds, "Jaime." She asks: "¿Quieres trabajo Jaime?" ["Do you want to work, Jaime?"] ("Sorrowsworn" *The Bridge*). It is clear that Eleanor purposefully picks a vulnerable man to work for her. It will be easier to manipulate him. Eleanor and Jaime then drive to the butterfly sanctuary where Jaime's job is to remove the barrel from the trunk of the car. He manages to do so but with difficulty, as the barrel contains Kyle's dead body. The entire time Eleanor is on the phone. Her blood, Jaime's disability, and Kyle's body are all part of this scene.

A similar encounter is portrayed in a later episode called "Rakshasa," which is the name of a demonic being in Hindu mythology who is also known as a man-eater. This episode opens with Jaime sitting on a pail in a tent city while we see legs walking across the screen, and a truck rolls by. These movements, contrasting with Jaime sitting there, accentuate his vulnerability. He sniffs glue. The scene suggests that his addiction and his disability have deprived him of his life force. Then we see César driving Eleanor through El Paso; they come to a group of day laborers one of whom is Jaime. Eleanor says: "I prefer Jaime because he's very good at following instructions." She then holds out a small container of glue and Jaime smiles. Eleanor is luring him in order to use him. César then yells at Jaime, "Súbete atrás . . . Ándale" ["Get in the back . . . get moving"] ("Rakshasa" *The Bridge*). César and Eleanor are not seeking a human being, for them, as many others in the capitalist system, day laborers are not human beings but interchangeable products. Interestingly, there are parallels between Eleanor and Jaime: just as Jaime was sitting alone behind the other men so Eleanor sits alone in the car; also, both wear unusual clothes. Jaime's clothes are even older than those of other day laborers and Eleanor's turtleneck underneath her blouses must be sweltering in the Texas heat. Maybe these parallels give Eleanor a sense of kinship with Jaime as well as confidence that she can overpower him.

Eleanor's power becomes evident as she makes Jaime commit violent acts on her behalf. It begins when we again see César driving Eleanor. She asks him if he knows how to use a machete. César is surprised by this question and replies: "Why? Because I'm Mexican?" She answers, "No . . . so you can show Jaime." ("Rakshasa" *The Bridge*). She wants Jaime to do something violent but it is not yet clear what this will entail. Several scenes later, Eleanor and César arrive at the Red Ridge Housing Development where we also see Jaime. Eleanor and César step inside a model home and meet the real estate agent, Chip Díaz, who immediately asks Eleanor, "What's up with your gardener?" ("Rakshasa" *The Bridge*). Chip refers to Jaime who, at that moment, is sharpening his machete with his hands and eating cookies that Chip has set out for an open house to attract buyers. Eleanor explains that the gardener's name is Jaime and he is going to do some clean-up work. Then, suddenly, César grabs Chip from behind and Jaime grabs him from the front. As the three men walk across the screen, Jaime strangles Chip with a plastic bag. Throughout the process, Jaime remains expressionless. Still, after they kill Chip, Eleanor asks César to look after Jaime. The camera pans to the other side of the entryway and we see Jaime bent over Chip's body. Instead of checking for signs of life, Jaime is about to take Chip's wallet. Seeing this, César yells at Jaime, "Dame eso güey . . . Hablo, eh . . . Hay que tener respeto" ["Give me that dude . . . I'm speaking . . . We must have respect"] ("Rakshasa" *The Bridge*). César is willing to teach Jaime how to be a murderer in order to keep his own job as the cartel's driver and also tries to teach Jaime basic respect. If César left, he would be killed. But Jaime killing Chip precipitates a mass shooting involving police officers, including Sonya's boss Hank, DEA agents, and cartel members. As such it suggests a connection among Jaime's precarious economic situation, the Galván cartel, real estate agents, and their financial backers.

The next episode is called "Eidelon," a name from ancient Greek literature that refers to a spirit-image of a dead person. In this episode we see Jaime driving a van with dead bodies from the crime scene described earlier, and César driving Eleanor and a very injured Hank to an unlicensed doctor. Jaime's van is labeled "Clark and Sons Heating and Air Conditioning" and there is so much blood in the bed of his truck that it spatters onto the windshield of the car behind it. That car's passengers then scream and call the police. Suddenly, *The Bridge* shows Jaime and the "Clark and Sons" van at the side of the road in a restaurant parking lot. The screen briefly shows a close-up of Jaime, hunched over in the driver's seat, eating and looking sheepish. Just then, Sonya and Marco, the two detectives arrive at the scene and, after ensuring that Hank is not among the dead, only the missing, they attempt to mitigate Eleanor's power over Jaime. Marco yells: "¿Tú mataste a alguna de estas personas? ¿eh? . . . ¿Quién te pidió que llevaras estos cuerpos de la casa? ¡Contéstame!" ["Did you kill any of these people? . . . Who asked you to take these bodies from the house? Answer me!"] Jaime begins to cry and Marco yells: "Cómo te metiste en esta desmadre? ¿Vas a llorar? No llore. Ay que ma . . ." ["How did you get involved in this fucking mess? Will you cry? Don't cry. Oh what a . . ."] ("Eidelon" *The Bridge*). We barely hear the end of the final insult but it means sucker and alludes to blowjobs. Marco dislikes Jaime because he is weak. Sonya, more gently, gets down to his level and says, "You're Jaime, right?" He nods. She continues: "You help Eleanor sometimes, with jobs?" He nods. Sonya continues and asks, "Do you know where you're supposed to go next?" ("Eidelon" *The Bridge*). Jaime smiles and his hands fill the screen. They are covered in blood and in handcuffs but Sonya can read his destination. Eleanor has inscribed him with a bloody temporary tattoo, making him more like her and reflecting her power over him. He almost belongs to her and she will fight to make sure he comes back.

Eleanor, who no longer has what *The Bridge* understands as grace, is like a soul-sucking monster who seeks for what she has lost in others. This becomes evident again when, after the shoot-out, Monte drives her to an unlicensed doctor who drinks near-constantly. She is unconscious, lying on a table in a room full of golden and reddish shadows. When she regains consciousness, she punches the doctor, and says, "don't touch me" ("Eidelon" *The Bridge*). Her clothes are coated with blood and her head is so bloody that her hair is slicked back. Shortly thereafter, Sonya's boss Hank is placed on a similar table. As the doctor operates on the police officer, all we see are the lights at the edge of the doctor's glasses. Then, Eleanor makes the doctor wake up Hank. The doctor tells Eleanor that Hank will die if she does that; however, he gives her the syringe that will briefly make Hank conscious. She sticks it in his arm and tells him that he has something of hers. Hank, ever the Texas police officer, tells her to go to hell. He continues to be as stoic as he can, until she puts her finger into his wound. He then screams in pain. Eleanor's action suggests that she is a perverted version of Jesus' disciple, Thomas, who refused to believe that Jesus was resurrected until he puts his finger into his wounds (John 20: 25–27). Eleanor and Hank, Monte, and the doctor are also seen as connecting via blood and other bodily fluids but the power emanating from them is destructive, not life-giving.

The blood calls to mind other fluids we have seen in this show, which have revealed themselves in interactions between characters that represent law enforcement, cartels, day labor, and bystanders. These fluids are present in a variety of interactions, and I read them to figuratively point to broader connections between law enforcement, cartels, and other entities. In other words, they show how different types of power and violence are connected. The excessive blood implicates every group and thus conflates good and evil.

They root Eleanor's cruelty in her own experiences in the Mennonite community and so that community is implicated in the drug-related violence that pervades the US–Mexico borderlands. The scholarly perspectives we considered at the beginning of this chapter did not specifically mention Mennonites, but this representation on television certainly makes that suggestion. The Mennonite character, Eleanor, is not as central in *The Bridge* as she is in this analysis; yet, what we see of her is complex. Having moved from the Mennonite community to the community of people involved in the drug business, she uses her power, including her sexuality, to manipulate, threaten, control, and even to kill. The series also invites the viewer to connect her negative traits to her Mennonite origins, including abuse suffered there, to the failure of that community to acknowledge finally the way it shunned her.

Los héroes del norte

The other television series I examine in this chapter was significantly more popular. It began in 2010, ran for four seasons, and also enjoyed an exceptionally wide viewership. Being a comedy, it is quite different from *The Bridge*; it tends to make light of drug violence, cartels, and law enforcement. Still, an underlying insecurity is evident. The series features a musical group made up of most unusual characters. One is a gifted oboe player who has lost both his position in a prestigious conservatory and his girlfriend. Uncertain about what to do, he meets a drummer and a guitarist who have been performing heavy metal music but are not gaining a following and are also uncertain about what to do. The three decide to form a band but end up in prison. There they meet the local chief of police, Zacarías, who, it turns out, has been dreaming of being a singer in a band. He then joins them. But first they have to get their instruments back; a Mennonite man is holding these instruments because the others refused to pay for cheese they bought from him. Then, noticing that this Mennonite is also a musician, they ask him to join them. Sometime later the Mennonite man's niece, a young Mennonite woman called Prisca, becomes part of the show. The group has all kinds of adventures: they travel and sing in almost deserted towns; get kidnapped by a drug lord who has them give him a private session; deal with changing relationships among themselves; travel into the US to perform. Mennonite colony life, though not central to the show, is more visible than in *The Bridge* but it tends to be mocked in subtle ways. In *Los héroes* Mennonites are portrayed as similar to other Mexicans and as drawn toward larger society.

Figure 5 "Me dicen el Menona" ["They Call me the Menno"]

The main Mennonite character is named Friedrich von Bowell, though usually he is called *el Menona*, a common Mexican nickname for Mennonites. In the opening credits, he introduces himself as "Friedrich, pero me dicen el Menona" ["Friedrich, but the call me the Menno"] ("Comienza la historia" *Los heroes del norte*). He maintains the Mennonites' stereotypical overalls, but they are red. To become a rock star, he has grown out his hair, wears sunglasses, and walks, aloof, through crowds of adoring fans. His first name, Friedrich, though German, is not used among the Mennonites; they might use Heinrich, Abram, Cornelius, Johan, or Peter. It reminds us of two famous nineteenth-century

Friedrichs, Friedrich Nietzsche and Friedrich Engels, both of whom made very elaborate critiques of the existing social and political order. His last name, von Bowell, is unusual, too. It alludes to his bowels and to the fact that, due to his lactose intolerance, he cannot eat the cheese for which Mennonites in Mexico are so widely known. This sets him apart from the Mennonite community. Likewise, the name of his niece, Prisca, is different from the common Mennonite names like Helena, Katharina, Sara, Susannah, Justina, Anna, or Maria. It is short for or equivalent to Priscilla, a female leader in the early Christian church (Acts 18: 1–6). Because conservative Mennonites do not allow women in leadership, this name carries a subtle critique. This suggests that there may be a female leader underneath Prisca's traditional Mennonite clothes who is eager to get out. Her name also alludes to the famous church of Santa Prisca and San Sebastián in Taxco in the state of Guerrero. Today this church is at the center of a booming jewelry industry; at one time, it was the center of silver mining operations in Mexico. This associates Prisca with wealth and suggests that she belongs to Mexico, not just to the Mennonite colony. Thus, both their names, Friedrich von Bowell and Prisca, and their characters, critique the Mennonite community.

"Duelo de los talentos" ["Talent Duel"], an early episode, introduces us to the Mennonite characters. It opens with preparations for a duel between Friedrich, *el Menona*, and Zacarías. Zacarías, who always has an eye for women, has taken someone else's wife as his lover. In response, the woman's husband has taken *el Menona* as a hostage; kidnapping him was a way of pressuring the band. Then, for reasons that are not clear, Zacarías is obliged to fight *el Menona* in a duel before *el Menona* can be reincorporated into the group. This is illogical. *El Menona* is innocent and is forced to fight in a duel for comedic purposes. The duel takes place in a ghost-like colonial town. There are makeshift stands in front of the church and a now-unused municipal building. Few people come, though *el Menona*'s unnamed Mennonite wife and his many children are there, as is someone who protests the duel by holding up a sign that says John 3:16, a well-known verse in the Bible.[10] But the duel itself, like the TV series, is light entertainment. Once it is over, *el Menona* has reintegrated into the group and his kidnapper, don Procopio, has become the group's manager. In other words, the duel is portrayed as having little consequence. In effect, the show belittles hostage taking and kidnapping, playfully destroying boundaries between the purportedly legal and illegal realms.

Further in this episode the group enters a musical competition, and here the series intersects with the so-called war on drugs for the first time. It also takes place in an almost deserted town and there are playful allusions mass migration from the country to the city, and from Mexico to the US. When the group registers for this competition, they have to pick a name for themselves. They choose *Sicarios*, a term that refers to young men recruited by drug cartels to work as hitmen and assassins. This suggests that they may perform *narcocorridos* or admire the genre.

When the group leaves the registration desk and goes backstage to get ready, Prisca appears, wearing traditional Mennonite garb. She will also compete. In order to increase her chances of winning she makes herself look sexier by putting on a miniskirt and flipping up her blouse.[11] She is the niece of Friedrich, that is, *el Menona* and when he sees her in this outfit he is not happy. This is hypocritical, because no one was upset that he has left his family or that he has changed his dress style, albeit from plain overalls to a fancy pair of overalls. Then when Prisca goes on stage, the announcer says "que Menona Menoníssima" ["what a Mennonite Menno"] ("Duelo de los talentos" *Los héroes del norte*).

Figure 6 "Que Menona menoníssima" ["What a Mennonite Menno"]

She begins to sing, in front of a backdrop that suggests a much bigger location than this small-town musical competition. She struggles to remember all the Spanish words, and tilts her head back and forth with awkward enthusiasm. Prisca moves this way because she cannot dance, alluding to the long-standing teaching of traditional Mennonites against dancing. The camera then shifts back-and-forth between her, on stage, and the musical group, off-stage, fighting with their instruments about whether she should be allowed to sing at all.

After Prisca's act is over, the *Sicarios* take their turn; both performances integrate the Mennonite characters into the broader Mexican context. As they are singing, we see Prisca's eyes peer over the edge of the stage. The announcer deems that Prisca and the Héroes could both win the award, so both have to perform again. After a back-and-forth competition between Prisca and the Héroes, Prisca is declared the winner because one of the Héroes, Faquir jumps into the crowd, landing face first on the dirt. Meanwhile, Prisca receives the trophy, which has a phallic-like appearance. This suggests a potentially fluid connection that she could have with a man. Later, she and Friedrich then discuss her clothing and the trophy and she explains that she has been kicked out of the Mennonite community ("Faquir, levántate y anda" *Los héroes del norte*). This has left her in an uncertain world but she opts to follow her uncle to find a place in that world, as does the opportunity to participate in this contest.

Friedrich eventually returns to his home in a Mennonite colony. The episode, "Un nuevo amor" ["A New Love"] shows that he no longer belongs in his home community. "Un nuevo amor" opens and we see an adobe house as well as a barn. Inside the barn, four Mennonite men watch some older clips of the Héroes on television. This mocks the Mennonites in a subtle way because they are known to have rules against television but people are shown here as not really following the rules.[12] Also, these men speak Spanish among themselves and with Friedrich. They ask him if their eyes will fall out if they keep watching. In all likelihood, this is what Mexican society perceives as the reason that Mennonite leaders discourage television watching. *El Menona* assures the men that their eyes will not fall out. They also offer him some cheese but he declines, saying that it gives him gas. Throughout this scene, as Friedrich hangs out in the barn watching television with these men, he acts like a child or teenager. This means that he is not living up to his role as a Mennonite father; also, his inability to eat cheese means that in one sense he does not belong to the Mennonite community because cheese is what Mennonites are known for. His body has rejected his community; it implies that he has had to go and do something else.

This episode also represents *el Menona*'s family that we first saw at the duel, as if it, too, is questioning its role in the Mennonite community. His children ask him why they sing boring songs in school, that is, referring to the singing that takes place in Mennonite village schools ("Un nuevo amor" *Los héroes del norte*). After this complaint, we hear singing that would be heard in an Old Colony Mennonite Church. The camera then films low over what appears to be a Mennonite colony, due to land-use patterns. It is close enough that it seems to come from a low-flying plane or drone, and settles on a plain building. Later in the episode we hear a young girl's voice singing in the background. Eventually the camera rests on a girl sitting on a hay bale with a guitar. This girl has somehow learned how to play the guitar, something that would not have been permitted in most colonies, especially in families where the girls wear long dresses and hats when they go outside. The girl then tells her father that she would like to leave the colony, as he has. The scene would appear to mirror Prisca's early life. It also suggests that Mexican society is preferable, especially for Mennonite women, and evokes the inclusion of women we saw in the first chapter.

Friedrich, in spite of these earlier misgivings, tries to reintegrate into the Mennonite community. In the next episode, "Tocando fondo" ["Reaching Rock Bottom"], he has a meeting in what appears to be an Old Colony Mennonite church building. He confesses to the unnamed minister and his associates, Cornelio Letkemann and Cornelio Wall, common first and last names among the Mennonites. In this meeting, Friedrich also tells the church leaders about what happened to Prisca, after she had left her fiancé, Johann Cornelius, at the altar. This story is strange in several ways. In conservative Mennonite churches, including the Old Colony Church, weddings are not large separate occasions but rather small ceremonies at the end of a Sunday morning worship service. No Mennonite minister would wear all white clothes; this is probably taken from images of television preachers. In many Mennonite churches in Mexico, their clothes would be black and they would not wear a tie. Also, in Old Colony churches, ministers wear a particular kind of boots when they stand in the pulpit. Nor would any Mennonite ever be made to swear on a Bible as part of his confession, as Friedrich was. Mennonites have long taught that it is wrong to swear, that they should simply affirm (Matt 5: 34–37). Thus, the Mennonite community, to which Friedrich returns, is portrayed inaccurately; some of the elements appear to be drawn more from Mexican and US culture. This reflects the ambivalence that a Mennonite who has gone into the broader society would feel upon returning to his colony.

Friedrich then talks about other aspects of Prisca's life to the ministers, suggesting that she has gone further from the community's values than he has. In this discussion, he connects Prisca to Mexico and the broader world. He mentions that Prisca stars in a soap opera called "Heart of Cheese" ("Tocando fondo" *Los héroes del norte*). This title makes fun of the purported heart of the Mennonite community, which takes place in a soap opera, the most popular television genre in Mexico. Then, in the clip inserted into the middle of the confession, Prisca wears a perfect Mennonite hat but also a very short skirt. Evidently, she is in love with someone, and milks a cow in a way that is very sexual, before getting into bed with him. Yet, in bed, they wear a lot of undergarments and go to sleep. This suggests some prudishness on the part of the Mennonites. This allusion to sexual temptation concludes with a table full of apples. This clip implies that the so-called heart of cheese is a soft one, suggesting that the boundaries around what it means to be Mennonite may be that way, too.

These boundaries, porous though they may be, show that Prisca and *el Menona* are different from other members of the musical group. After the musical group is invited to play in LA, they get passports and visas. But, as shown in the slightly later episode "Welcome to Elei" ["Welcome to L. A."], it is hard for Prisca and Friedrich to get the same documents as the rest of the group because they do not have official birth certificates. Indeed, the Mexican bureaucrat initially does not believe these two characters are Mexican. Once the official associates them with the band, the paperwork gets done quickly. Then they have an easy time entering the US; they even offer the US border patrol officials some cheese. *El Menona* and Prisca are just different enough for it to be helpful.

This difference is not enough to protect them from the dangers faced by many migrants in their attempt to enter the US. As the group travels back from LA, they get lost in the desert, and other dynamics from the border region enter their story ("Cruzando fronteras" ["Crossing Borders,"] *Los héroes del norte*). Aliens from outer space appear on the scene and change the groups' bodies and voices in ways that evoke the tens of thousands of migrants who die in the desert or are deported. We see that these aliens have caused the characters to ooze out of their bodies. Prisca's body has Zacarías's voice and then her body gets really excited about her breasts, adjusting them constantly. Prisca's voice, however, is in Botarga's body, and her voice describes her increasing nausea and constant desire to vomit, meaning that she is pregnant, but her voice also affirms her virginity. This multifaceted mixture and dissociation reinforces the show's representation of border crossing because it refers to the rape and sexual assault many women experience as they cross into the United States. To cure this dissociation, the group first goes to a Catholic priest, and then to a woman who works with unorthodox saints and remedies. Neither can help, so eventually they find a veterinarian who puts electrodes on the men's penises and Prisca's breasts and shocks the characters' voices back to their rightful bodies ("Este cuerpo no es mío" ["This Body is Not Mine"] *Los héroes del norte*).

Los héroes del norte does not show as much of the blood and violence of the drug trade, as *The Bridge* does but the allusions are clear, particularly to the challenges associated with documented migration. It is noteworthy that *Los héroes* ties Prisca and Friedrich's Mennonite-ness to a specific way that their bodies exist in the world. Milk, cheese, and allusions to semen, which accompany Prisca's performance of exceptional innocence, and Friedrich's lactose intolerance, suggest that these characters' individual bodies are a border between Mennonite and Mexican communities. The show's playful nature implies that these Mennonite characters, though they may have some of their own cultural traits and practices, are not significantly different. Their lives are affected by hostage taking, violence, and mass migration north just as are the lives of other Mexicans, with all the accompanying risks.

MacBurro

The webcomic, *MacBurro*, is a short work with only two installments published on a Tumblr-based website between 2013 and 2015. Like *The Bridge*, it has a lot of blood and violence; at points it ridicules the violence. In this fictionalized world, a tsunami caused by the San Andrés fault, created a new world from what was Baja California Norte, Baja California Sur, and Washington, DC, now called Babel's sanctuary (Ruiz). This also alludes to the Biblical Babel where it is said that God imposed linguistic diversity so as to confuse humans and thus thwart their effort to defy God. Thus, the bar and Babel are symbols of defiance, diversity, and confusion. In the bar, the human characters encounter mutant robots and humanoid lizards, which are also called "squidheads" and "three-eyes," alluding to the idea that there may be unusual dynamics not evident to normal eyes (Glaubitz and Ruiz 2.1).[13] In addition, there are allusions to informal economic networks: the main character is a *taquero* [a man who makes tacosz] called Chente. There is also a robot-*vendedor ambulante* [a street-seller] called "Big Joe." In the comic, the *yakuza* call Chente a *ronin*, a Japanese term for a young person in between jobs, or one who is looking for his first job, that is, for getting into a network.[14] This suggests that Chente may become part of their group. In common usage in Mexico, Chente is short for Vicente. In the second installment, there are allusions to the state that allow for such an interpretation. Each minority has a shorthand label. The Mennonites, for instance, have mustache-less beards and the Russian security guards wear stars on their heads.[15]

The comic, unlike *The Bridge* and *Los héroes del norte*, focuses on violence committed by people who sit at the margins, the Mennonites, or clearly don't belong, like the *yakuza* and Russian mafiosos. I believe this text portrays violence as the product of foreigners as a way to access something so common it can be ignored. The comic's backstory is also illuminating in this regard. According to Giancarlo Ruiz, they included these characters because they exist in Tijuana. He believes there has been an Amish group there for about thirty years, and they are part of the area, although they marginalize themselves. Since they are not well-known:

> en el imaginario de uno siempre existe el potencial de la ficción. Por lo tanto, Que hacen allá dentro? queso? galletas? cantan canciones? juegan? que? . . . Entonces en Macburro pense que los Amish podrián ser como una ganga; pandilla; controlando el queso como primera orden [sic].

> [in one's imagination there is always the potential for fiction. At the same time, What do they do there? Cheese? Crackers? Sing songs? Play? What? . . . And so in *MacBurro* I thought that the Amish could be like a gang, a street-gang, which controlled the cheese market most of all]. (Ruiz)

He believes that they must have a mafia, because every group has a mafia.

This webcomic was unlikely to have had a large readership; yet, it was part of an online platform that was accessed by millions of people. This expansive readership may reflect what historian Anne Rubenstein has said about Mexican print comics in *Bad Language, Naked Ladies and Other Threats to the Nation* (1998). She argues that comics are read by large numbers of people because they are portable and vulgar (Rubenstein 8). Certainly, that description fits

MacBurro. If anything, *MacBurro* amplifies *The Bridge* and *Los héroes del norte*, in the way it portrays the problems associated with organized crime and the devastating effects of migration. Moreover, it conforms to Bruce Campbell's *¡Viva la historieta!: Mexican Comics, NAFTA, and the Politics of Globalization*. Campbell states that late twentieth- and early twenty-first-century Mexican comics reflect neoliberalism without explicitly critiquing it (46). The comic thus follows some conventions of its genre and commented on Mexican society for its limited audience.

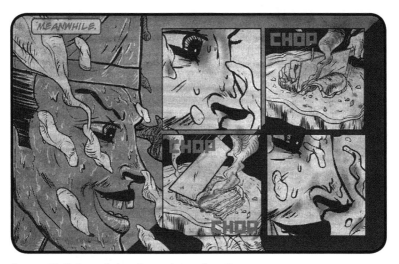

Figure 7 "Meanwhile, chop, chop, chop."

This comic places blood on center stage when it introduces us to Chente, the taco maker. Three parts of the first chapter are divided in vertical thirds where the left-most third represents Chente's face, and the subsequent thirds are divided in half, to explain the steps involved in chopping taco meat. In the left-most panel, blood made up of red dots over white beads of sweat is reduced to white beads of sweat (Glaubitz and Ruiz 1.5, 1.6). As Chente becomes sweatier from chopping meat, he also becomes more violent. Then the bright red meat, cut up in cubes, becomes a bloody, grid over Chente's face. This fragmented narration reminds us that in comics, as McCloud has pointed out, the individual panels leave a lot unsaid, and that is why the space in between the panels, called the gutter, is so significant. Viewers fill in this space with their imagination to complete the story. McCloud calls this reaching closure, which, in his view, "allows us to mentally construct a continuous unified reality" (67). In the situation at hand closure means that over the course of these three installments, Chente becomes less ugly. We also imagine that the tacos are moist and, according to the comic itself, delicious, because of Chente's blood, sweat, and other bodily fluids. This fluid emphasizes violence; it also expands beyond the page to embrace other characters.

At points in the comic, blood comes squirting out from one character to another, suggesting that, in a sense, the several minorities stand on the same ground and have certain connections, even as they inflict violence on one another. Toward the end of the comic's first installment, the Mennonites enter the bar. As they arrive, one patron runs away, exclaiming: "Keep the change I'm outta here" (Glaubitz and Ruiz 1.9, emphasis in original). Evidently, the Mennonites are identifiable even after they have left their communities, because of their speech, dress, or cultural mannerisms. The Mennonites are called the "Three Bearded Brothers." can place them into Ahmed's heterogeneous network of criminals, security, intelligence, and government, because they are connected to other minorities and to criminal activity. The brothers give the main character, Chente, their cheese and as payment, they demand that the *obayun* process their meat (Glaubitz and Ruiz 1.10). But Chente is busy so he cannot do this.

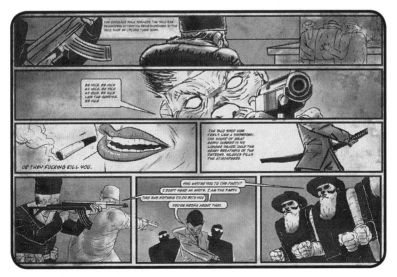

Figure 8 "Be nice."

The Mennonites then get angry and threaten him and the others in the bar. At this the Japanese *yakuza* and the Russians become angry. An armed Russian, with empty eyes and a pointed gun, commands:

Be nice. Be nice
As mice. Be nice
As rice. Be nice
Like the sunrise.
Be nice (Glaubitz and Ruiz 1.11)

The rhyme plays on the Mennonite stereotype of meekness; instead of connecting the "Amish" to their traditional food, the Russian man mentions rice, which evokes the stereotyped *yakuza*.

This encounter involving the Mennonites, the *obayun* and the Russians continues in the comic's next line of graphics. This one is divided into three frames. In the right-hand frame, the Mennonites ask the *obayun*: "Who invited you to the party." In the middle frame, he responds: "I don't need an invite. I am the party." On the left, the Russians, whose guns surpass the dividing frame, explain: "This has nothing to do with you," and the *obayun* correctly replies: "You're wrong about that" (Glaubitz and Ruiz 1.11). Like the gun pointed at the Mennonites and the gun that crosses the frames, these minorities stand on the same ground even if they are not bound together. The *yakuza* and the Russians collaborate. In spite of this opposition, I consider the three groups together because without the Mennonites, the other two groups would not have an alliance with one another. Moreover, in the broader context of drug trafficking, nothing is outside of the system.

Indeed, the next part of the webcomic represents this tension as the Russians and the *yakuza* work together to eliminate the Mennonite threat.

Yakuza: I ain't moving an inch
Russian: Don't push your luck
Yakuza: Luck!? You moron!
Russian: We should've done you in when we had a chance. (Glaubitz and Ruiz 1.12)

MacBurro's criminal characters. There is some preexisting conflict that points to a dog-eat-dog world. Then, the robot, Big Joe, dissipates the tension and the narrator in the final panel explains: "Everyone laughs, the tension is no longer palpable. The *yakuza* leave. The Russians leave. The Amish are still demanding their trade but they are visibly calmer" (Glaubitz and Ruiz 1.12). It appears that the situation has resolved.

Then, even stronger divisions appear between the minorities. The *yakuza* give Chente a saw and later in the chapter, Chente ends the conflict by using it to remove one of the Mennonite men's hands. The violent amputation, I believe, is a sign for a new way of doing business in the dog-eat-dog economy where Mennonites were naive enough to think that they might get paid in a traditional way and make deals with a handshake. The blood from this hand and Chente's sweat I would argue into the taco meat metaphorically cement these groups to one another. In spite of the clear divisions between characters, there is still more shared experiences than differences between them.

The comic's second installment connects Chente to the Mennonites. It focuses on Chente's nihilistic reflections on his own life. He wears a read hoodie and wanders around a postapocalyptic landscape holding on to the gaping wound that, according to the comic's narrator, is "[w]rapped in an old handkerchief . . . [and] is dripping blood" (Glaubitz and Ruiz 2.4). This image, a caricature of a Depression-era unemployed man—in black and red—reminds us of the Mennonite man's black clothes and his now-missing hand. The Mennonite man's blood pours out of the severed hand, and Chente takes it "and draws a blood circle around him[self]" (Glaubitz and Ruiz 2.6).

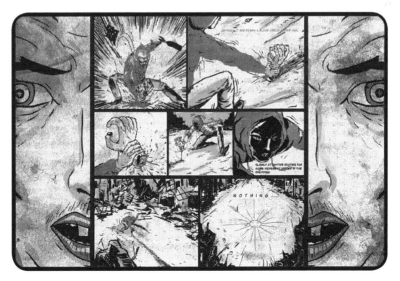

Figure 9 "A circle of blood."

Through these musings, *MacBurro* goes deep into Bowden's second Mexico with its rampant and meaningless violence. Here the comic reminds us of Zavala's observations regarding Víctor Hugo Rascón Banda's novel *Contrabando*. Its unlikeable characters, as Zavala states, mean that the novel more easily exposes and denounces "the decades-long symbiosis between the state and drug cartels" (350). Chente is similarly unlikeable and I argue that his wanderings also critique the effects of the state, which, arguably, is the largest drug cartel. The Mennonites are an integral part of the world that is bleeding its inhabitants until they die.

In the next panels, we see Chente walking through what appears to be a sunken riverbed, past what may have once been a harbor. This almost empty space shaded black, green, and red, with a few old blimps that rest over a decaying city street. In the sky, we read: "Old signs and billboards in the streets of Babel's sanctuary are a wasteland of memories" (Glaubitz and Ruiz 2.1). The shadows of grim-color boat-like objects create a solemn scene. This further evokes the criminal state, because, in line with Nordstrom's assertions about the global drug trade, borders and ports best demonstrate the close relationship between the state and cartels (191). The comic also refers to the drugs and pharmaceuticals that pass through porous borders by asserting that: "Everyone is sick and needs their medicine. The filth must be cleansed into oblivion ..." (Glaubitz and Ruiz 2.2). We imagine that these goods are exchanged for money in an informal commercial relationship. Yet, they do not alter the wasteland. As Chente observes: "Another day another coin. For what!? Dead metropolis just rotting away. Everyday. Cause' [sic] we can't snap coys [fish] from the bay!?" (Glaubitz and Ruiz 2.2). In an earlier time they probably were able to get fish there. This suggests that the chaos—a clear allusion to networks of legal and illegal commerce along the Mexico–US border—gives Chente some money. In other words, his business in the bar and taquería as either laborer or owner depends on this commerce. However, his surroundings have deteriorated so significantly that he cannot use his money to buy anything of use. For Chente, "without chaos there is no order and without order there is no community and without community there is no society and without society there is no Babel's sanctuary" (Glaubitz and Ruiz 2.2). This idea of order strongly evokes the US, and implies that its ideal of order depends on places like the hellhole Chente walks through, and his bar-taquería. Thus, in some sense, Chente's experiences facilitate people elsewhere living what they understand to be normal lives.

The comic concludes with an image that echoes our introduction to Chente chopping meat, in pages divided into vertical thirds. This time, the left and middle thirds of the page are divided into two squares each that portray him chopping onions. The right-hand third sketches Chente's body holding the Mennonite man's bloody hand and the saw he used to cut it off (Glaubitz and Ruiz 2.5). This final bloody image connects the tacos to a grotesque act of violence. Something that appears so simple is, in my reading of the comic, part of a broader system and that system is perverse. The Mennonites are subject to the whims of organized crime and neither they, nor the government, that protects the cartels, can exist independently. The characters' experiences also point to ways that some types of power, such as those of legal drugs, or commerce in ports and borders, relate to individual characters. They may form alliances to eliminate others. Blood is a key marker for these conflicts and ultimately nothing escapes it.

Los güeros del norte and México: 45 voces contra la barbarie

The two works, Javier Ortega Urquidi's *Los güeros del norte* and Lolita Bosch's *México: 45 voces contra la barbarie*, about polygamous non-LDS Mormons, are different. Ortega Urquidi and Bosch simply calls the LeBarons Mormons, but LDS church members in northern Mexico are quite clear to distinguish themselves from the LeBarons. Ortega Urquidi and Bosch portray the LeBarons as perfect victims, in sharp contrast with *The Bridge*, *MacBurro*, and *Los héroes del norte*. These television shows and comic portrayed Mennonites and criminals or deviants. An additional contrast is that the works about Mennonites are popular entertainment, this writing about Mormons seek to portray an actual kidnapping, of a young teenager, Eric LeBaron, his subsequent release, and then the killing of his brother and brother-in-law. They also portray the way the family and community responded and how they came to see the structures of power.

The two works deal with the same developments, so I discuss them together. The first is the book *Los güeros del norte* (2010) by Javier Ortega Urquidi. Ortega Urquidi is a writer who has gained a certain prominence in the state of Chihuahua. One of his earlier books, *Tierra de siete culturas* [*Land of Seven Cultures*] (3rd ed., 2012), which deals with Mormons, Mennonites, and others, won a prize from the Chihuahua Cultural Institute in 2008. The book we look at here, *Los güeros del norte*, focuses only on the LeBarons and portrays the events around the kidnapping of Eric LeBaron. The other piece I want to focus on is a small part in a larger collection by Lolita Bosch, an internationally recognized Catalán journalist based in Mexico City. The collection consists of interviews with human rights activists, journalists, and victims of the violence in Mexico. One of the interviews, the one I focus on, is with Eric LeBaron's older brother, Julián. The collection has also received acclaim. It was reviewed in the Mexican online press and was publicly presented in the Biblioteca Vasconcelos in Mexico City February of 2015 (Secretaría de Cultura). The journalist Carmen Aristegui, writing in *Aristegui Noticias*, said that this work: "reúne una serie de testimonios que narran la experiencia, enfoque y posible solución a la fallida 'guerra contra el narcotráfico' " ["collects a series of testimonies that narrate the experience, focus and possible solution to the failed 'War on Drugs' "] ("45 soluciones"). Judith Flores adds that Bosch's work is the result of collective indignation that could stop the massacre. Flores admires its different voices from different generations. Flores quotes Bosch and concludes that her collection: "Es un esfuerzo de muchos meses y de muchas personas para contestar, juntos, qué está pasando en México, cómo llegamos hasta aquí y qué sigue. Juntos, juntas, sabemos muchas cosas" ["It is an effort of many people over many months, who together, answer: what is happening in Mexico, how did we get here, and what comes next. Together, together, we know many things"] (Flores).

Ortega Urquidi's book and Bosch's interview describe the kidnapping of Eric LeBaron and the way his family, and others in the Mormon community, lobbied the government to have him released. In fact he was eventually released but the cartel, because of the lobbying, then murdered his brother, Benjamin LeBaron, and his brother-in-law, Luis Carlos Widmar. The book lauds the way that the family lobbied the government, thereby reflecting an unusual faith in the government. Most people in Chihuahua would not appeal to the government; they would say that that would only make things worse. They would either accept their losses or look for other ways of addressing them. Ortega Urquidi's *Los güeros del norte* portrays the LeBarons' belief in government as a mythological goal to which all Mexicans should aspire. In doing so these Mormons become the perfect victims and their blood becomes almost sanctified. The interview with Bosch portrays them in a similar way, as innocent victims working for peace. We get the sense that the people who protested about Eric LeBaron's kidnapping did so because it went against the prevailing myths about LeBarons; they are considered such good people that this should not be happening to them.

There are many forced disappearances and kidnappings in Mexico and many women are forgotten. All we see are their pictures fading on the outside of buildings. But according to Bosch, Eric LeBaron, was an exceptional victim. His situation was more publicly acknowledged. Also, unlike many other people, his family believed in the law and in the responsibilities of the state and also in himself. In my view, Bosch's description of their trust in the law is somewhat similar to the allusions about grace in *The Bridge*. We can imagine Eric being kidnapped by Eleanor, as Kyle and Dex, because he was also an adolescent with a lot of potential. Eric's grace, that is, his life force, did not drain away. It connected him to his family and to the government. This belief may have contributed to his exceptional release. Others have different views on why he was released. In the interview with Bosch, Julián explains that "Eric está convencido de que fue liberado sin previo pago porque, en un suceso inédito en este marasmo de violencia que sacude al país, logró convencer a sus secuestradores de que lo soltaran" ["Eric is convinced that he was liberated without payment because, in an unprecedented event in this paralysis of violence that is wracking the country, he convinced his kidnappers to release him"] (Bosch 31). Julián LeBaron adds that "aunque hay quien piensa que la presión al gobierno logró su liberación" ["although there are people who think that government pressure led to his liberation"] (Bosch 31). So, Eric was not an entirely hapless victim; he was able to challenge his captors and he had people on the outside putting pressure on those in the government. In this portrayal it is Eric's belief that leads to his release.

Julián explains that this pressure by outsiders on the government may have worked, because "inclusive hay quienes creen que hubo complicidad de los secuestradores con el gobierno del estado" ["there are those who believe that there was complicity between the kidnappers and the government of the state [of Chihuahua]"] (Bosch 31). The government's complicity could have involved yielding to public pressure, a deal with the cartel to have Eric released and then promising not to investigate if the cartel would decide to take other actions against Eric's community. This could have led to killing Eric's brother and brother-in-law. They also could have been killed because their involvement in the movements for peace and human rights made the government and the cartel uncomfortable. Julián reflects that the experience led him to a much more critical view of the government. He states: "los servidores públicos en México nunca han sido servidores públicos y nosotros siempre hemos asumido que somos sus feudos. Creo que hoy ya no queda un solo mexicano que crea en sus instituciones" ["public servants in Mexico have never been servants of the public and we have always assumed that we were their serfs. I think that today there is no longer any Mexican who believes in their institutions"] (Bosch 33). This implies that Julián sees Mexico as a feudal society, and that he positions himself as a fellow serf within it. In all likelihood, because his family became a victim, he realized the extent of governmental corruption. Thus, even though the Mormons lobbied the government in a way that suggested that they had faith in it, in reality they identified more with the very critical attitude held by most Mexicans. In the end, Julián's views support Nordstrom's claims, that there is a high level of complicity between criminals and the government, that the Mexican state is what Ahmed calls, a criminal state. Julián also develops a perspective on the issue of kidnapping:

> Si vivimos en una sociedad donde un chavo cree que la única forma de prosperar en el mundo es secuestrar a otro ser humano, y nosotros como ciudadanos colaboramos . . . nomás por el hecho de vivir en el mismo país . . . de cierta forma estamos participando [en el secuestro].

> [If we live in a society where a young man thinks that the only way to prosper in the world is by kidnapping another human being, and we, as citizens, collaborate . . . only because we live in the same country . . . in a certain way we are participating (in the kidnapping)]. (Bosch 34)

This statement underscores the notion that Mexican society is part of the problem; that society is a collaborative project that is failing. The Mormon boy was an exception to the rules and for this reason he was saved.

Ortega Urquidi also portrays the Mormons as exceptional, but not because of their belief, as in Bosch's interview. He attributes it more to the LeBarons being an almost perfect minority and to their ability to organize marches and speak with members of state of Chihuahua's and federal congresses. These actions were, in Ortega Urquidi's view, "un exhorto para que el Ejecutivo estatal implementara una estrategia eficaz antisecuestros en la entidad [del estado de Chihuahua]" ["a way to force the state executive to implement an effective anti-kidnapping strategy within the entity (the state of Chihuahua)]" (Ortega Urquidi *Los güeros* 115). He mentions that Benjamín LeBaron, Eric's brother who was later murdered, personally asked for security from the governor and the attorney general (Ortega Urquidi *Los güeros* 180, 197). In Ortega Urquidi's view, this was a positive development because it showed that the community had faith in the government. The governor gave these assurances but the cartel killed Benjamín anyway. This, from Ortega Urquidi's perspective, shows that the state simply needs more pressure and that with enough resistance, it might change.

The belief in government does not stop sadness for the LeBaron family. The scenes that portray Benjamín and Luis Carlos' deaths and funerals include multiple mentions of tears and blood and the description of these funerals is particularly moving. Ortega Urquidi speaks of how these occasions brings together the living, the formerly kidnapped, and the dead. "La sangre de los mormones humeaba, bajo la piel del sol" ["The Mormons' blood smolders under the sun, under the surface"] (Ortega Urquidi *Los güeros* 173). And all of their blood is the same under the sun. He adds "que con mirada triste los veía marchar, la pena martirizaba su sentir de astro rey, la saliva se atragantaba en su garganta, lágrimas de impotencia nublaban el suelo chihuahuense" ["with a sad look I saw them walk away, sorrow martyred their feelings of being as important as the sun, saliva stuck in their throats, tears of impotence blocked the sun from the Chihuahuan soil"] (Ortega Urquidi *Los güeros* 173). We can easily imagine the LeBarons walking to their cemetery carrying the coffins of the deceased and we can imagine that their salty tears meld with their blood. Their salty tears figuratively moved the broader community; throats were stopped; and, their sadness was so great it was as if the sun was no longer shining. In Ortega Urquidi's retelling, these events metaphorically bring the LeBarons into the Chihuahuan soil. The bodies of Benjamín LeBaron and Luis Carlos Widmar belong there as much as anyone else. So, when this kidnapping escalated into murder, everyone weeps together. They are all profoundly rooted in the state of Chihuahua and are somehow nobler, because Eric's kidnapping motivated his relatives to work for justice in their state.[16]

Ortega Urquidi's view of the Mormons as exceptional continues until the end. His panegyric echoes patriotic discourse that generally accompanies the fallen soldier as he memorializes the life and death of Benjamín LeBaron: "puso su vida sobre el altar de la libertad y luchó por el bien de sus semejantes . . .

su recuerdo pertenece a la memoria universal . . . ¡Nadie lo puede borrar!" ["he put his life on the altar of liberty and fought to help others . . . his memory is part of a universal memory . . . No one can erase it!"] (*Los güeros* 160). This is similar to some nineteenth-century poetry, written after Mexico lost significant territory to the United States. Poets like Guillermo Prieto worked to reconceive of the nation's distinctiveness after this catastrophic loss (J. J. Rodríguez 169).[17] With this in mind, Ortega Urquidi's elegy of the young Mormon places him as belonging in Mexico; in this framework, LeBaron died as a victim of the overall climate of violence he was more than a single murder victim.[18]

Julián LeBaron, in the interview with Bosch, is more matter-of-fact. He observes that "el problema más grande es que la gran mayoría de las soluciones que se proponen tienen que ver con la autoridad, pero la autoridad no es la herramienta correcta para resolver el problema del miedo" ["the biggest problem is that the majority of proposed solutions have to do with authority and the authorities, but the authority is not the correct tool to resolve the problem of fear"] (Bosch 32). He also critiques the government's violence. In his view, the only way they could enforce the law would be to put a soldier at every street corner. And, he sadly observes, "el problema es que los soldados no producen nada y que lo único que provoca un ejército es destrucción" ["the problem is that soldiers do not produce anything and the only thing that an army provokes is destruction"] (Bosch 34). The fact that the soldiers' violence, that is, the potential for destruction, is somewhat invisible: "no significa que se haya atendido el miedo que causa, porque entre más aplastas con el temor la inclinación hacia violencia, más violencia vas a tener eventualmente" ["does not mean that anyone has addressed the fear that they cause, because the more that fear is quashed with an inclination towards violence, the more likely it is that there will eventually be more violence"] (Bosch 34). State violence will only lead to more violence, and, this violence could take any number of the forms Pansters has enumerated. Thus the interview with Bosch implies that addressing fear and avoiding the use of government force is one way to get out of the criminal state. Ortega Urquidi's work plays a part in addressing this fear. He portrays connections between the LeBarons and other Mexican. They have a common experience with violence; and in the end, when they die, they will all go into the earth. Still, the Mormons are distinguished by their belief and hope.

What we see in these two works is a remarkable identification of this small minority group with Mexico. Like other Mexicans, the Mormons experienced kidnapping and murder; their blood, sweat, and tears fell onto the same soil as that of other Mexicans. The Mormons had begun with a different view of government, one that believed that the government could be persuaded to act on its basic duty to protect its citizens, but their experience brings them close to the more skeptical view held by most Mexicans. This is indicated particularly when Julian says that all Mexicans, including the Mormons, are basically serfs. Still, the Mormon belief and hope, which led them to activism for human rights and peace, despite the uncertainty of success, enhances their image at least among portion of Mexican society.

In each of these examples of popular culture, then, the characters' existence as religious minorities marks them. It affects how they act, either in response to something particular in their own lives, or in the world around them. These actions place the represented Mennonites and Mormons are perceived to be part of the networks of power and violence along the Mexico–US border. Some Mennonites ally with cartels. Eleanor, for example, is part of the Galván cartel and takes advantage of other vulnerable people to such an extent *The Bridge* ends with an incredible amount of violence. Prisca, on the other hand, is hypervirginal and is more likely to be taken advantage of because of her Mennonite background, even though she claims to have left it behind. Many representations of her involve fluids—or allusions to it. The "Three Bearded Brothers" characters in *MacBurro* suffer brutal consequences because of their involvement in the drug trade. One of their members has is blood spurting from a disembodied hand toward the end of the comic. The LeBarons, who are portrayed in direct response to historical events, become figuratively more Mexican as they become victims of kidnapping and murder. This representation opposes their self-representation in the documents that describe their conflicts with ejidos, and that in these conflicts, they were accused of not being Mexican enough. In many of these portrayals, fluids complement intangible forces of grace and hope, to cement the places of these minority figures in networks of power along the border.

5

Contact Zones in *Stellet Licht [Silent Light]* and *Las Mujeres Flores/The Flower Women*

In the summer of 2015, when I was conducting research among Low German Mennonites in northern Mexico, I visited relatives of mine in the La Honda colony, which we learned about in chapter three, together with my dad. One night my dad and I had supper with one of his cousins at a local Mennonite restaurant, arriving there by car. Our conversation included Low German, Spanish, and English. Then his cousin, using his smartphone, showed us pictures of his family, including one of his first wife, who had died earlier that year. The picture was of her in her coffin and it focused on her head and shoulders. She was dressed in white and her hair was covered with a traditional dark kerchief.[1]

To share a picture of a deceased person might seem unusual but in the Low German Mennonite community it has long been fairly common. The use of the technology of a phone for doing so has gained acceptance in recent years. And in this instance the exchange involved several languages. These three aspects of this encounter—the representation of death, the use of technology, and the exchange of languages—are themes explored in this chapter, specifically in relation to two cultural portrayals of the Mennonites in Mexico by Mexican artists: Carlos Reygadas' film, *Luz Silenciosa* (2007), called *Silent Light* in English and *Stellet Licht* in Low German, and Eunice Adorno's collection of photographs, *Las Mujeres Flores/The Flower Women* (2011).[2] I examine how these works portray technology, linguistic exchange, and death, and consider whether these portrayals can be seen as zones of contact as well as examples of connections and boundary crossing, between the Low German Mennonite culture and larger Mexican society.

Few Mexican cinematic ventures have directly engaged with Mennonite culture. Critic Ignacio Sánchez Prado explains that there was a significant change

125

in Mexico's art cinema field in the 1990s (126). This may have created space for the representation of the Mennonite community. Sánchez Prado states that, "up to the mid-1990s, art cinema was mostly a State-run affair," in terms of funding sources, distribution channels, and related policies. He further observes that these favored the promotion of an ideology that envisioned a strong state and an integrated society. In this understanding of Mexico, rural regions would be anything outside of Mexico City (Hind "Provincia" 26). These areas were seen, condescendingly, as antimodern, backward, and overtaken with religious beliefs (Sánchez Prado 126). By the late 1990s, however, this urban and state-centered vision had been greatly weakened because of financial problems following the implementation of NAFTA in 1994, and other markers of globalization. As Andrea Noble argues, by this time period, Mexican films appropriate rural and indigenous elements to advance a national culture; at the same time, the films continue to ignore rural and indigenous people (126). Emily Hind adds that in films from the 1990s and 2000s, this rural setting has been a "laboratory for social liberation," an unreachable place where dreams remain unfulfilled ("Provincia" 26–28). In some ways, then, she concludes that this is the site for ideas about what Mexico is, as the representation of rural areas can illustrate ideas about Mexico's past and future (Hind "Provincia" 43).

Reygadas used these new openings. According to Sánchez Prado, Reygadas "disrupt[ed] the continuity of nationalist film tradition," deliberately "under-min[ed] the marks of the national," and "insert[ed] himself into the limits and margins of Mexican cinema" (129). In *Silent Light*, he focused on "a community that had never been represented as an organic part of the Mexican nation" (Sánchez Prado 132). In addition to changes in Mexican cinema, Reygadas' work, and Adorno's, was also made possible by changes among the Mennonites. Admittedly, the Mennonites continue to live in separate colonies and use the Low German language, even though Spanish words had entered their vocabulary. By this time, most colonies in Mexico have accepted electricity and telephones, including cell phones, and cars and trucks have replaced horses and buggies. What this means is that changes in both the Mennonite way of life and in Mexican culture has led both to become slightly more open toward the other and this would be reflected in more commonalities, connections, and boundary crossing.

These two works are quite different from one another. Adorno's one-hundred-page book consists of photographs of women from La Honda colony in the state of Zacatecas and the Nuevo Ideal colony in Durango. It shows them in their daily lives, following traditional ways, but we also see them having cameras and cell phones and using multiple languages. Adorno's collection also has several photographs relating to death, including some that her subjects shared with her. That she included them indicates that she recognized the importance that these people attached to these photographs. Reygadas' film, *Silent Light* runs for two-and-one-half hours and is set in what is called "the Manitoba colony" near the city of Cuauhtémoc in Chihuahua. It shows how a Mennonite man, Johan Voth, struggles with the fact that he, though married to Esther, is having an affair with another Mennonite woman, Marianne. Johan continues to be with his family, even going to a swimming hole with Esther and their children to bathe them, but his affair causes Esther enormous grief. Eventually she dies of a broken heart and then, as her body is laid out for a funeral at their home, the film portrays her being resurrected when Marianne kisses her. While presenting this story, the film shows the use of various kinds of technology and of different languages.

I examine these works from the perspective of zones of contact, but this is, of course, not the director or photographer's stated goal. Reygadas' purpose was to produce a particular kind of film, and describe what he perceived as an idyllic community. For this, the Mennonites and their colony life provided a suitable setting. Not surprisingly, later on some Mennonites felt that he had used them. In 2016, I met with Irene Teichroeb, a woman in Chihuahua who works for Servicios Integrales Menonitas, an organization that has a library in the Mennonite colonies, about resources for my research. This film came up and she described how in 2007 she was a teacher and that Reygadas' film crew had come to her school seeking actors. The crew suggested that they were looking for assistance with a documentary. As there have been many documentaries made of different Mennonite colonies in Mexico, the children and their families were open to this.[3] Luna notes that Mexican film follows the literary and artistic tradition of equating women and rural areas. She claims that by the 1990s, rural areas are represented as spaces to contest and debate rights, particularly of women (210–11). However, at the premiere for the film the children's parents were aghast when they realized that the *Silent Light*'s plot revolved around adultery. Alfredo Thiessen, who plays one of Johan and Esther's children on the film, echoes this statement in an interview with Will Friesen. Alfredo explains that he thought that the film was simply showing the lives of Low German people in a documentary. Will, the interviewer, then goes on to explain some differences between the subtitles and the dialogue, and Alfredo offers more examples. For them, this suggests a further distance between the film and the lived experience of Low German people (Friesen "Unjahoolinj"). The Low German community received Adorno's work more positively in the initial stages. She began by building trust; yet, over time, she was similarly viewed with suspicion. According to rumors in Nuevo Ideal, she did not explain that the photographs were going to be exhibited so widely. Yet, I would argue that these photographs portray the community in a way that is more similar to their lives because Adorno's photographs stay closer to the lived reality of their subjects than Reygadas' film, which involves actors who play roles and follow a script. Even though these two works are different and were not produced to show zones of contact, they feature current Mennonite life and in doing so, I claim, they reveal such zones.

Both Reygadas' film and Adorno's collection of photographs have received critical acclaim. Adorno's was awarded Mexico's Fernando Benitez National Culture Prize in 2010 and it has been exhibited in Europe, the United States, and Mexico, and part of *Las mujeres flores* was recently featured in a collection called *México a través de la fotografía, 1839–1910* [*Mexico through Photography, 1839–1910*] (2013). Reygadas was given the Cannes Film Festival Best Director Award in 2012 and his film was selected as Mexico's entry for the Best Foreign Language Oscar at the 80th Academy Awards. It has enjoyed "national circulation and strong festival presence" (Sánchez Prado 133). Along with this prominence there have been many commentaries from film critics, some of which provide insights for my analysis.

CONTACT ZONES, PHOTOGRAPHY, AND THE REPRESENTATION OF DEATH

I have alluded to contact zones throughout this book, that is, spaces where Mennonites, Mormons, and other Mexicans encounter one another. This chapter addresses the concept in detail. It was coined in Mary Louise Pratt's 1991 address to the Modern Language Association and her subsequent and now highly famous work, *Imperial Eyes: Travel Writing and Transculturation*. She used the term to refer to "social spaces where disparate cultures meet, clash, and grapple with each other, often in contexts of highly asymmetrical relations of dominance and subordination—such as colonialism, slavery, or their aftermaths as they are lived out . . ." (7). One of Pratt's examples is a 1,200-page letter written by an Andean man, Felipe Guaman Poma de Ayala, to King Philip III of Spain in 1613, just forty years after the Spanish conquest. The letter appears never to have reached King Philip; indeed, it was "discovered" only in 1908, in Danish archives, and made readable in the 1970s (Pratt 5–9). Now it is recognized as an extraordinary example of early intercultural dialogue.

Guaman Poma de Ayala, who may have been of noble descent, had accepted some major elements of Christianity, and acquired a Spanish education. His letter outlined a Christian picture of the world with Andean peoples at the center, not Europeans. His Biblical creation story of Adam and Eve incorporated indigenous people and he drew elaborate parallels between Christian history and Andean history, describing them as separate but equal trajectories that diverged with Noah but reintersected at the time of Saint Bartholomew who, it was said, came to the Americas before Columbus (Pratt 9). Guaman Poma de Ayala concluded that but for Spanish greed, the conquest could have been a peaceful encounter of equals with benefits for all. What Pratt found so significant is that this man, while still rooted in his own heritage, had accepted the language and some of the ideas of his conquerors and then used them to explain his own people to them (Pratt 9). Thus, his work is an example of a contact zone. The examples in this chapter are of interpretations of contact from outside, from the majority culture.

In the years since Pratt's address, and the undeniable influence of her work, the idea of zones of contact has been adapted and used in many fields of study. Rather than fixed and confined, it is a concept that opens possibilities for imagining and understanding what happens when different cultures come in contact with each other. I do not claim that Mennonite relations with Mexican society involve a substantial power differential. Nor do the works of Adorno and Reygadas represent an effort on the part of the Mennonites to explain themselves to Mexican society, as Guaman Poma de Ayala tried to do with the Spanish colonial power.[4] But in a sense when Adorno came to Nuevo Ideal and La Honda, she was asking these Mennonite women, "who are you; what are you like; and how can I portray you to larger Mexican society?" Of course, her subjects were not necessarily aware of the final product or its widespread exhibition. Reygadas' approach was different, and his film introduced his large audience to the Mennonite community. For these reasons, the concept of contact zones can be used to examine these works, even if the interactions they portray are quite different from those of Guaman and his people with the Spanish crown.

Photography, as a contact zone, needs to be explained in further detail, in order to understand the unusual nature of Adorno's work. These observations also relate to Reygadas' film because it is so slow that I view it as a series of photographs joined together. The critic, Roland Barthes, has written that "the age of photography corresponds precisely to the explosion of the private into the public, or rather into the creation of a new social value, which is the publicity of the private" (98). This observation is most appropriate because the work of Reygadas and Adorno has contributed to bringing the lives of these private and isolated Mennonites more into the Mexican public sphere. In a Mexican context, critic Olivier Debroise has observed that photographs also facilitate an appropriation, classification, and evaluation of things, which, in turn, helps to make the world understandable for us (243). John Mraz writes that in Mexico, photography has been used to classify people by their racial or ethnic groups, their social class, or according to their origins within the country. He observes that this has related directly to the way power works in Mexico, where the whiter men at the center of power, Mexico City, perceive those from other backgrounds and from other parts of the country, as inferior ("Technologies of Seeing" 73). The photographic tendency toward classification in Mexico, Mraz observes, began in the late nineteenth century, when photography captured the activities and pastimes of the elite, while workers, or campesinos, were portrayed on the margins. Indeed, photographs showing people from lower social classes usually showed them in settings where they were overshadowed by machinery or by crops. This continued throughout the twentieth century.

Photography can also be used to overcome categorizations. I posit that Reygadas and Adorno do that in relation to the categories in which Mennonites have been perceived. One way that Reygadas does this is by using an exceptionally slow tempo and by having his actors speak relatively little, and when they do, in a language that few people understand. Sánchez Prado elaborates on this point of Reygadas' slow film. He draws on the early cinematic theorist Tarkovsky and states that:

if a take is lengthened, boredom sets in for the audience. But if the take is extended even further, something else arises: curiosity. Tarkovsky is essentially proposing giving the audience time to inhabit the world that the take is showing us, not to *watch* it, but to *look* at it, to explore it. (Sánchez Prado 128)

Thus, *Silent Light*'s slowness encourages a certain curiosity in Low German Mennonite culture. Sánchez Prado then goes on to state that "the curiosity elicited by boredom not only allows for the aesthetic contemplation … but, perhaps more importantly, it also suspends the ideological and cultural meanings present in received cinematic traditions" (128). In other words, Reygadas' slow tempo serves to open the mind of his viewers to perceiving rural Chihuahua and his Mennonite subjects in new ways. As we see, that is also the effect of Adorno's photography. It draws viewers to her subjects as people; the categories in which they may have been perceived traditionally become less significant. It is not that they are suddenly seen to be just like everyone else. Their distinct way of life, marked by sparseness, restraint, and many particular characteristics, remains. They are understood in more authentic ways by the connections and commonalities they have with the larger society.

A third key issue to be placed in context is the representation of death. In fact, there are two contexts, that of the larger Mexican society and that of the Mennonites. Historically, the place of death in Mexican culture, which is the context from which Adorno and Reygadas work, has been quite different from its place in the dominant culture in the US, Canada, and western Europe. This culture, it is often said, tends to deny death while Mexican culture, historically, is said to have embraced it. In Mexico City and states in southern Mexico, the annual Day of the Dead celebrations in November are marked with elaborate festivities including altars with *calaveritas* or white sugar skulls and marigolds as decoration, special food and prayers for departed loved ones. This annual observance is rooted in precontact cultures, but during the colonial period, certain Christian elements were incorporated and it began to be celebrated during the Catholic feasts of All Saints and All Souls. Twentieth-century governments continued to support it; indeed, by making the Day of the Dead a national holiday and promoting it in public schools, they used it to nurture a national identity and to bolster the state. The anthropologist Claudio Lomnitz, who has studied it extensively, concludes that in Mexico, "the political control over dying, the dead and representation of the dead and the afterlife has been key to the formation of the modern State, images of popular culture, and a properly national modernity" (*Death and the Idea of Mexico* 483–84).

In recent decades, however, the state's ability to use death in this way has weakened substantially. One reason for this relates to the state's reduced capacity for running the economy and controlling institutions that promote the national narrative, which, in turn, is related in part to the forces of globalization, as noted earlier by Ignacio Sánchez Prado. Aside from the human tragedy of increasing death due to ongoing violence, which we saw in the previous chapter, the situation indicates that many deaths are outside the purview of the state. In this context, says Lomnitz, the official promotion of the Day of the Dead as a national tradition has a hollow ring to it in many circles (*Death and the Idea of Mexico* 483). Lomnitz also highlights the appearance, in some areas, of a cult focused on *La Santa Muerte*, a hooded figure, sometimes dressed as a bride, carrying a sickle. In other incarnations, she is a skeletal version of the Virgin of Guadalupe, wearing a similar shawl over her head and shoulders as the images of the Virgin popular in Mexico. People, particularly those most marginalized, such as trans people, people with addictions, undocumented people, and so on, gather to pray to this figure to seek protection. Drug cartel members and the police, two groups whose members come from lower social classes, participate in such observances (Lomnitz *Death and the Idea of Mexico* 492). The emergence of this devotion lends support for the claim that the understanding and representation of death, as somehow solemn and joyful, has eroded and broken down. Pedro Ángel Palou adds that in Mexico death is no longer relevant (193). This decline in broader society might lead to a certain interest in Mennonite practices relating to death and the representation of Mennonite death in the works of Adorno and Reygadas reflects openness or an alternative.

The Mennonite approach to death is different. They have never had celebrations comparable to the Mexican Days of the Dead but neither is there a denial of death. Funerals are very important in their communities, wrote Calvin Redekop about the Old Colony Mennonites in Mexico in 1969 (33). This remains true today. Funerals will not necessarily be held in churches; they may be in homes or village schools and they will be quite well attended. There will be a sermon by an ordained minister and some familiar hymns and the religious service will last at least one hour. There will likely be comments about how the deceased is now released from the trials and hardships of this earthly life. After the funeral there will also be a meal, though this could be as simple as coffee and buns with sugar cubes, or dessert breads with syrup, cheese, and peanut butter. A man in the village makes the coffin; likewise, local women prepare the body, which will be laid out on white cloth in the coffin. The bodies will also be dressed in white though a woman will wear a dark kerchief (Buhler "Part One" 51).[5] There would be no flowers and the burial will be in the village's cemetery. After death, few people will visit the cemetery and it is unlikely that they will return to the graves with flowers.

There is not a lot of writing about Mennonite funerals but the Canadian journal, *Preservings*, published by the Plett Foundation to preserve Low German Mennonite history and identity, includes quite a few stories about cemeteries, funerals, and deaths, usually accompanied by a photograph.[6] The *Saskatchewan Mennonite Historian*, which deals with a part of Canada where many Mennonites in Mexico originally came from, presented a two-part series in 1995 and 1996 on death. In two articles, Linda Buhler explained various customs and noted that sometimes people would take a family picture of them standing behind the open coffin of the deceased. ("Part One" 51). In another article, Roland Sawatzky, the curator of the Mennonite Museum in Steinbach, Manitoba, Canada, claims that there was even some encouragement for taking photographs of deceased loved ones because in the early years the Mennonites did not always mark the graves in their cemeteries.[7] The photograph would then be the *momento mori*. This Mennonite acceptance of photographs of their deceased loved ones parallels what Nigel Llewellyn found in nineteenth-century England, namely, that postmortem photographs became significant markers of death for the survivors, at least for those who could afford the photographs. These then are elements in the context for Adorno's photographs, for my father's cousin's photograph of his deceased wife, and for those in Reygadas' film (Buhler "Part Two" 49; B. Fast 13).

REYGADAS' *SILENT LIGHT*

This chapter has already indicated Reygadas' unusual approach to *Silent Light*. By briefly examining his two preceding films, *Japón* [*Japan*] (2002) and *Batalla en el Cielo* [*Battle in Heaven*] (2005), we gain further understanding. The 1955 Danish film, *Ordet*, which, it appears, served as Reygadas' model for *Silent Light*, is also worth studying for the same reason. Reygadas' *Japón* features an unnamed middle-aged man leaving Mexico City for a remote area with the intent of dying by suicide there. While there he meets a devout, old, indigenous woman. Her name is Ascen but she explains that it is short for Ascensión. Her name refers to the Biblical ascension of Christ into heaven after his miraculous rising from the dead, and not the more typical Asunción, which refers to the miraculous assumption of the Virgin Mary into heaven. Ascen agrees to let the man stay in her barn. He then lives there but continues his solitary wanderings in the area. As he does so he begins to hesitate about his plans to take his own life; he also develops sexual feelings for this woman. Eventually he asks her to have sex with him, stressing that he needs it for spiritual reasons and accepts. The film ends with her dying in an accident. What stands out is how she, a devout, rural, indigenous woman, has diverted this man from suicide and serves as a means for his spiritual regeneration (Luca).

The film, *Battle in Heaven*, features Marcos, a working-class, obese, indigenous-looking man in his mid-thirties. Together with his wife, he kidnaps his friend's child, but the child dies in the process and he becomes wracked with guilt. Eventually Marco confides in his boss' daughter, Ana, who is rich, light skinned, and therefore considered beautiful, and who secretly works as an upper-class prostitute. They occasionally have sex and they carry each other's secrets, hers, of her double life, and his, of his involvement in the kidnapping. Early on, Marcos had been dismissive of religion but his guilt leads to spiritual turmoil, which intensifies during the celebrations for the Virgin of Guadalupe in Mexico City in the week surrounding her feast day on December 12. When he inexplicably stabs Ana to death, he is overcome with remorse; he then joins a flagellation ritual in a religious procession, ultimately collapsing dead in the Basilica of Guadalupe in northern Mexico City. The film then shows him in the country walking into the woods, receding further and further away from the camera until a mist descends and he disappears completely, as if he has ascended to heaven like Jesus or Mary. A few shots later he reappears, reaching the top of a hill where a wooden cross overlooks the countryside.

The most obvious themes in these films relate to sexual desire, betrayal, guilt, killing, death, religion and redemption, which are both universal and personal (Sánchez Prado 127). In Reygadas' films these themes cause deep inner struggles for his characters. Reygadas lifts up these struggles in a particular way. In fact, this is why he chooses not to use professional actors. He believes that with ordinary people these struggles will be conveyed more authentically and that viewers will not be distracted by remembering roles that professional actors might have played in other films. That he has his actors talk relatively little and that his films have an unusually slow tempo help to convey these struggles, or spiritual journeys into their inner lives.

It is less obvious is that these films give positive meaning to rural parts of Mexico. Critics Ignacio Sánchez Prado and Ilana Dann Luna have noted this. Luna notes that Mexican film follows the literary and artistic tradition of equating women and rural areas. She claims that by the 1990s, rural areas are represented as spaces to contest and debate rights, particularly of women (210–11). Sánchez Prado observes that Reygadas represents rural Mexico in a unique way. According to this critic, "*Japon* extricates it [the rural] from the cinematic traditions of Mexicanism and reconfigures it as a space that confronts the modern individual with . . . the spiritual and the sublime" (Sánchez Prado 124). Reygadas film, *Battle in Heaven*, brings out Mexico's closely related class and racial divisions. Marcos and Ana are on opposite sides of both of those divides. According to Mexico's social norms, it should not have been possible for them to have an intimate personal relationship, but in Reygadas' film they do. In this way, according to critic Tiago de Luca, *Battle in Heaven* "exposes an abyssal social divide by bridging this gap and making this couple *in reality*, refusing to acknowledge its incongruity within the social establishment." If *Japón* challenges Mexico's established image of the rural and if *Battle in Heaven* challenges its race- and class-based divide, it is but a small step to think of *Silent Light* as challenging the perception of the Mennonites. Even Sánchez Prado, who has been quoted at length, continues to believe that they are a community that is still not "an organic part of the Mexican nation" (132).

We glean further insight into Reygadas' approach by considering the Danish film *Ordet*. Carl Dreyer directed the film in 1955, though it is based on a play written by Kaj Munk, a Lutheran priest who was later murdered by the Nazis, in 1932. *Ordet* involves a farming family headed by Morten Borgen who has three sons: Mikkel, Johannes, and Anders. Mikkel, the oldest, who claims not to have a faith, is married to a very devout woman called Inger, who is pregnant with their third child. His second son, Johannes, is said to have gone insane from reading Kierkegaard, and believes himself to be Jesus Christ; and Anders, who would like to marry a young woman called Anne, though Anne's family, belonging to a more evangelical group, is opposed to their marriage. The two fathers then argue about the marriage but as they do so, Morten receives word that Inger has gone into a difficult labor. A doctor is able to save her but not the baby. Johannes now says that she too will die unless Morten has faith in him. Morten refuses and Inger dies. As they prepare for Inger's funeral, the fathers reconcile and allow the marriage of Anders and Anne to go ahead. Then Johannes proclaims that Inger will be resurrected if the family asks God. Inger's young daughter then asks God for help and Inger comes back to life.

Silent Light adopts many of *Ordet*'s characteristics. Both films move slowly and show wide landscapes, rooms with little furniture and are generally sparse. *Ordet*'s actors in both films seldom speak; in this way, the landscape overtakes the dialogue. The Danish language, moreover, has similarities to Low German. Both films show the rhythms and concerns of domestic life. In both films a lead actor, called Johannes in *Ordet* and Johan in *Silent Light*, stop a big ticking clock on the wall with an almost identical gesture. In both death scenes the body of the deceased rests in a white coffin on a small table set on a carpet with a tall candle on either side. And at the represented funerals, people gather and sing religious songs. However, there are differences. In *Ordet* the name, Johannes, evokes John the Baptist in the Bible who announced the coming of Christ but Johan in *Silent Light*, who appears to have been named after Johannes, has no messianic aura. An even sharper difference involves the resurrection scenes. In *Ordet*, Inger's young daughter asks God to raise Inger and in *Silent Light*, Marianne's kiss brings Esther back. Tiago de Luca says that instead of suggesting religious faith, this evokes the fairy-tale scene where the prince awakens sleeping beauty with a kiss.

Silent Light differs from *Ordet* in significant ways. Tiago de Luca holds that whereas *Ordet* was genuinely religious, *Silent Light* is not. In his view: "*Silent Light* is filled with discernible Christian signifiers which are either twisted or else presented with an indifference to the moral codes inscribed in them" (Luca). This is to create "a destabilizing ambivalence" (Luca). After the film was shown in the Manitoba colony, there was a radio debate between a minister from the Old Colony church, Rev. Jacob Dyck, and Cornelio Wall who played the lead role of Johan in the film.[8] Rev. Dyck claimed that the film did not reflect the Mennonites accurately, not even in matters of clothing. In accordance with Will Friesen's interview, George Reimer, who discusses the debate in *Kurze nachrichten*, establishes that other Mennonites who had allowed their homes to be used as sets, said the film was not what the prior explanations had led them to believe (G. Reimer). So, why then did Reygadas make this film in a Mennonite colony? Jonathan Foltz quotes Reygadas:

> The idea for choosing the Mennonites as a context for the love story was that I wanted something as timeless and placeless as possible. If you drive

around on Mennonite land, you wouldn't know where you are or what era you're in, if not for the cars.... I wanted to keep out all those things like interest, ego, jealousy, to keep only the archetypes, as in fairy tales or myth. (165)

Reygadas' purpose was not simply to portray the Mennonites as fully and accurately as possible. He wanted to produce a particular kind of film. And he found, in the Mennonites and their colony way of life, the setting for doing so. This was not quite fair to them; nevertheless, his film had the effect of introducing the Mennonites to new and much broader audiences.

CONTACT ZONES IN *SILENT LIGHT*

Voth Family Breakfast, Johan's Conversation with a Friend, and Radio Music

The film opens with a very slow moving portrayal—five-and-a-half minutes—of a sunrise in a rural Mennonite village in Mexico. There are trees, fields, and some distant buildings. Everything is peaceful and quiet except for the sounds of farm animals and birds. Viewers become drawn in. A scene of Johan at the breakfast table with his wife and children follows this long opening scene. In one instance in the film that is true to the custom of Low German Mennonites in the Old Colony Church, the family bows for a silent prayer. After eating, the film departs from the custom of this church, as the family simply leaves without praying. After Esther and the children leave the room, Johan gets up to stop the clock on the wall; then he sits down again. For a moment, he plays with a spoon; then he pushes it away and begins to weep. This scene of him weeping is long. It shows that he is in turmoil, though the film has not yet explained the reason for doing so.

Eventually we see Johan getting up and driving his pick-up truck to a nearby mechanic shop that, it appears, is run by his friend, Zacarías. As he drives to the shop, along the straight dirt roads in the colony, the camera switches back and forth from the inside of the truck and showing the side of Johan's face, to the outside showing the roads and fields. This switching tends to reinforce the sense of Johan having an inner struggle in the midst of what, according to the tradition, should be a straight path. The shots of the outside allude to Johan's connection to his farm work in rural Mexico.

At the shop, we hear Low German radio featuring Christian music, Bible stories, devotional talks, and certain news stories.[9] In this setting, Johan yells for his friend, Zacarías. The camera shifts back and forth between Zacarías

Figure 10 "Johan and Zacarías." Image courtesy of Carlos Reygadas/ Mantarraya films.

and Johan and then Zacarías, then leaves his welding and walks over to Johan. Helpers, probably his children, follow Zacarías. Then, in a shot of a field and the truck, Johan, Zacarías, and another man carry a heavy metal implement to Johan's truck, whereupon the camera focuses on the truck-bed. The men speak briefly.

The other man then leaves and Johan and Zacarías, now by themselves, begin talking. Zacarías tells Johan: "A powerful thing's come over you. You've found your natural woman. Very few know what that means. You'll have to carry on . . . if that is your destiny, then you'll have to be brave." Johan responds: "My woman is called Esther, Zacarías." Zacarías explains: "It's only for you to decide, but be careful not to betray yourself." Johan responds: "It's true that Marianne is a better woman for me. At least that's my feeling." Zacarías then says: "And that feeling may be founded in something sacred, even if we don't understand it." Then someone inside the shop switches the radio to Spanish music and Johan begins to sing what Foltz calls the "Country Roland" cover of Pedro Infante's song "No volveré" ["I will not return"] (Foltz 159).

This song brings Johan into contact with Mexican cantina culture and jukebox music, as Pedro Infante is a famous musician. The song also calls to mind, at least for Mexican viewers, a space in machista cultura that lets Mexican men cry alone with their beers, particularly over women. Critic Cynthia Tompkins argues that "No volveré," together with the surrounding scene, shows Johan's *joie de vivre* and eager anticipation of his imminent tryst with Marianne (181). Johan begins to sing along, with abandon, even as he gets into his truck and starts driving. Pedro Infante's lyrics are noteworthy:

te lo juro por Dios que me mira
te lo digo llorando de rabia
no volveré
no pararé
hasta ver que mi
llanto ha formado
un arroyo de olvido anegado
donde yo tu recuerdo ahogaré. ("Letra 'No volveré' ")

[I swear to you before God (who is watching me)
I tell you crying with rage
I won't come back
No, I won't stop
Until I see that my tears have formed
A stream of flooded oblivion
Where I will drown your memory.] (trans. Foltz 160n4)

At first, Johan drives in circles, quite fast, on the yard by the shop but by the last line of the song he drives away, leaving Zacarías in the dust, while he continues to sing.

fuimos nubes que el viento apartó
fuimos piedras que siempre chocamos
gotas de aguas que el sol resecó
borracheras que no terminamos. ("Letra 'No volveré' ")

[We were clouds that the wind separated
We were rocks that collided
Water droplets dried by the sun
Drunken nights that did not end.]

These lyrics, coming from outside Mennonite society, resonate with Johan. Indeed, they provide a measure of legitimacy for his desire to continue seeing Marianne. They are a contact zone. Further, the references in Pedro Infante's lyrics to water and stones have many religious connotations: Jesus spoke of himself as "living water" (John 4:14); he is also said to be the cornerstone of the church (1 Cor. 3:11). Christians generally, including Mennonites, are baptized with water. They are also called to be "living stones" that were rejected by other people but chosen by God (1 Peter 2: 4–5). Water is to be life-giving, but, in these lyrics, tears form a stream to drown out a memory. In some ways, this foreshadows how Esther will die while being drenched in a rainstorm. Also curious is the reference to swearing; generally Mennonites do not swear, not even in a court of law.[10] For Johan to enjoy these words in a song is another indication that he no longer follows his church's teachings and that he has accepted certain Mexican ways.

These scenes show the role of technology and linguistic exchange in providing zones of contact. The truck and a radio are vital, as is the exchange from religious radio programming in German to Pedro Infante's song. The music is a "zone of contact" with Mexican society. Also to be noted is the remarkable filmography, which moves from prolonged stillness, to Johan driving in circles and then to him in forward motion, which is alluded to by the words in the song, "I won't come back" and "No, I won't stop." Viewers are encouraged to imagine a trajectory of him moving forward though at this point in the film, it is not clear that he is moving toward Marianne.

Technology Overtakes Johan's Conversation with his Father and Esther Working in the Fields

Other scenes show Johan discussing his concern about by his relationship with Marianne; these scenes contrast with others where he is shown farming with his wife and children. Both aspects of his life include significant emphasis on the outdoors and show that he, and his Mennonite community, are firmly grounded in the Mexican context. He is so troubled, in fact, that he seeks his father's counsel. We first see Johan's parents in the barn—but, before we even see them we see a cow being prepared for milking, in a somewhat rudimentary milking system. The barn is quite small, and alludes to a time period when most Mennonites in Mexico produced milk for cheese production. Johan and his father speak in the barn and he confesses his adultery. They step outside of the barn into a snowy winter scene. The camera moves in a circle, and we see several outbuildings in their farm, echoing Johan's wild drive in his truck.

Figure 11 "Johan and Marianne." Image courtesy of Carlos Reygadas/ Mantarraya films.

It comes to rest on Johan and his father's faces and upper bodies. They talk about how this will affect Johan's mother and then the camera cuts to a scene inside of Johan's parents' home. We see several trademarks of a Mennonite home—more than one German calendar on the wall from a local business.

As the camera shifts to the two men together, we see that Johan looks anxious and his father stares straight ahead, giving advice without seeking any kind of relationship. Johan is displeased, claiming that he comes to his father to get fatherly advice, not to get advice from a preacher. Then Johan states that this relationship is in God's hands, the camera follows him across another part of the room—we see a cabinet that holds all of Johan's parents' china and other beautiful trinkets. We also notice flowered curtains covering the doorway between the main room and kitchen from the parlor and bedrooms. Johan's father says "Esther is the wife God gave you," but then he adds, "I can understand your situation." Johan went to his father seeking to confess and receive absolution, in a Mennonite version of the Catholic sacrament of confession. His father's soft response almost gives Johan permission and his mother enters from the kitchen and wishes him good day. Then, Johan thanks her, and she leaves the room. This snippet shows a few ways that traditional Mennonite culture interferes with the Mexican film. The calendars and traditional home are one small way that the film somewhat accurately represents Mennonite culture.

The film then shifts to Esther driving a big combine. We see the blades massacring the dead corn and the machine's noise overtakes the scene. As the camera then moves to Esther, we realize that in some ways, even among the Mennonites, technology overtakes people. The combine's windshield simultaneously reflects the fields, the sky, and Esther's face and this further suggests that machines are becoming more important than humans, and the machine itself is a contact zone. The film shifts to the field and we follow as if we were in her eyes and we briefly feel powerful in the face of the field. It is as if we stop the machine with Esther. The camera moves outside of it and focuses on the machinery slowing down. Esther gets the combine and has some difficulty keeping her skirt down, as she is not wearing a slip underneath her dress. She has a basket and a cooler with food for Johan and their two oldest children to whom she then eats a mid-day meal out in the field in the back of Johan's truck. Off-screen, Marianne drives onto the field and parks her car some distance away. The camera then zooms out and we see that Johan leaves Esther and the children as they eat and walks over to Marianne. The car, truck, and combine are portrayed as small in comparison to the fields and hay bales. Esther then stares defiantly at the camera, and at Marianne. This scene is remarkable for showing Esther as a very capable woman—operating a combine as it eats the fields—while still living in a traditional way and not showing her emotions. This scene also shows that Mennonite rural people are producing corn, a valuable product in Mexico, with modern machinery, and suggests that even though they may be reticent about some forms of technology, it also affects them to a significant extent. They also produce this corn for the benefit of their community and other Mexicans, and suggests that their traditional way of life may benefit others. This evokes the documents in the agrarian reform archive that implied or stated outright that the Mennonites were either perfect or deeply alienated from Mexican society and that the Mormons were excellent economic contributors and considered foreign American invaders.

Johan's Tryst with Marianne, and the Voth Children in a Stranger's Van

The next scene is of an entirely white room in what appears to be a restaurant. We soon realize that Johan has taken his children out to an ice-cream shop run by Marianne—likely a good distance from his home village. Johan and Marianne then go to a back room in the hotel next door and have their tryst.

The film does not show them actually making love. The film suggests that this is not a joyous erotic encounter. Indeed, there are tears streaming down Marianne's face, which suggests emotional anguish and that she is wracked with guilt. After a significant time lag, where the camera continues to focus

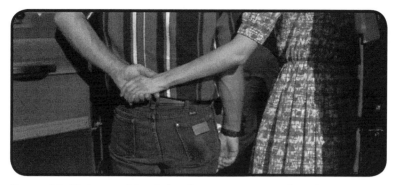

Figure 12 "Johan and his father." Image courtesy of Carlos Reygadas/ Mantarraya films.

on Marianne's tears, she says, to herself or also to Johan, "poor Esther." This delves into the moral and social implications of adultery. Then Johan gets up and goes out to check on the children. Marianne follows him. They are told that the children are in the parked van of an American man, Bobby.

Johan then finds the van and the children in it though they are hard to see because the van has darkened windows. The van has a small TV inside and on it the children are watching the Belgian singer, Jacques Brel, singing in French. We see Brel sweating on screen but the children are laughing loudly. Marianne and Johan talk briefly with the men who have been watching the children. The camera then shifts to their backs and we see that she then holds Johan's hand, in a romantic way, behind his back. Then Johan gets into the van as if to be with his children and then the cameraman inside the van tells Marianne, in English, that it is time to leave. He then closes the door in front of her and she walks away. Johan remains in the van, watching Brel together with his children, appearing remarkably happy to leave his other woman behind. This happiness belies a certain unease when we realize that a man left his children in a white van, stereotypically used by child kidnappers. The film does not encourage our unease, as it emphasizes the happy-sounding singing, but we cannot ignore this parental neglect.

I see these scenes as zones of contact; they involve technology and linguistic exchange. The van, with a TV and darkened windows suggests sinfulness by Mennonite standards and its windows, connects Johan's children with the outside world. Also, there is a new language, namely French, even if it is used only for this one song. That Brel, the singer, comes from Belgium, may be noteworthy because these Mennonites have sixteenth-century roots in that part of the world and the Flemish language in Belgium is similar to the Low German used by these Mennonites. The song that Brel sings is what critic Nils Niessen calls the "breakup version" of "Les Bonbons" ["The sweets"] (Niessen 45). I believe that this version suggests the creation of a new space with possibilities for the relationship of Johan and Marianne. Brel's tone is at once nostalgic for young love and hopeful for the future. Brel sings:

> Je vous ai apporté des bonbons
> Parce que les fleurs c'est périssable [sic]
> Puis les bonbons, c'est tellement bon [sic]
> Bien que les fleurs soient plus présentables
> Surtout quand elles sont en boutons
> Mais je vous ai apporté des bonbons . . . ("Les bonbons")

> [I have brought you candy
> Because flowers perish
> But candy is so good
> Even though flowers are more presentable
> Especially when they are buds
> But I have brought you candy . . .]

We can imagine Johan singing this to Marianne, either to signal that he is finally bringing her something more lasting than an affair, or to indicate that "it's over." The latter is more likely given the way the cameraman told Marianne that it was time to leave. In the latter case, we can imagine Johan thinking of ice cream as a form of candy, thus building on the image of the ice cream in Marianne's store. We suspect that the love between them, for which Johan almost sacrifices everything, will last only as long as an ice-cream cone in the summer.

Esther Dies and a Doctor Gives the Bad News to Johan

These scenes begin with Esther and Johan driving their car on the dirt roads through the Manitoba colony, past fields with growing crops.[11] The speedometer shows that they are going fast, about 80 km/h, as if they are trying to get away from their troubles. They do not talk much but when Esther asks about the strain between them, Johan admits that he has seen Marianne again, saying that he was not able to restrain himself. Esther then refers to Marianne as "that damned whore," to which Johan replies that the situation is very hard for her, too. Some moments later Esther says:

> Remember when we loved traveling like this? We wouldn't stop singing. We were always happy. . . . However it was, just being next to you was the pure feeling of being alive. I was part of the world. Now I am separated from it. . . . How I wish it was all just a bad dream. (Niessen 31)

Eventually, Esther makes Johan pull over and stop even though by this time it is raining heavily. She gets out of the car, reaches back for her umbrella, walks into a field to a tree for what limited shelter it can provide, and begins to weep, even as she is being drenched. Eventually she collapses and dies; the wind carries her umbrella away, suggesting that this is what is happening to her spirit. Before long, the film shows Johan slowly carrying Esther's body back to the road, indicating that her body is in Mexico even if her soul may be elsewhere.

Then a flatbed truck with two truckers pulls off the road and stops. Though Johan is not perfectly fluent in Spanish, he interacts with them, which signifies a type of contact with the outside world that goes beyond singing along with a Pedro Infante song on the radio or using an occasional Spanish word in a Low German conversation. The driver says: "Buenas tardes" ["Good afternoon"], and then commands Esther, "Levántese, levántese" ["Get up, get up"]. This comment reminds us of the film, *Ordet*, where Johannes tells Inger to get up. In *Ordet*, Inger does indeed come back to life though only after her young daughter asks God to bring her back. It also reminds us of the story of Jesus saying, "get up" to the daughter of Jairus and raising her from the dead (Mark 5:40b-42; Luke 8:54). However, the man's call does not bring Esther back.

After this, the other trucker observes, in a way that brings the film back to represented reality: "Está bien teso" ["She's very stiff"]. He asks Johan: "Dígame que le pasó a su mujer. ¿Chocaron? ¿Qué le pasó?" ["Tell me what happened to your wife. Did you crash? What happened to her?"] Very, very slowly, Johan responds: "Yo me llamo Juan, ella es mi esposa, se llama Esther" ["I am called Juan, she is my wife, her name is Esther"]. Johan never explains what happened to her. But the three men manage to place Esther's body into the car—a piece of technology—in the context of rain and their different languages. Then the Mexican men drive away with their truck and John drives away with the car and Esther's body.

This interaction in relation to Esther's body suggests a contact zone and an alternative space. These two helpful men speak in Spanish with Johan, and, in their work lives, they may regularly come into contact with Low German–speaking truck drivers who work for Mennonite businessmen. They talk about the death of this Mennonite woman in a respectful manner. The question of what caused her death is not answered but their joint work of putting her body into the car illustrates their cooperation and how these two groups can create a new space in Chihuahua. In relation to Bowden's two Mexicos referred to earlier, one where deaths are commemorated and the other with the massive number of violent deaths, Esther's death is different from both. She does not belong to the traditional Mexico, but neither is her death meaningless. There is a certain human respect and caring, including from those outside of her community, making this a remarkable contact zone.

This connects to other zones of contact. For instance when Johan and Esther are driving, the road, the land, and the rain, all connect them to Mexico, despite the historic Mennonite separateness, and the particular organization of Mennonite colonies. When the camera is focused on the side mirror, as it does for a time, even filling up the screen, it reflects various vehicles and other parts of the outside world. The windshield wipers serve to mark time as they drive and pass a truck. They also mark time when Johan is sitting in the car, waiting, as Esther is outside in the pouring rain, dying. This marking of time, Tompkins claims, correlates to Esther's reduction to a catatonic state (183). The camera also focuses on the car's dashboard and other technical features, thus highlighting the way technology of all kinds connects a representation of the Low German Mennonites to the world outside their community.

The peaceful pastoral comforts of the living contrast sharply with his inner turmoil, as Johan drives back into the heart of the Manitoba colony, with Esther's body. Things move so slowly that viewers stop paying attention. The film then presents a doctor's office.[12] In it, a near mime of a nurse calls patients from the waiting room to the examination room. The film does not portray Esther's body being brought into the examination room. It only shows Johan in a waiting area and the doctor coming and sitting down next to him to confirm to him that Esther has died. Johan, a lowly farmer, is now in contact with the educated world of medicine. This, added to the fact that places him as a Mennonite who is having an affair, he is further on the outside of his community. Still, the scenery we see through the window behind him, as well as the bilingual Spanish-German signs on the walls, has him rooted in Mexico.

The camera focuses on Johan's face and its sad expression. He is a typical Mennonite man in overalls. The film then switches to the outside of the office building where we see the window behind Johan from another perspective, and we see how this window reflects the fields. The image of the fields is superimposed on the window of the doctor's office and also over Johan's body. We had seen the fields earlier, when Johan drove to the shop to talk with his friend Zacarías, when Esther was driving the combine, and in the drive of Johan and Esther that ended in Esther's death. The image here reminds of us of those earlier images, connecting them in the minds of viewers and they become zones of contact.

The doctor embraces Johan in front of the same window and Johan begins to cry. This is unusual between two men. The doctor is a Mennonite and speaks Low German. But he is not a *Trajchtmoaka* [traditional chiropractor] that many people will see to have bones set or for complementary care. The doctor has a very high level of formal education so he represents contact with the outside world and he is fluent in Spanish. The scene also reminds us that medicine is a difficult connection for Low German Mennonites. Many Mennonite women, because of their sizeable families, will need to see doctors quite often. If they have husbands who are employed in the formal economy, as opposed to being self-employed, or employed "under the table" in the informal economy, they had the right to visit doctors affiliated with the *Instituto Mexicano del Seguro Social* (IMSS) [Mexican Social Security Institute]. If they are employed in the formal or informal sector, the same would apply. Mennonites in Mexico who do not meet these requirements would be eligible to buy subsidized insurance through the *Sistema de Protección Social en Salud* (*Seguro Popular*) [Social Protection through Health (Popular Health Insurance)] to visit low-cost public health centers, or to visit private clinics. In most of these scenarios, they would face significant challenges in communicating with their doctors or nurses because of their limited Spanish, not to mention the financial barriers.

This difficulty is in the background along with the Mennonite fields of corn there in Mexico. This is then a contact zone that is rife with the possibility of linguistic colonization, that is, for Spanish to overtake Low German as a type of linguistic communication among Mennonites, or for Spanish to enter their schools, and privileging a certain view of health care.[13] However, the way this doctor embraces Johan suggests that there is a certain level of integration between Mennonites and the world around them, and that this is helpful. The automobile technologies that facilitated Esther's death, the truckers that helped bring her body to the car, and the windows in the combine and the car that suggest connection between Mennonites and the fields, could, on a broader scale, bring Mennonites and Mexicans together.

Esther's Funeral and Unlikely Resurrection

This set of scenes begins with one where Esther's body is laid out, in a casket, in a spare room in her home. No one else is present in this initial scene. Everything is quiet. Esther's body is dressed in white except for the somewhat elaborate black head-covering, crafted to suggest the Old Colony Mennonite tradition. Then we see Johan slowly coming into the room, together with his father and his sons; they carry Esther's casket to a table in the center of the room, as if to prepare for the funeral service.

The camera then shifts to show outside the house to where several men are standing but now an image of Esther's body is superimposed over a field reflected in a window. This reminds us of the scene with Johan and the doctor where the reflection of a field was prominent, too. But here the image connects Esther with the land; her body is almost as grounded in the Mexican soil as the corn she was harvesting in a previous scene. According to custom, her body would be buried in a Mennonite cemetery on land donated by a farmer in her village. We also notice that the fields are straight, as an allusion to the straight and strict way that the Mennonites view the world.

Figure 13 "Esther's coffin." Image courtesy of Carlos Reygadas/Mantarraya films.

The film then returns indoors, into the room with Esther in the casket. Here we notice that almost everything is white. The casket and the cloth with which Esther is dressed, and the material on which her body is laid, but even the walls and the curtains and the floor are white, and contrast with her black head-covering. The whiteness helps to create a silence and a reverence. It may also suggest purity, for example, that of Esther in relation to her unfaithful husband. The slightly different shades of white may also be taken as variations in purity, which are present here; not all the Mennonites are totally pure. The whiteness may also allude to the white sugar skulls, the *calaveritas*, widely displayed in Mexico's Day of the Dead festivities, thus connecting with that part of Mexican culture.

As the camera focuses on the casket and on Esther in it we are reminded of Sawatzky's comment that historical photographs taken at Mennonite funerals of a deceased person carefully laid out in a casket can become a sole *momento mori*. But we also notice a tall candle on a silver holder on each side of the casket, and that the casket is above a red patterned rug. Candles are not used in Mennonite funeral services. They are Catholic. The candles and rug emulate the scene in *Ordet*, and allow for the Mennonite funeral to be understood by that broad Mexican audience, making this a contact zone between the two cultures.

Singing familiar hymns is an important part of Mennonite funerals as it provides an interpretation of death and helps to make death acceptable for the deceased's loved ones. The particular hymn that the people here sing is curious. It is an eighteenth-century hymn, number 726 in the *Gesangbuch* [hymn book] used by the Old Colony Mennonite Church, and it is announced by a *Vorsaenger* according to custom, but it is for engagements, not for funerals.[14] It is in the section of the hymn book called "*Gebetslied zur Verlobungsfeier*" ["A Prayer Song for an Engagement Celebration"]. The hymn asks:

Herr zu diesem wichtigen Schritte leuchte uns den Angesicht. O verschmähe unsere Bitte, unser Flehen um Segen nicht. Diese Zwei, die

sich verloben, hätten salben gern von oben, und wir andern alle stehen ihnen bei in ihrem Flehen.

[Lord, on this important step shine your face. Oh do not despise our plea or our supplications and grant us Your blessings. These two, who are betrothed, long to be anointed from above, and we hold them in supplication to You.]

This hymn would normally have been sung at a couple's engagement, celebrated on a Saturday; the wedding—a simpler affair—would take place on the Sunday one week later, at the end of the worship church service.[15]

It signals that, with Esther dead, Johan could become engaged to Marianne, that the community sought to re-create a sense of Johan's commitment to Esther even though he had betrayed her, or it could foreshadow Esther's resurrection. These different possibilities may point to the "destabilizing ambivalence" Tiago de Luca notes in his comment on Reygadas' films.

Soon thereafter we see Marianne, who has now reentered the story. She and Johan go outside the house by themselves. Johan says: "I'd give anything to turn back time . . . go back to things as they used to be." Marianne responds: "That's the only thing in life that we cannot do, Johan" (Niessen 32). Then they embrace, and, while doing so, Marianne looks at the sun and stretches her arm out. It appears that she touches the light, connecting with divine power; this action and her previous comment certainly connect her with the temporal symbols, like the clock, and the cycle of seasons, within the film. Then, Marianne goes into the immaculately white room. No one else is with Esther's body. Marianne stands in front of the casket, then slowly walks around it and carefully caresses the cloth and then kneels, close to Esther's face. Then, in a series of slow movements, she rises, bends over Esther's body, and gives her a long kiss on her lips, echoing the way that some Mennonites in Mexico might kiss a body in a casket on the cheek, which reinterprets *Ordet* in this context. When Marianne backs away, we gradually see one tear gently flowing down Esther's cheek though at first we wonder if it might be from Marianne, echoing Marianne's tears from the hotel where she and Johan had sex. Moreover, this parallel is underscored when, after a while, Esther's lips part, her eyes begin to open and, her first words back from the grave are, "Poor Johan." This suggests that she is joined with Johan, and may be ready to forgive him. Marianne says: "Johan will be all right now." Esther then says, "Thank you Marianne."

While Esther is still in the casket, though obviously alive, her two young daughters come in. They stand beside Marianne right beside the casket and they look at Esther. What is striking is that they show no astonishment or surprise at the miracle of their mother having come back to life. This could represent a normalization of the miraculous, as Niessen suggests (27–28). It could also mean that because the resurrection and this response are outside of normal time and space, beyond any one culture and they become accessible to all. Finally, Marianne's action of raising Esther represent her response to Johan's expressed hope about being able to turn back time and go back to things as they used to be, with Esther.

After Esther has clearly come back to life, we see Johan coming back into the room. Marianne has disappeared but the film does not show Johan and Esther together. This improbable resurrection—without a tearful embrace or Johan apologizing—represents the fulfillment of a sense of longing developed after watching the long, slow film in its entirety. This challenges the Mennonite theological emphasis on forgiveness and the idea that resurrection does not happen on earth. The Mennonites in Mexico typically believe that resurrection will only occur when Jesus Christ returns to earth. This thus integrates them into a positive narrative that is outside of their culture, and is likely outside of most understandings of redemption in Mexico as well. It moves the characters from a contact zone into Reygadas' unexpectedly hopeful project.

EUNICE ADORNO'S *LAS MUJERES FLORES/THE FLOWER WOMEN*

Adorno's Approach to Making the Collection

Eunice Adorno's one-hundred-page book, with eighty seven photographs, is a much smaller project than Reygadas' film; it also shows remarkable examples of contact zones. Her photographs come from the colonies of Nuevo Ideal and La Honda, in the states of Durango and Zacatecas, respectively, and most of them are about women and girls in their daily lives. These two colonies are slightly more conservative than the Manitoba colony, and there is a different type of contact with the outside world in these colonies. La Honda is very isolated from most surrounding towns, and so wealthy businesspeople have set up stores on the colony. In Nuevo Ideal, Mennonite people regularly drive to the nearby town for errands. This is in contrast with the Manitoba colony, and surrounding areas, where the wealthy businesspeople attract significant interest from the outside world through a commercial highway in the center of their colony. Life would likely be similar for most poor people in each area, but they are farther away from the highway and surrounding area in the Manitoba colony.

It is thus exceptional that Adorno was able to garner this type of access to women in La Honda and Nuevo Ideal. Her photographs show women doing up their long hair, young girls jumping on a trampoline in their dresses, a group of teenage girls standing around somewhat self-consciously, as well as freshly baked cookies on a table, dresses hanging on a clothes line to dry, the hands of a young woman held by the hands of a young man in a romantic way, the back of a woman in her bra, a woman milking a cow, decorative things in a kitchen, a woman dressed in the traditional way but driving a car and enjoying an ice-cream cone, a little girl standing on a chair beside her mother "helping" to wash dishes, several bodies of deceased people prepared for burial, and so on. Many of the photographs are close-up and intimate. Some reveal a sense of playfulness. Everything is relaxed and unforced. Some photographs were taken on the women's kitchen tables so that they appear to be sharing them with us, the viewers, as if we were friends enjoying *faspa*—a light mid-afternoon meal of coffee, bread, and dessert—together. It appears that these women welcomed Adorno into their lives.

That Adorno was able to get such close-up pictures, some of which were given to her by the women, is extraordinary. She states that she arrived to gain their trust and eventually, also that of the colony leaders, although it has been said that she did not appropriately explain what she hoped to do with the photographs after she had taken them. She was drawn by a desire to understand the girls and women and their daily life at a deeper level, as is suggested by her introduction. She met the women as they were selling things under some trees. Adorno grew fascinated with them, particularly with the contrast between their almost all black or dark-colored clothing and the brightly colored, sometimes even neon, embroidery on their head coverings. Adorno explains that over time, she began to better understand them, and the contrast between their public and private lives; that is to say that the contrast between how they present themselves to the outside world and are, in turn, understood by it, and the way that they understand themselves and present themselves to their own community. Adorno explains that:

> The houses, particularly the kitchens, constituted a kind of secret on the horizon where the[y] . . . take refuge, for hours on end, among objects and trinkets full of personal meaning. Separated from work and from their husbands, the women forge their own universe, fashioned out of chats, memories, secrets, friendships, pleasures, and diversions, and they hide

this universe beneath their cumbersome and unrevealing clothes and a reserved gaze directed at the world. (17)

In other words, to the outside world, and to Adorno's initial perspective, these women appear to be repressed. As she goes on to observe, there is one element that allows for significant personal expression: flowers. Adorno observes that they "are a common denominator among these women; the flowers appear in their dresses, in their objects, in their names, and in their gardens; the flowers have thus provided a title [for this book]" (Adorno 17). The flowers grace the homes of most Low German Mennonite people that I met and are a common print in many women's dresses. If at all possible, a woman will grow flowers outside of her home. I did not meet any women with flowers in their names— most Low German names follow traditional naming conventions within the community and are typically biblically based; it is possible that because there are a limited number of first and last names that women gain nicknames from the names of their favorite flowers. Adorno also makes it clear that the flowers initially drew her to the Low German women, but that they were not the reason that she remained connected to the community. She adds that "our real point of connection has been human feeling, which we share as women, feelings documented, now, by these photographs . . . the emotional relationships that they construct are part of a series of images, and they reveal tranquil and joyful moments that moved us away from the rigid and stereotypical idea of a conservative life" (Adorno 17). This essentialist view of women is troubling because it implies that emotions, like the flowers and kitchens she mentions earlier, are the exclusive domain of women. At the same time, this connection allows her unprecedented access to the community and leads to the production of a breathtakingly beautiful book. Moreover, this last phrase, about the photographs leading viewers beyond the rigid and stereotypical idea of a conservative life, is similar to the claim about Reygadas noted earlier that his exceptionally slow tempo leads viewers beyond boredom to curiosity and to "a suspension of received ideological and cultural meanings" and thus to an openness to consider the subjects in new ways. It is because of this that we can see the works of both Adorno and Reygadas as contributing to "zones of contact" between these fairly separate cultures.

It is worth focusing on Adorno's photographs of death in some detail, as they are unique in the history of Mexican photography and in the photography of Low German Mennonites. The closest in the study of Mexican photography would probably be some of those studied by John Mraz in *Photographing the Mexican Revolution: Commitments, Testimonies, Icons* (2012), particularly the photographs of people killed during the Mexican Revolution by the Zapatistas fighting the Villistas, two separate factions during the Mexican Revolution (98). The Villistas put their corpses in coffins, took photographs of them and then displayed the photographs to inspire anti-Zapatista sentiment. These photographs were graphic. It is also common to see the photographs of disappeared people in Mexico, particularly those of women, pasted on walls in northern cities. In Mexico City, it is quite common to see ID-style photographs of missing people on some public buses, and of the forty-three disappeared students from Ayoztinapa.[16] Adorno's photographs differ from these historical photographs of death, and these contemporary searches for the disappeared. Hers do not sanitize death but were taken and published with a different purpose.

The closest in terms of photographs of Low German Mennonites would probably be Larry Towell's *The Mennonites*, which covers Mennonites who have moved from Mexico to Canada and includes some photos of their life in Mexico; it shows their ordinary life and the difficulties of migration, but the focus is not exclusively on women. Mexican photographer Itzel Aguilera has also exhibited photographs of Mennonite life in Chihuahua ("La exposición"). Her website includes several dozen images of daily life in various communities near Ciudad Cuauhtémoc (Aguilera). An interesting comparison involves the La Honda colony's fiftieth anniversary commemorative book published in German in 2014, and in Spanish in 2016. It has more than four hundred photographs; they highlight land and farms, including farm work and farm machinery, as well as homes, schools, and churches, roads, water systems, and other tangible accomplishments. It also has many photographs of people but most of these show them in a somewhat formal way as, for example, family members lining up for a photograph or school children lining up for a class photo. Certainly, these are valuable but one does not get a sense of people living their daily lives or how they feel about things in the way one does from Adorno's photographs.

This relates to the question of power, which Pratt mentions as she discusses the idea of contact zones. In my view, the La Honda fiftieth anniversary collection reflects the perspective of the community's exclusively male religious and secular leaders. Adorno's collection is different not only because her focus is on women and girls but also because she interacted with people outside of their official roles in schools, churches, businesses, or NGO offices. Moreover, as she was taking the photographs, she shared her power as the photographer and as a representative from the majority culture with her subjects. Moreover, she gained the trust of the colony leaders, who could have prevented the women from cooperating with her. In this way, she freed the women to share their lives with her in ways of their choosing. That she, in her book, included photographs that the women shared with her confirms that the women had allowed Adorno to photograph them. The fact that Adorno came as a young soft-spoken woman surely also helped prevent a defensiveness on the part of both the women and the community leaders, as will her evident personal interest and appreciation of them. In this regard, Adorno concludes her introduction by saying: "Looking at these Mennonite women is also to be looked at by them" (17).

PHOTOGRAPHS OF TECHNOLOGY AND LINGUISTIC EXCHANGE AS CONTACT ZONES

I turn now to photographs showing particular zones of contact, starting with technology. It was only in the late-1990s that these two colonies officially accepted cars and trucks and the national electricity system. This represented an increased openness toward technology but many restraints remained.[17] That is the context for considering the technological devices in Adorno's photographs. These devices include digital cameras, cell phones, and a tape player. One of her photographs shows a girl with a disposable Kodak camera taking a picture (Adorno 38). This results in the curious sensation of being captured even as we are viewing the girl being captured by Adorno's lens. One wonders if this girl was shy and if Adorno playfully proposed: "will you let me take a picture of you taking a picture of me, if I let you take a picture of me taking a picture of you?" This stance may have helped her capture this and other images. This girl wears a modern fleece jacket over her traditional dress and stands in front of evergreen trees and dry land, the epitome of a person between cultures. The fleece and evergreens, although in Mexico, remind us of the Mennonites' Canadian origins, and the fact that many people in the two communities

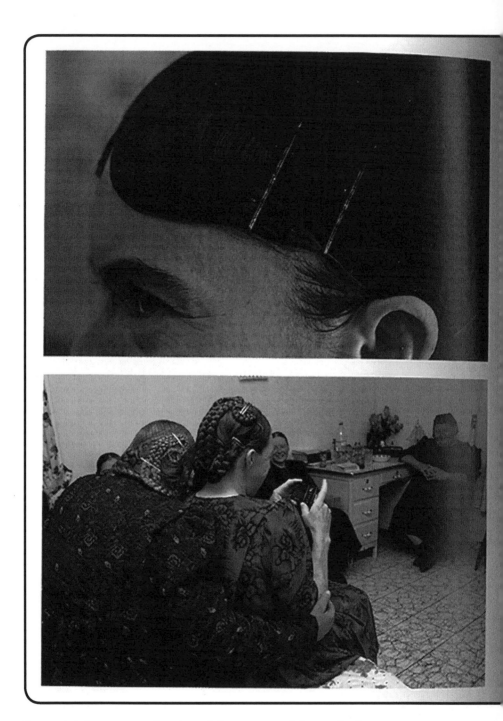

Figure 14 "La reunión de solteras/The meeting of the singles." Image courtesy of Eunice Adorno.

Adorno photographed migrate to Canada for summer farm work, and live in Mexico primarily during the winter months.

Elsewhere in the collection, Adorno moves from the outside world of children to the inner world of women. A set of four photographs arranged over two pages is significant, too, in terms of technology and language (Adorno 60–61). Three of these photographs are untitled and one is called "La reunión de solteras/Meeting of the Singles." It appears, from decorations on the wall, the china cabinet, and some of the dresses, that all these photographs were taken in the same woman's home. In the top right photograph, a woman stands and braids another woman's hair. This is a weekly process for women in the more conservative churches who never cut their hair and need to find some way to arrange it. In the lower left photograph, the women who were braiding each other's hair are now seated and one of them holds a digital camera while the other leans over her shoulder. Together, they look at photographs on the camera. In the same image, an older woman sits at a desk on the other side of the room and smiles, amused at this use of technology (Adorno 60). What is noteworthy here is the role of technology; it has brought these women together; it preserves their experience; but, in a sense, it also places them in the outside world.

The bottom right photograph portrays a woman's hands holding a Nokia phone (Adorno 61). Its pink background picks up on some of the colorful flowers on the women's dresses and in the curtains in the room. But here we notice a bilingual text message on the phone from someone called "Susch" (Low German for Sarah). The message reads: "Pos no se. Schreibst du medio mir? Wie" ["Well, I don't know. Can you write me in half (an hour)? As"]. This example of colloquial or texting Spanish, with "pos no se," instead of "Pues no sé," suggests that these women are somewhat familiar with the language of the outside world. The replacement of a specific time with "Medio" instead of the Spanish "Media Hora" ["Half an Hour"] or "Una y Media" ["One-thirty"] also suggests an interesting combination with German, as time in German begins with the world "Halb" ["Half"], such as "Halb Zwei" ["One-thirty"].

Women in these colonies purport not to know much Spanish but here we see them using common phrases and filler words from that language. For other parts of their lives, they still use standard German, a language they heard during their six years of school and continue to hear on Sundays at church. Because colloquialisms are dynamic and evolving it is likely that these Mennonite women will gradually come to use more Spanish terms. But even these few words suggest a contact zone where Mennonites cross over, using the same technology as other Mexicans and some Spanish colloquial language. Their phone, although an older style, was likely current when Adorno took the photograph, and is still widely used by people of lesser economic means in Mexico. At the same time, they also claim a certain agency over this technology in the sense that they use it on their own terms, as part of the female-dominated rituals of doing their hair.

This linguistic exchange is evident also in photographs of romantic longing. One such photograph, "I love you, Peter" is spread over two pages (Adorno 56–57). It shows four female forearms, from the inside, with various words written on them. The arms appear to be those of teenage girls, because they are wearing bracelets and what we can see are conservative dress sleeves. Older girls, who have formally joined the church, would not be allowed to wear such jewelry. Moreover, their hands do not show evidence of years of hard physical labor. But the main detail that draws our attention is the writing on their arms. From the left, the first of four pale arms reads: "I love you [unreadable name]," and the second, where the writing is in red, says, "I love you," surrounded by

Figure 15 "I love you, Peter." Image courtesy of Eunice Adorno.

six small red hearts. The third, wearing two bracelets, displays, inside a larger heart, "I love you Peter un Mary. Te amo" ["I love you Peter and Mary, I love you"]. This trilingual sentence includes a small grammatical error, saying "un," instead of the German "und," which could be a written version of the Low German spoken "onn" or "enn" [and]. The writing on the fourth arm, with only one bracelet, says, "Te amo, I love you, Johan un Tina. Te [amo] . . ." [I love you, I love you, Johan and Tina, [I love] you"]. The girls' arms show that they use three languages, English, Spanish, and German, on their own terms. They are drawing on the outside world to express something of themselves. Admittedly, they will be careful about who they show this to; they can easily pull down the sleeves so that their mothers won't notice and, in all likelihood, the ink is washable.

One other picture showing romantic longing and linguistic exchange in the collection is an untitled photograph, also from Nuevo Ideal (Adorno 69). The outside is taken from a pink-colored chocolate bar wrapper with the words, "Real Milk Chocolate." This wrapper has a heart-shaped window that, in its original form, probably showed an attractive person enjoying a chocolate bar, or, a heart-shaped chocolate sold for Valentine's Day. Now, however, someone, probably a Mennonite girl, has inserted the photograph of a young man into it. The photograph is not a perfect fit for this window but the wrapper's pink color, filled with many small silver hearts, helps to give the arrangement a romantic appearance. Maybe this young man gave the girl this chocolate bar and she then wanted to keep his picture connected with that gift. Or maybe she was too poor to buy a frame for this picture or could not get to a store to buy one. Maybe she wanted to keep it all a secret.

Whatever the reasons for this arrangement of frame and photograph, the presence of a chocolate wrapper hints at the exchange between Mennonites and the outside world. The label on the wrapper is in English. It is said to weigh 2.5 ounces. This means that it came from the United States, because both Mexico and Canada use the metric system, not ounces. This raises another possibility. This young man is working in the US and has sent this chocolate bar, along with other gifts, to his girlfriend or wife in Durango, who has then arranged the photograph and frame in this way. It is clear that this arrangement brings in something from the outside world and that it represents something meaningful in this woman's sacred place, her home.

These examples of love and longing cement our understanding of their community as a place where different cultures meet, and where we are not always sure which one dominates. The women live in a less powerful place in their religious community. They are disadvantaged also because of their inability to speak Spanish fluently. Yet, they create symbols of love and longing that draw on the outside world and thus become intercultural zones of contact.

Photographs of Death as a Zone of Contact

Adorno's representations of death among the Mennonites also engage with the outside world, in a metaphorical way. They may not offer direct connections but are likely to draw viewers, given that death is universal and that most people will reflect at least a little on their own eventual death and the rituals that they would like for that occasion, and given also that, as noted earlier, the historic understanding and representation of death in Mexico has eroded and broken down. In Adorno's images, the messiness of death relates to light and peace, and can be sublimated through ritual.

Adorno's collection has six photographs related to death. The first photograph, spread over two pages, is of a deceased woman whose body has not yet been prepared for burial (Adorno 94–95). Her body is laid out on the floor,

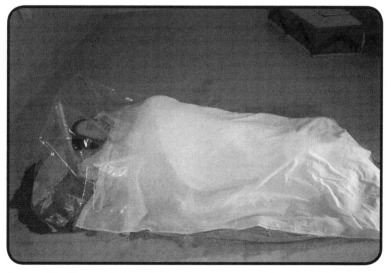

Figure 16 "Sin título/untitled." Image courtesy of Eunice Adorno.

on a thick blanket, which is probably wrapped over ice; underneath is a layer of sawdust, probably to absorb the water from the melting ice as well as blood and other bodily fluids; over top is a low plastic canopy to help keep the cold around the body and to contain odors. There is considerable blood on the floor. But it is not like an abandoned body published in a newspaper or shown on Mexican television. It shows human care. There is a white cloth covering over this woman's body and a black kerchief on her head. In the background we see, albeit faintly, part of the casket into which the body will probably be placed. The picture, which is quite dark, does not sanitize death. It is graphic and it shows that these Mennonites do the work of preparing the bodies of their people for burial. That they allowed Adorno to take this photograph indicates that they did not feel a need to hide their practices relating to death. They accept death as part of their community's life.

Figure 17 "Sin título/untitled." Image courtesy of Eunice Adorno.

Spread out on the following two pages is a photograph centered on the casket of which we saw only a part in the preceding picture (Adorno 96–97). Almost certainly this is the same room; the floor has the same turquoise color. We do not see the body, nor is there any blood on the floor. It is probable that the body has been prepared for burial, placed into the casket, and the lid closed, while people wait for the funeral. When the photograph was taken, however, the room is flooded with light. We also see two pieces of furniture in the room. One is a bench and the casket will be placed on this bench and then opened for a viewing. The other item is a refrigerator, which may have been used to make the ice. The walls and the curtain on the one window, though not entirely white, are all in light colors, conveying a starkness that reminds us of the scene of Esther in the coffin in *Silent Light*. It represents a sharp contrast to the stereotypically colorful Mexican representations of death. The only indication that we are in Mexico is the Spanish-language calendar on the wall.

On the subsequent two pages, there are two photographs on each page. The ones on the bottom half of the first page and on the top half of the second page are photographs of photographs that these women shared with Adorno. Each of these shows a coffin with the body of a man carefully laid out in it. It is as if things are ready for the funeral service and the burial. On the first page, the coffin sits on a bench on a mottled floor and in front of everyday objects including a stool, a chair, a coatrack, and a refrigerator (Adorno 98). Above this photograph on the same page is an untitled image of three ducks on a wall, arranged so that they appear to be flying away—this is a common decoration in Low German homes. In the case of Adorno's collection, it alludes to the idea of the soul flying away when a person dies.

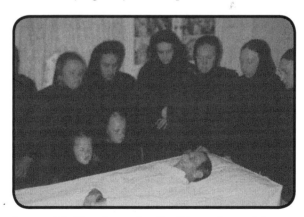

Figure 18 "Las fotos de ellas/Their photos." Image courtesy of Eunice Adorno.

In the photograph on the facing page, a group of female mourners—seven women, of all ages, and two young girls—surround the coffin with the deceased man. They may belong to this man's family (Adorno 99). They are formally dressed, in dark colors, with more formal black kerchiefs carefully crafted according to their tradition. They appear ready for the funeral. However, the women's dresses show small spots of purple and dark burgundy, the edge of beauty that their church would allow. In the background, we see the curtains over a window as well as a few other photographs, which, given their size and shape, are calendars from years past. This, and the color of the walls suggest that it is in a home rather than in a church. The image on the bottom half of this page shows a clock hanging on the wall; the wall has an off-white color but the ceiling is painted in turquoise; on one side of this photograph we see a small part of what is probably a refrigerator. Clearly, what we have in these photographs is a community's acceptance of death. It is not celebrated as in Mexico's Days of the Dead festivities but neither is a deceased person left without human care, mourning, and community ritual.

These images of technology, love, longing, linguistic exchange, and death suggest widespread contact zones between broader Mexican culture and the Mennonite minority. Reygadas' film presents transportation, technology, and music that lead to death as he portrays the Low German Mennonite community in Mexico and grounds the Low German Mennonites into Mexican soil. The first scenes I examined, involving the Voth family breakfast and Johan stopping the clock suggested that Johan was troubled by his decisions. When he then went to speak with his friend Zacarías and hear Pedro Infante's song on the radio, we saw the extent of his contact with the outside world. Technology then almost overtook his conversation with his father, and Esther combining. The machines appear more important than the human beings or their interaction with any outside context. The next scenes, where Johan has a tryst with Marianne while his children sit in a van and listen to Jacques Brel, suggest further contact with other cultures. Then, as Johan and Esther drive in the colony, and she dies in the greenery in the rain, they have further contact, this time, with kind truckers. The way the doctor announces Esther's death and the hymn at Esther's funeral, moreover, suggest further points of contact and leave us with many unanswerable questions.

Adorno's photographs present a different kind of contact zone. They also reflect the ways Low German Mennonites celebrate death, interact with technology, and their intricate linguistic exchange between Spanish, German, Low German, and English. Technology invites us into the women's homes, through their own photographs. It captivates us and, as we saw with Adorno's photograph of the women surrounding a digital camera, it connects the women to each other. Similarly, the photographs of longing and love suggest that Mennonite women engage the world on their own terms. Adorno's work demonstrates that they select the language best suited to communicate specific ideas. These photographs show that Mennonite women refashion symbols and objects in ways that are meaningful to them, including those pertaining to death.

CONCLUSION

Liminal Sovereignty considers the Mennonite and Mormon communities in Mexico; it explains that they have existed as ministates with official or unofficial exceptions from several aspects of Mexican law. Leaders in these communities have negotiated special terms with various levels of government in order to maintain some level of separation from broader society at the same time, Mennonite and Mormon people have modified some aspects of their lifestyles to live in Mexico. Similarly, over the course of the twentieth century, the Mexican state modified its expectations regarding secular public education, agrarian reform, and mestizaje, some of its central tenets, to include Mennonites and Mormons.

I often encountered portrayals of this mutual accommodation—and, in some cases, conflict—in unusual places. Mennonite and Mormon people told me about their experiences and their stories shaped how I sought out information and drew conclusions from the archives, television, film, webcomics, and novelized histories.

This led to this book's loosely chronological story that analyzes some of the most significant ways that Mennonites and Mormons have interacted with broader Mexican culture. The chapters, windows into the experiences of Mormons and Mennonites in Mexico, describe some of the religious communities' significant challenges in Mexico. *Liminal Sovereignty* began by exploring how recent immigrant Mennonites and newly returned Mormons fit early twentieth-century concepts of Mexico, when it was understood fundamentally along racial lines, and related such an understanding to theories of mestizaje. This complicated entrance of religious minorities into Mexico continued throughout the twentieth century. Part of this was denoted by documents that allude to another central tenet of the Revolution, and thus, to post-Revolutionary Mexico: agrarian reform. Documents, such as memos between bureaucrats, and materials printed in the *Diario Oficial de la Federación* [*Mexican Federal Register*] allude to the Mennonite and Mormon role in this process. The decisions relating to Mormons in these processes portrayed them as land-hungry foreign invaders and as strong economic contributors to the northern part of the state of Chihuahua. The representation of Mennonites also shifted between foreigners opposed to the Revolutionary goal of agrarian reform and as a group of people who fulfill the goal of education. Both the second and third chapters showed ways that the religious groups worked with local and state governments to find mutually beneficial solutions. The fourth chapter, about crime and violence, exemplified misunderstanding. The results of this misunderstanding, as we saw in the fourth chapter's treatment of sources, including the webcomic *MacBurro* and Javier Ortega Urquidi's accounts of Eric LeBaron's life, ranged from humorous to heartbreaking. The belief that Mennonites are criminals and non-LDS Mormons are victims are then two sides of the same coin; the exceptional communities combine to shed light on different parts of Mexico's current status as a state of exception. The final chapter interpreted representations of love, death, and technology in Carlos Reygadas' *Silent Light* and Eunice Adorno's *Las mujeres flores*, and suggested that these were contact zones that could lead to paths of understanding across cultures. It encourages us to move beyond

Figure 19 Mormonen, ihre Damf Muhle. Image courtesy of Mennonite Heritage Centre Archives.

stereotypes to encounter the richness of the lived experiences of these minority religious communities.

This photograph gives an example of mutual understanding between Mennonites and Mormons. It was taken by Cornelius Krause, a Mennonite man visiting Mexico in 1923. And, as far as I know, it is the earliest example of interaction between Mennonites and Mormons in Mexico and is, essentially, the gaze of a Mennonite outsider in Mexico on a member of another minority group there. The photograph shows a three-story brick building, which occupies most of the frame. A few of its windows are broken, but the awning over the door is intact. There are two cars parked in front of the building, and five men stand in the foreground. According to the caption from the archives, it is of "Mormonen ihre damf [sic] Mule [sic]" ["Mormons and their Steam Mill"]. That is, it portrays Mormons working at their steam mill in Chihuahua. Krause was visiting Mexico to see if it would be a suitable home for him and members of his religious community. He belonged to a conservative group of Mennonites called the Chortitzer Mennonites; this group, like other Mennonites from Manitoba and Saskatchewan, planned to emigrate from Canada for reasons of religious freedom. In 1923, however, their plans had not yet been finalized and they were still seeking a new home (Stoesz). The Mormon presence would have helped Krause understand that other groups of foreigners could flourish in Mexico; they would also have been able to mediate between the Mennonites' technological restrictions and broader society.

In the century or so covered in *Liminal Sovereignty*, there are few instances of meaningful contact between Mennonites and Mormons beyond the hints we can see in this photograph. The Mormons I met in Colonia Juárez were curious about Mennonites and I was fortunate to hear stories where curiosity turned into mutual understanding. According to a Bishop in Colonia Juárez, in the past, at Christmastime, a local choir and a choir from a nearby Mennonite *El Valle* [The Valley] colony, most of whose members belonged to the *Kleine Gemeinde* church, sang together. Both groups reached beyond their own communities and created something beautiful.

I would like to end with another story, also from Colonia Juárez, about the possibilities for better understanding. Another LDS couple in Colonia Juárez had become part of a Mennonite family. They had had a son with disabilities and, given the lack of education and social programs for people with disabilities in the state of Chihuahua, they had started a school for children with disabilities and their parents. Through this work, they had gotten to know a Mennonite family, who also had a child with disabilities. Their relationship was so important that the LDS couple even had a picture of the Mennonite family on their wall with family photographs—something that moves from kind to incredibly significant because family is one of the cornerstones of the LDS faith. They also went to the weddings and funerals of that Mennonite family and were given a place of honor when they stayed there overnight. Other Mennonites now came and visited and played in their beautiful backyard in Colonia Juárez, which is a beautiful and green area in the midst of a very dry region. The relationship that came out of a challenging situation transformed both families and their communities. Would that all of the interactions between these religious groups and the outside world lead to such conclusions.

NOTES

INTRODUCTION

1. This book calls the Mennonites in Mexico "Low German Mennonites," or "Mennonites." They might refer to themselves as "Dietsch," or Low German, the language that they speak. The largest church group is the Old Colony Mennonite Church. There are more than 30,000 Mennonites in Mexico who have been baptized as adults into various church groupings. They tend to have large families, so there are likely between 80,000 and 100,000 Mennonites in Mexico ("Mexico: 2013 Update"). For more information about the Low German language see Cox, Driedger, and Tucker's article.

2. For more information about conservative Mennonites, see Donald R. Kraybill's *Concise Encyclopedia*.

3. Scholars debate the exact dates of the Mexican Revolution. This book concurs with most scholarship, dating it to 1910 and referring to the 1917 Constitution as a significant end-point. Others note that fighting ended in 1920 so that is when the Revolution ended. For more information on these debates see John E. Dean's *How Myth Became History*, p. 174n4.

4. For an explanation of these concepts in the US context see Amanda B. Edgell's "The State of Exception, Sovereignty, and the National Emergencies Act."

5. For further explanation of the 1912 experience see Joseph Barnard Romney's MA thesis, "The Exodus of the Mormon Colonists from Mexico, 1912."

6. See, for example, Gareth Williams' *The Mexican Exception: Sovereignty, Police and Democracy*.

7. The Mexican government gave Mormons and Mennonites similar exceptions but they only published the exceptions for the Mormons, because these exceptions did not contradict the then-prevailing government ideals.

8. Other agreements from the time period allow for the same flexible definition of family, and for some foreign participation within colonization ventures. See, for example, agreements with foreign immigrants regarding colonization near the Yaqui river from 1885, reprinted in *Legislación de tierras baldíos*, pp. 75–79.

9. Early Mormon immigrants in Mexico were polygamous and belonged to the LDS church. Before immigrating, church leaders had met with then-Mexican president Porfirio Díaz and then-secretary of public works, Carlos Pacheco, who assured them they could have the kind of families they wanted as they did it *quietly* (emphasis in text) (Hardy 176).

10. Only one Mormon, Benjamin Teasdale LeBaron Mcdonnal, was prosecuted for polygamy in Mexico. One of his fathers-in-law, a US-based Mr. Ogden, complained, and this complaint eventually reached the *Dirección de Investigaciones Políticas y Sociales* [secret police] (J. Reuben Clark's "Dear Mr. Ambassador" and César Pérez Aldama and Miguel Ángel Rivera's "Carta al Jefe").

11. More information about these exceptions can be found in almost any historical survey of Mennonites in Mexico. Will explains that the exceptions do not constitute a contract of colonization: "In 1933 the Department of Migration of the Secretariat of Government inquired of the Secretariat of Agriculture's Department of Colonization as to whether such a document existed, and found that it did not" (357n5). Barragán Cisneros reproduces this information in Spanish (116).

12. Rondal R. Bridgemon's article "Mennonites and Mormons in Northern Chihuahua, Mexico," also compares the two groups but his analysis is less academic than Glenda Miller or Janet Bennion's work.

13. In earlier years the Old Colony church encouraged leaving land in each village so that landless people could cultivate it. This is no longer common in Mexico.

14. For more information about Low German Mennonites and water use see Victoria Burnett's "Mennonite Farmers Prepare to Leave Mexico, and Competition for Water." The archive for the Comisión Nacional del Agua [National Water Commission], which collects information about water use and water rights in Mexico, does not yet have information from the late 1980s to the time of publi

15. Liliana Salomán Meraz's *Historia de los menonitas radicados en Durango* is based on interviews and archival work. It offers an excellent survey of this history in Spanish.

16. David M. Quiring has also written about Old Colony people. *The Mennonite Old Colony Vision: Under Siege in Mexico and the Canadian Connection* (2003; rev. 2009) applauds the Old Colony Church for their commitment to a faithful Christian existence.

17. For more information about Mennonite history see Sawatzky, *They Sought a Country*, pp. 1–31. Information about the early years of Mennonite settlement in Mexico is found in the same monograph, pp. 31–97.

18. Kraybill provides an overview of these groups. More information about the Conferencia Evangélica Menonita can be found at "Mexico: EMMC Mexico" and the "Conferencia Menonita de México" on the website of the same name. Other information is from personal observation.

19. For more information about the history of the LDS church, see *Our Heritage: A Brief History of The Church of Jesus Christ of Latter-day Saints*. For more information about Mormon polygamy from the perspective of a faithful member of the LDS church, see Brian C. Hales' "Chronology" on his website, *Mormon Polygamy and Mormon Fundamentalism*.

20. LaVon Brown Whetten's uncritical history is more appropriate because she is writing a commemorative work for Colonia Juárez.

21. For more information about LDS church practices, including topics such as "Baptism for the Dead," Temple Garments," and a detailed description of the church's beliefs about the family, see *The Church of Jesus Christ of Latter Day Saints | Newsroom: The Official Resource for News Media, Opinion Leaders and the Public.*

22. This surname is spelled as LeBarón, Lebaron, Lebarón, or LeBaron. I use "LeBaron," except in direct citations.

23. Byron James McNeil's MA thesis, *The History of the Church of Jesus Christ of Latter-Day Saints in Mexico*, provides excellent historical context regarding Mormons in Mexico, including the LeBaron group (16–17). He, however, mistakenly argues that this church no longer exists (McNeil 24–25).

24. Lindsay Hansen Park interviews Brian Buchanan, a faithful LDS member, about polygamous marriages that took place among LDS church members in Utah after it was officially prohibited by the church by looking at personal papers and family genealogies and discusses ("Episode 129"). Bennion mentions some of these marriages in her own family history (*Polygamy in Primetime* 25). George Ryskamp's "Mormon Colonists in the Mexican Civil Registration" discusses the ways polygamous families lived in the late nineteenth century but does not allude to new polygamous relationships.

25. For more information see Brian C. Hancock's entry, "Reason and Revelation," in the *Encyclopedia of Mormonism*.

26. Some groups, like the AUB (formerly Allred group) welcome converts; the LeBarons have a longer history of actively proselytizing. For more information on converts to the AUB see *Bennion Polygamy in Primetime* 34.

27. All translations from Spanish or German to English are the author's, unless

otherwise noted. Any translations from Low German to English reflect the author's best understanding of Low German Mennonite code-switching.

28. Andrea Dyck's MA thesis, which examines a Mennonite newspaper in the early 20th century to establish Mennonite understandings of their Mexican counterparts, is analogous to my project. Michael Hunter's *Mormons and Popular Culture: The Global Influence of an American Phenomenon*, and Randy Astle's discussion of Mormons in cinema, also relate to my project.

29. Amish and Mennonite people have similar religious roots in the radical Anabaptist (re-baptizer) wing of the Protestant Reformation in Europe. The Amish began in 1693 when a leader, Jakob Amman, believed that the Mennonites were not strict enough in certain matters. Today, Amish people maintain strong lines of separation from the outside world by carefully monitoring their interactions with technology. Some Mennonites also eschew cars, drive only black cars, or wear simple clothing. For more information, see Donald Kraybill's *Concise Encyclopedia*.

30. Luann Good Gingrich's *Out of Place: Social Exclusion and Mennonite Migrants* in Canada is an example of feminist engaging with the lives of Low German Mennonites.

31. Whetten's history of Colonia Juárez states that it will not deal with this situation (xii).

CHAPTER 1. MENNONITES, MORMONS, AND
THE REGISTRATION OF FOREIGNERS IN THE 1930S AND 1940S

1. The registry was created by the "Ley de Migración de los Estados Unidos Mexicanos" ["Migration Law of the United Mexican States"] on April 19, 1926.

2. Thanks to Bruce Wiebe for providing information about these documents.

3. In the 1930s and '40s a majority of the Mennonites lived near Cuauhtémoc, Chihuahua and Mormons near Nuevo Casas Grandes, Chihuahua. The registration required them to travel to the Immigration offices in Cuidad Juárez, a distance of 200–400 km.

4. The 1917 Mexican Constitution restricted Catholicism in Mexico by, among other things, prohibiting religious education. In 1926, when the government moved to enforce these provisions, the Catholic Bishops suspended mass. The three-year Cristero War followed and the fighting was particularly intense in

west-central Mexico. The government closed most religious schools and hospitals in Mexico during this time period. For more information, see, for example, Ángel Arias' *Entre la cruz y la sospecha: los cristeros de Revueltas, Yáñez y Rulfo*.

5. There were Asian and Afro-descendent people as well; they are seldom included in Mexico's founding mythology. For more information see "Now Counted by their Country, Afro-Mexicans Grab Unprecedented Spotlight."

6. Alexandra Stern adds that in Mexico in "the late 1800s prominent *científicos* promoted whitening the population through European immigration and colonization and uplifting the Indians through civic assimilation and education" ("Mestizophilia" 189).

7. See also Stern "Mestizophilia" 190.

8. For more information about phrenology in Mexico see, for example, Gabriela Castañeda López's "La frenología en México durante el siglo XIX." These categories also imitate categories developed for criminals under Spanish colonial rule and in early decades of Independence throughout Latin America. See, for example, "Documento original de filiación del soldado" for Honorato Barriga, Jesús Blanco Sandoval, Jacinto Bermudez Saldaña and others who deserted the army in the nineteenth century in the Archivo General de la Nación in Bogotá, Colombia.

9. See also Stern "Eugenics" 152.

10. For more information about hybridity and mestizaje, see Dalton's *Mestizo Modernity: Race, Technology, and the Body in Post-Revolutionary Mexico* (Gainesville: University Press of Florida, 2018). For further information on hybridity, see, for example, Joshua Lund's *The Impure Imagination: Toward a Critical Hybridity in Latin American Writing* or Pedro Ángel Palou's *El fracaso del mestizo*.

11. See, for example, Johann Loeppky's, "Journal on a Trip to Mexico, 1921." The Mormons appear to have faced less conflict around education and their flagship Academia Juarez was never closed by the government.

12. For more information see, for example, Amos Morris-Reich's *Race and Photography: Racial Photography as Scientific Evidence, 1876–1980*.

13. See, for example, "José Flores Ramos," which presents a man, his wife, and their child. These passports present examples of misclassification only in that they include more than one person with the head of household's description.

14. Louis Kaplan argues that photography has been linked with a sense of haunting since the nineteenth century when there was a desire to uncover spirits in a scientific way (211).

15. See, for example, Margo Glantz's *La Malinche, sus padres y sus hijos*.

16. For more information about whether Mennonites are Dutch or German see T. D. Regehr's "Of Dutch or German Ancestry? Mennonite Refugees, MCC and the International Refugee Organization."

17. Mormon modesty restrictions have changed over time; today they are clothing that would be worn over temple garments. Temple garments are an expression of some devout Mormons' faith, and cover from knees to the neck and shoulders ("Temple Garments").

18. According to Russell Cluff, many Mormons used the category of student when they entered the country as missionaries (Re: Mennonites and Mormons in Mexico). Indeed, because of Mexico's anticlericalism, there was a very limited missionary presence of Mormons or any other religious group in the early decades after the secular Revolution. Boanerges Rubalcava states that missionaries came to Mexico in the mid-nineteenth century but mostly served the colonies. His article in the *Encyclopedia of Mormonism* acknowledges that missionaries returned in greater numbers after 1946 once the ostensibly secular country was more open to religion.

19. In 1932, 1933, and 1935, Leonora, Elmo, and Douglas Farnsworth Neilson were also listed as students. They were 17, 15, and 17, so this designation makes more sense ("Farnsworth Neilson Elmo," "Farnsworth Nielson Leonora," and "Farnsworth Nielson Douglas").

20. For more information about the complicated process through which the LDS church abandoned polygamy, see Lindsay Hansen Park's *Year of Polygamy* podcast. For example, she has interviewed Denver Snuffer, who claims Joseph Smith was never a polygamist ("Episode 128").

21. The Mormons also had a small colony, Colonia Morelos, in the state of Sonora until 1912.

22. A woman's children were typically listed on her documents but their photographs were seldom included. This was the case for Mexican women (as demonstrated in passports at the Archivo de la Secretaría de Relaciones Exteriores) and for foreign women (those studied in this chapter and others in the same collections of documents).

23. One of her relatives, Ralph Clarence Farnsworth, also has a foreign resident document even though he was born in Idaho and lives in Arizona ("Ralph Clarence Farnsworth").

24. There are typos on most of these cards. In some cases, there are various spellings for the surnames, and so I have left them as they appear on the cards, in others, I have corrected the spelling.

CHAPTER 2. WHOSE LAND IS IT

1. For more information about the law and the LDS church in the US, see Nathan B. Oman's "International Legal Experience and the Mormon Theology of the State, 1945–2012."

2. Palomares Peña notes the Chihuahua state government wanted the Mennonites to be like the Mormons (30).

3. The most recent histories, such as Dormady and Tamez's, do not reach this time period.

4. See, for example, Pete Brown's "Institutions, Inequalities, and the Impact of Agrarian Reform on Rural Mexican Communities," which dealt with the then-current implications of the 1992 reforms to Agrarian Laws in Mexico. See also the ten-volume series *Historia de la cuestión agrarian en México* published from 1988 to 1990, which focused primarily on the relationship between the government and peasants. Rosario Robles B.'s "La participación estatal en la agricultura: veinte años de irrigación y crédito" in *Historia de la cuestión agraria mexicana: política estatal y conflictos agrarios 1950–1970* is an excellent example.

5. For more information see James J. Kelly's "Article 27 and Mexican Land Reform: The Legacy of Zapata's Dream."

6. By 1959, there is an ongoing problem. According to bureaucrat Elfego Piñon Cordoba, most of the land "se encuentra ocupado por personas ajenas a ese núcleo, encontrándose también algunas construcciones propiedad de las gentes que por muchos años lo han poseído" ["was occupied by people who are not from the area, although we also find some buildings that belong to people who have owned them for a long time"] (Piñon Cordoba).

7. This undated report draws on information from the three summaries of colony populations; it was likely written in 1956 or 1957.

8. Palomares Peña mentions the Casas Grandes conflict in passing (49).

9. The document states "El Inspector Federal del Tra-" and then does not continue the dash on the following line. I assume it would be del "Trabajo," as the letterhead states that it comes from that sector of the government.

10. The letter claims the man is a "ministro de culto" ["minister of religion"]. The LDS church has a male lay leadership and this could refer to a number of leadership assignments.

11. Rodríguez Villarreal had been an interim governor of Colima, and was involved in politics in Colima and in Tamaulipas, before moving to federal politics (Camp 1943).

12. This letter repeats most of a letter from May 2, 1972. The earlier letter includes the names of thirty-five heads of family and states that the land was invaded. It does not mention Mormons.

13. The CCI began in 1963 to challenge inefficiency in the CNC. For more information see Don M. Coerver's encyclopedia entry, "Confederación Nacional Campesina."

14. There is the option to contact the ejido, but they have not replied to my queries. This suggests that the website is no longer being updated. The most recent updates are from October 2012.

15. The ejido provides a reproduction of the first page of Teodoro de Croix's declaration, likely from the Agrarian Archive.

16. For information from the perspective of the members of the colony, see Ortega Urquidi *Los güeros del norte* 45–60.

17. García Paniagua would become the Minister of Agrarian Reform in the mid-1980s, and his actions reappear in chapter 3.

CHAPTER 3. MENNONITES AND AGRARIAN REFORM

1. Carolina Vargas and Martha García Ortega explain that Mennonites have now formed an ejido in the state of Quintana Roo (329). Closer study suggests that the Mennonites purchased land from an ejido (Hernández). I assume they are now living as a community in such a way that Vargas and García Ortega might understand as an ejido, as they have a central leadership that deals with the government on their behalf.

2. Scholars of Mennonites use the term *agraristas* to refer to ejidatarios. I maintain this word use in direct citations only.

3. Sawatzky claims they purchased 3,000 acres (1,214 hectares), and adds that in 1934 this colony purchased an additional 6,500 acres (2,630 hectares) (Sawatzky, *They Sought a Country*, 194). This number seems too small, given that it is estimated that between 950 and 1,000 Mennonites settled in Durango.

4. It is still difficult to find the text of these privileges in the archives today. I found a copy of it enclosed with other documents relating to agrarian reform in the collection relating to the J. Santos Bañuelos ejido, and not in the Archivo General de la Nación with other presidential declarations.

5. This mirrors my experiences—including a discussion with a professor of urban planning at the Universidad Autónoma Ciudad Juárez [Autonomous University of Ciudad Juárez], who wanted to encourage other Mexican people to emulate Mexican business practices.

6. The government retained 8,000 hectares for private landownership and another 4,000 was allocated for an ejido. Sawatzky says that the Mennonites paid for this 4,000 as a goodwill gesture (Sawatzky *They Sought a Country*, 182, 196). Elorduy also retained 1,000 hectares for the workers on his ranch (Bergen *La Honda*, 7).

7. For more information about the decades of industrialization and the "Mexican Miracle," see, for example, Héctor Aguilar Camín and Lorenzo Meyer's *A la sombra de la Revolución Mexicana*.

CHAPTER 4: MENNONITES AND MORMONS IN MEXICO'S DRUG WARS

1. In the Biblical account, people attempted to defy God by building a tower to the heavens. God then brought in a diversity of languages, sowing confusion among the people, and causing the failure of their project (Gen 11:1–9).

2. Most of Ortega Urquidi's works are now available as eBooks.

3. See, for example, Enrique Demond Arias' *Drugs and Democracy in Rio de Janeiro: Trafficking, Social Networks, and Public Security*.

4. Joy Langston's *Democratization and Authoritarian Party Survival: Mexico's PRI*, traces the PRI to 1929. She argues that it began as the National Revolutionary Party, which became the Mexican Revolutionary Party in 1940 and the Institutional Revolutionary Party in 1946 (Langston 2).

5. For further information about narcocorridos see César Jesús Burgos Dávila's "Narcocorridos: antecedents de la tradición corridística y del narcotráfico en México," James H. Creechan and Jorge de la Herrán Garcia's "Without God or Law: Narcoculture and Belief in Jesús Malverde," or Elijah Wald's *Narcocorrido*.

6. Writing in Mexico about crime and corruption is exceptionally dangerous, particularly in the state of Veracruz. For more information see Azam Ahmed's "In Mexico, 'It's Easy to Kill a Journalist'" or the Committee to Protect Journalists' report, "Mexico."

7. For more information about the fascination with Amish or plain-dressing religious groups, see Valerie Weaver-Zercher's *Thrill of the Chaste*.

8. Since the series ended, el Chapo has broken out of prison, and given an extensive interview with Sean Penn in *Rolling Stone* ("El Chapo Speaks"). He was recaptured and in January 2017 and extradited to the US.

9. For more information and a comparison between Catholic and Protestant notions of grace see, for example, Kirsi I. Stjerna's "Grace Only? Or, All is Grace?"

10. This popular Bible verse states: "For God so loved the world that he gave his only Son, so that everyone who believes in him may not perish but may have eternal life."

11. In a case of life imitating art, Itali Heide Schellenberg from Cuauhtémoc participated in the 2016 version of *La Voz de México* [*The Voice of Mexico*]. Her white skin, blonde hair, and Mennonite background, may have helped her get votes in the television competition ("Itali Heide").

12. Some Old Colony Mennonites in Mexico use televisions, and others do not.

13. I cite the pages in the comic by their chapter and page number. The events of 2.1 occur in chapter 2, page 1.

14. Traditionally a *ronin* was a samurai without a master; today in Japan it also alludes to unemployed young men.

15. This webcomic confuses Mennonites and Amish—the majority of Mennonite men in Mexico are clean-shaven; a small number have mustaches. They generally wear cowboy hats. Mennonite men are known for drinking in bars when they leave their colonies, and drinking beer on the streets of their colonies or in their barns and sheds behind their houses.

16. Julián LeBaron worked with Javier Sicilia's movement for peace in Mexico for a brief period. Then after some disagreements with Sicilia, he left the movement.

17. See, for example, Slavoj Žižek's *Violence: Six Sideways Reflections*, pp. 1–2.

18. For more information see Jaime Javier Rodríguez's *The Literatures of the U.S.-Mexican War: Narrative, Time, and Identity*.

CHAPTER 5. CONTACT ZONES IN *STELLET LICHT* [*SILENT LIGHT*] AND IN *LAS MUJERES FLORES/THE FLOWER WOMEN*

1. For more information about the photography of deceased women see Paulina Barrenechea, Carolina Escobar, Andrea Herrera, and Gabriela Rivera's

"Discusión: 'Ofrendas fotográficas contra el femicidio. Archivo por la no violencia a las mujeres'. Sobre prácticas, fotografías, política de los afectos y zonas de contacto feministas."

2. Adorno's book was published by La Fábrica, as part of a selective book-publishing workshop organized by the Festival Photo España and the Center for the Arts of San Agustin Etla, Oaxaca, Mexico.

3. National Geographic, for instance, made a documentary about the Sabinal and Capulín colonies in Northern Chihuahua called *Living in a Perfect World.*

4. There are few examples of this type of communication. Most communication from the Low German community is to others within the same community, in German or Low German, or it is colony leaders communicating with bureaucrats or politicians in Spanish.

5. Thanks to Helen Fast from the *Saskatchewan Mennonite Historical Society* for making these articles available.

6. Loewen's *Village Among Nations*, which portrays Low German Mennonites in great detail, does not detail their funerals or their relationship with photographic and cinematic technology. Similarly, Larry Towell's *The Mennonites*, a collection of photographs taken between 1990 and 1999, which demonstrates the hardships of the poorest Mennonites in heart-wrenchingly beautiful ways, has no photographs of death.

7. This is the case in cemeteries in Mennonite communities in Mexico. Graves in the early years after immigration to Mexico had no stones or had modest stones that have since deteriorated to the point of being unreadable. Those from the 1980s onward remain readable.

8. The Manitoba colony is closely connected to the city of Cuauhtémoc and several other colonies. Thus, this film was accessible by those Mennonites whose religion permitted viewing a film in a theater.

9. This radio station is likely *De Brigj* [The Bridge], run by Mennonite Community Services in Aylmer, Ontario, Canada, and broadcast throughout Latin America.

10. Most Mennonite groups follow Jesus' edict, "do not swear… Let your word be 'Yes, Yes' or 'No, No'; anything more than this comes from the evil one" (Matt 5:36–37). To avoid swearing in courts Mennonites usually affirm that they will tell the truth.

11. They are likely driving in the Manitoba colony, near the hotel and restaurant where the previous scenes were filmed.

12. Low German Mennonite health is an emerging area of research. For more information about Low German Mennonite health in Canada, see Luann Good Gingrich and Kerry Preibisch's "Migration as Preservation and Loss: The Paradox of Transnational Living for Low German Mennonite Women," Judith C. Kulig, Margaret Wall, Shirley Hill, and Ruth Babcock's "Childbearing Beliefs among Low-German-Speaking Mennonite Women" and Judith C. Kulig, Ruth Babcock, Margaret Wall, and Shirley Hill's "Being a Woman: Perspectives of Low-German-Speaking Mennonite Women." For more information about Mexico, see Islas-Salinas, Pérez-Piñón, and Hernández-Orozco's "Rol de enfermería en educación para la salud de los menonitas desde el interaccionismo simbólico."

13. The Old Colony Church sponsors village schools for six years of education in each village in the colonies in Mexico. In the Cuauhtémoc area, some Old Colony schools have grades and teach some Spanish. Other churches sponsor schools that teach in ways that follow government guidelines more closely.

14. In church services, be it a regular worship service or a funeral or wedding service, there would be a group of *Vorsänger* [song leaders] sitting on a platform in the front and announcing the hymn and leading the congregation. This service is in a home so they have only one *Vorsänger*.

15. Some church groups, such as the *Kleine Gemeinde*, the *Conferencia Evangélica Menonita*, and the *Conferencia Menonita de México* would have the wedding service as a separate celebration, which would then be followed by a reception.

16. For more information on missing and murdered students, see Francisco Goldman's "Crisis in Mexico: The Disappearance of the Forty-Three." For more information about the general representation of violence in Mexico, see Wil G. Pansters' "Zones of State-Making: Violence, Coercion, and Hegemony in Twentieth-Century Mexico."

17. Indeed, as late as 2002, La Honda colony leaders asked then-president Vicente Fox for special assistance to fund electricity infrastructure in their colony (Krahn Thiessen).

WORKS CITED

"45 soluciones a la guerra contra el narcotráfico." *Aristegui Noticias*, 1 Oct. 2014, aristeguinoticias.com/0110/lomasdestacado/45-soluciones-a-la-guerra-contra-el-narcotrafico/. Accessed 1 Dec. 2016.

Aboites, Luis. *Breve Historia de Chihuahua*. El Colegio de México; Fondo de Cultura Económica, 2006.

Acosta Chávez, Pedro and Porfirio Rivas. Telegrama al Presidente de la República. 25 Apr. 19[35]. Dirección General de Gobierno Collection, Archivo General de la Nación, Mexico City.

Acosta Morales, Rafael. "The State and the Caudillo: Legitimacy in Yuri Herrera's *Trabajos del reino*." Trans. Mariana Ortega Breña. *Latin American Perspectives*, vol. 4, no. 2, 2014, pp. 177–88.

"Acuerdo sobre inafectabilidad agrícola relativo al conjunto de predios rústicos denominado Fraccionamiento La Honda ubicado en el Municipio de Miguel Auza, Zac." *Diario Oficial de la Federación*, 1 Oct. 1979, 2nd section, pp. 2–13.

"Acuerdo sobre Inafectabilidad Agrícola relativo al predio rústico denominado Lote 4 de la Colonia Menonita Número 4, La Batea, ubicado en el Municipio de Sombrerete, Zac. (Registrado con el número 9020)." *Diario Oficial de la Federación*, 3 Mar. 1980, 1st section, pp. 51–52.

"Acuerdo sobre Inafectabilidad Agrícola relativo al predio rústico denominado Lote 19 de la Colonia Menonita Número 4, La Batea, ubicado en el Municipio de Sombrerete, Zac. (Registrado con el número 8188)." *Diario Oficial de la Federación,* 7 Feb. 1980, 1st section, pp. 18–19.

"Acuerdo sobre Inafectabilidad Agrícola relativo al predio rústico denominado Lote 20 de la Colonia Menonita Número 4, La Batea, ubicado en el Municipio de Sombrerete, Zac. (Registrado con el número 8996)." *Diario Oficial de la Federación*, 6 Mar. 1980, 1st section, pp. 11–12.

"Acuerdo sobre Inafectabilidad Agrícola relativo al predio rústico denominado Lote 1 de la Colonia Menonita Número 4, La Batea, ubicado en el

Municipio de Sombrerete, Zac. (Registrado con el número 10168)."
Diario Oficial de la Federación, 20 May 1980, 1st section, p. 9.

"Acuerdo sobre Inafectabilidad Agrícola relativo al predio rústico denominado Lote 12 de la Colonia Menonita Número 4, La Batea, ubicado en el Municipio de Sombrerete, Zac. (Registrado con el número 10700)."
Diario Oficial de la Federación, 12 June 1980, 1st section, pp. 41–42.

"Acuerdo sobre Inafectabilidad Agrícola relativo al predio rústico denominado Lote 8 de la Colonia Menonita Número 4, La Batea, ubicado en el Municipio de Sombrerete, Zac. (Registrado con el número 10934)."
Diario Oficial de la Federación, 25 June 1980, 1st section, pp. 22–23.

"Acuerdo sobre Inafectabilidad Agrícola relativo al predio rústico denominado Lote 22 de la Colonia Menonita Número 4, La Batea, ubicado en el Municipio de Sombrerete, Zac. (Registrado con el número 10896)."
Diario Oficial de la Federación, 11 July 1980, 1st section, pp. 42–43.

"Acuerdo sobre Inafectabilidad Agrícola relativo al predio rústico denominado Lote 21 de la Colonia Menonita Número 4, La Batea, ubicado en el Municipio de Sombrerete, Zac. (Registrado con el número 10894)."
Diario Oficial de la Federación, 15 July 1980, pp. 49–50.

"Acuerdo sobre Inafectabilidad Agrícola relativo al predio rústico denominado Lote 15 de la Colonia Menonita Número 4, La Batea, ubicado en el Municipio de Sombrerete, Zac. (Registrado con el número 11595)."
Diario Oficial de la Federación, 29 July 1980, 2nd section, pp. 1–2.

"Acuerdo sobre Inafectabilidad Agrícola relativo al predio rústico denominado Lote 11 de la Colonia Menonita Número 4, La Batea, ubicado en el Municipio de Sombrerete, Zac. (Registrado con el número 11998)."
Diario Oficial de la Federación, 28 Aug. 1980, 2nd section, pp. 1–2.

"Acuerdo sobre Inafectabilidad Agrícola relativo al predio rústico denominado Lote 5 de la Colonia Menonita Número 4, La Batea, ubicado en el Municipio de Sombrerete, Zac. (Registrado con el número 11997)."
Diario Oficial de la Federación, 28 Aug. 1980, 2nd section, p. 2.

"Acuerdo sobre Inafectabilidad Agrícola relativo al predio rústico denominado Lote 2 de la Colonia Menonita Número 4, La Batea, ubicado en el Municipio de Sombrerete, Zac. (Registrado con el número 12203)."
Diario Oficial de la Federación, 3 Sept. 1980, p. 10.

"Acuerdo sobre Inafectabilidad Agrícola relativo al predio rústico denominado Lote 17 de la Colonia Menonita Número 4, La Batea, ubicado en el

Municipio de Sombrerete, Zac. (Registrado con el número 12515)."
Diario Oficial de la Federación, 7 Oct. 1980, 2nd section, p. 20.

"Acuerdo sobre Inafectabilidad Agrícola relativo al predio rústico denominado Lote 14 de la Colonia Menonita Número 4, La Batea, ubicado en el Municipio de Sombrerete, Zac. (Registrado con el número 12929)." *Diario Oficial de la Federación*, 20 Oct. 1980, dof.gob.mx/nota_detalle. php?codigo=4860417&fecha=20/10/1980. Accessed 1 July 2016.

"Acuerdo sobre Inafectabilidad Agrícola relativo al predio rústico denominado Lote 16 de la Colonia Menonita Número 4, La Batea, ubicado en el Municipio de Sombrerete, Zac. (Registrado con el número 13147)." *Diario Oficial de la Federación*, 12 Nov. 1980, p. 13.

"Acuerdo sobre Inafectabilidad Agrícola, relativo a los predios rústicos denominados Lote 12 y 13 de la Fracción La Campana, ubicado en el Municipio de Riva Palacio, Chih. (Reg. 1856)." *Diario Oficial de la Federación*, 30 Dec. 1983, dof.gob.mx/nota_detalle.php?codigo=4842877&fecha=30/12/1983. Accessed 1 July 2017.

"Acuerdo sobre Inafectabilidad Agrícola, relativo al predio rústico denominado Lote 3 de la Fracción Arroyo de las Cartucheras, ubicado en el Municipio de Cuauhtémoc, Chih. (Reg. 13128)." *Diario Oficial de la Federación*, 7 Nov. 1980, p. 16.

"Acuerdo sobre inafectabilidad del predio rústico sin nombre, propiedad de Irvin B. Romney y Gordon M. Romney, en Casas Grandes, Chih." *Diario Oficial*, 2nd section, 28 Mar. 1950, pp. 11–12.

"Acuerdo sobre inafectabilidad ganadera del predio El Alamito, en Casas Grandes, Chih." *Diario Oficial*, 2nd section, 28 Mar. 1950, pp. 4–5.

"Acuerdo sobre inafectabilidad ganadera del predio predio rústico sin denominación, propiedad del señor Claudius Bowman, ubicado en Nuevo Casas Grandes, Chih." *Diario Oficial*, 2nd section, 28 Mar. 1950, pp. 6–7.

"Acuerdo sobre inafectabilidad ganadera del predio rústico sin denominación, propiedad de Samuel J. Robinson en Nuevo Casas Grandes, Chih." *Diario Oficial*, 2nd section, 28 Mar. 1950, pp. 12–13.

"Acuerdo sobre inafectabilidad ganadera del predio rústico sin nombre, propiedad del señor Roy J. Adams, ubicado en Nuevo Casas Grandes, Chih." *Diario Oficial*, 2nd section, 28 Mar. 1950, pp. 5–6.

Adorno, Eunice. *Las mujeres flores/The Flower Women*. La Fábrica, 2011.

Agamben, Giorgio. *State of Exception*. Translated by Kevin Attell, U of Chicago P, 2006.

"Agrario. Resoluciones dotatorias o ampliatorias de ejidos. Procedencia del juicio de amparo de acuerdo con el artículo 66 del código agrario." Segunda Sala. Sexta Época. Vol. 132, 3rd part, 13 Apr. 1966, p. 128.

Aguilar Camín, Héctor and Lorenzeo Meyer. 1989. *A la sombra de la Revolución Mexicana*. Cal y Arena, 2003.

Aguilera, Itzel. "Tiempos de sol." Brainahead, 29 Nov. 2010. www.itzelaguilera.com/?p=169. Accessed 1 Nov. 2017.

Ahmed, Azam. "In Mexico, 'It's Easy to Kill a Journalist'." *The New York Times*, 29 Apr. 2017, www.nytimes.com/2017/04/29/world/americas/veracruz-mexico-reporters-killed.html. Accessed 1 June 2017.

Ahmed, Nafeez Mosaddeq. "Capitalism, Covert Action, and State-Terrorism: Toward a Political Economy of the Dual State." Wilson, *The Dual State*, pp. 51–81.

Alcerreca, Luis G. Letter to Sadot Garces de León, 2 Mar 1970. Ejido Galeana Collection, Archivo General Agrario, Mexico City, Mexico.

———. Memorandum to the *Cuerpo Consultivo Agrario*, 13 June 1964. Ejido Casas Grandes Collection, Archivo General Agrario, Mexico City, Mexico.

Alfaro-Velcamp, Theresa. *So Far from Allah, So Close to Mexico: Middle Eastern Immigrants in Modern Mexico*. U of Texas P, 2007.

Alizal Arriaga, Laura del. "Re: Historia de Zacatecas." Email to author, 7 Aug. 2016.

Álvarez Zapata, José and José Parra Barajas. Letter to C. Lic. Luis Echeverría Álvarez. 15 Dec. 1973. Ejido Casas Grandes Collection, Archivo General Agrario, Mexico City.

Anguiano Hernández, Mario. "Feudalismo menonita." Un atento contra México 3. *Nosotros* no. 754, 14 June 1965, pp. 24–29.

———. "Las autoridades cómplices." Un atento contra México 2. *Nosotros* no. 753, 31 May 1965, pp. 20–23.

———. "Sin título." *Nosotros* no. 748, 15 Mar. 1965, pp. 34–35.

———. "La república menonita de Chihuahua." Un atento contra México 1. *Nosotros* no. 752, 17 May 1965, pp. 20–23.

Arias, Ángel. *Entre la cruz y la sospecha: los cristeros de Revueltas, Yáñez y Rulfo*. Iberoamericana; Vereuvert, 2005.

Arias, Enrique Desmond. *Drugs and Democracy in Rio de Janeiro: Trafficking, Social Networks, and Public Security.* U of North Carolina P, 2006.

Astle, Randy. "What Is Mormon Cinema? Defining the Genre." *Dialogue: A Journal of Mormon Thought*, vol. 42, no. 4, 2009, pp. 18–68.

Badcock, James. "Sixty Mass Graves Found in Search for Missing Students." *Telegraph*, 27 July 2015, www.telegraph.co.uk/news/worldnews/central americaandthecaribbean/mexico/11765246/Sixty-mass-graves-found-in-search-for-missing-Mexico-students.html. Accessed 3 Dec. 2015.

Baggett, Sam G. "Article 27 of the Mexican Constitution: The Agrarian Question." *Texas Law Review*, vol. 5, no. 1, 1926, pp. 1–9.

Bailey and Godson. "Introduction." *Organized Crime and Democratic Governability: Mexico and the U.S.-Mexican Borderlands.* Edited by John Bailey and Roy Godson, 2000, pp. 1–29.

"Baker Elena Farnsworth y Martineau." Servicio de Migración, Registro de Extranjeros. 25 July 1933. Migración Collection, US Series. Archivo General de la Nación, Mexico City.

"Banman Dyck, Margaretha." Servicio de Migración, Registro de Extranjeros. 8 June 1936. Migración Collection, Canadian Series. Archivo General de la Nación, Mexico City.

"Banman Friesen Isaac." Servicio de Migración, Registro de Extranjeros. 10 Dec. 1941. Migración Collection, Canadian Series. Archivo General de la Nación, Mexico City.

"Banman Lepki Katarina." Servicio de Migración, Registro de Extranjeros. 18 Feb. 1935. Migración Collection, Canadian Series. Archivo General de la Nación, Mexico City.

"Banman Tiechroeb, Bernhard." Servicio de Migración, Registro de Extranjeros. 3 Oct. 1940. Migración Collection, Canadian Series. Archivo General de la Nación, Mexico City.

Baray, Pedro. "1ª acta de defunción." 8 Sept. 1922. Plaque in Mennonite Museum, Ciudad Cuauhtémoc, Mexico.

Barragán Cisneros, Velia Patricia. *Los mennonitas* [sic] *en la historia del derecho: un estatuto jurídico particular.* Universidad Juárez del Estado de Durango; Instituto de Investigaciones Jurídicas; Consejo de Ciencia y Tecnología del Estado de Durango, 2006.

Barrenechea, Paulina, Carolina Escobar, Andrea Herrera and Gabriela Rivera. "Discusión: 'Ofrendas fotográficas contra el femicidio. Archivo por la no violencia a las mujeres'. Sobre prácticas, fotografías, política de los afectos y zonas de contacto feministas." *Revista Transas: Letras y Artes de América Latina*, 28 July 2016, www.revistatransas.com/2016/07/28/ ofrendas-fotograficas-contra-el-femicidio-archivo-por-la-no-violenci a-a-las-mujeres-sobre-practicas-fotograficas-politica-de-los-afectos-y-z onas-de-contacto-feministas/. Accessed 1 Aug. 2016.

Barthes, Roland. *Camera Lucida: Reflections on Photography.* Translated by Richard Howard, Farrar, Straus and Giroux, 1981.

Basauri, Carlos. *La población indígena de México*, vol. 2. Secretaría de Educación Pública, 1940.

Batalla en el cielo. Directed by Carlos Reygadas, performances by Marcos Hernández, Anapola Mushkadiz and Bertha Ruiz, No Dream and Matarraya Films, 2005.

"Beecroft Jannice Farnsworth Donnal de." Servicio de Migración, Registro de Extranjeros. 5 June 1933. Migración Collection, US Series. Archivo General de la Nación, Mexico City.

Bennion, Janet. *Desert Patriarchy: Mormon and Mennonite Communities in the Chihuahua Valley.* U of Arizona P, 2004.

———. *Polygamy in Primetime: Media, Gender, and Politics in Mormon Fundamentalism.* Brandeis UP, 2012.

"Berg Loewen Heinrich." Servicio de Migración, Registro de Extranjeros. 8 July 1933. Migración Collection, Canadian Series. Archivo General de la Nación, Mexico City.

"Berg, Aganetha." Servicio de Migración, Registro de Extranjeros. 27 Feb. 1950. Migración Collection, Canadian Series. Archivo General de la Nación, Mexico City.

"Bergen Friesen Helena." Servicio de Migración, Registro de Extranjeros. 24 Dec. 1949. Migración Collection, Canadian Series. Archivo General de la Nación, Mexico City.

Bergen, Peter T. *Historia de los menonitas en tierras zacatecanas.* La Honda, Mexico, 2015.

———. *La Honda: 50 Jahre, 1964–2014.* [*La Honda: 50 Years, 1964–2014*]. La Honda, Mexico, 2014.

———. *La Batea: 55 Jahre* [*La Batea: 55 Years*]. La Honda, Mexico, 2017.

"Bergen Thiessen, Helena." Servicio de Migración, Registro de Extranjeros. 19

Sept. 1935. Migración Collection, Canadian Series. Archivo General de la Nación, Mexico City.

Biale, David, Michael Galchinsky, and Susannah Heschel, eds. *Insider/Outsider: American Jews and Multiculturalism*. U of California P, 1998.

Blum, Ann S. "Breaking and Making Families: Adoption and Public Welfare, Mexico City, 1938–1942." Olcott, Vaughan and Cano, pp. 127–44.

Bosch, Lolita. *México: 45 voces contra la barbarie*. Océano, 2014.

Bowden, Charles. *Murder City: Ciudad Juárez and the Global Economy's New Killing Fields*. Nation Books, 2010.

"Braun Thiessen, Peter." Servicio de Migración, Registro de Extranjeros. 30 Mar. 1940. Migración Collection, Canadian Series. Archivo General de la Nación, Mexico City.

Bridgemon, Rondal R. "Mennonites and Mormons in Northern Chihuahua, Mexico." *Journal of the Southwest*, vol. 54, no. 1, 2012, pp. 71–77.

"Brigham A. Farnsworth." Servicio de Migración, Registro de Extranjeros. 25 Jan. 1937. Migración Collection, US Series. Archivo General de la Nación, Mexico City.

Brown, Pete. "Institutions, Inequalities, and the Impact of Agrarian Reform on Rural Mexican Communities." *Human Organization*, vol. 56, no. 1, 1997, pp. 102–10.

"Bueckert Epp Katharina." Servicio de Migración, Registro de Extranjeros. 15 July 1933. Migración Collection, Canadian Series. Archivo General de la Nación, Mexico City.

"Bueckert Siemens, Jacob." Servicio de Migración, Registro de Extranjeros. 7 Aug. 1933. Migración Collection, Canadian Series. Archivo General de la Nación, Mexico City.

Bueno G., Víctor Manuel. "Carta de la Vieja Guardia Agrarista de Chihuahua al Lic. Javier García Paniagua." Ejido Galeana Collection, Archivo General Agrario, Mexico City.

Buhler, Linda. "Mennonite Burial Customs – Part One." *Preservings*, vol. 7, 1995, pp. 51–52.

———. "Mennonite Burial Customs – Part Two." *Preservings*, vol. 8, no. 2, 1996, pp. 48–50.

Burgos Dávila, César Jesús. "Narcocorridos: antecedents de la tradición corridística y del narcotráfico en México." *Studies in Latin American Popular Culture*, vol. 31, 2013, pp. 157–83.

Burnett, Victoria. "Mennonite Farmers Prepare to Leave Mexico, and Competition for Water." *New York Times*, 16 Nov. 2015, www.nytimes.com/2015/11/17/world/americas/mennonite-farmer s-prepare-to-leave-mexico-and-competition-for-water.html. Accessed 19 Nov. 2015.

Camp, Roderic Ai. *Mexican Political Biographies, 1884–1934.* U of Texas P, 1991.

Campbell, Bruce. *¡Viva la Historieta!: Mexican Comics, NAFTA, and the Politics of Globalization.* UP of Mississippi, 2009.

Cárdenas, Lázaro. Carta a los señores John P. Wall y A. A. Martens. 19 June 1936. Ejido J. Santos Bañuelos Collection, Archivo Agrario, Mexico City.

———. Carta al Señor General Severino Ceniceros, Gobernador del Estado de Durango. 19 June 1936. Ejido J. Santos Bañuelos Collection, Archivo Agrario, Mexico City.

"Card Tips: Metamorphosis." *Yu-Gi-Oh! A Fandom Games Community.* 8 Apr. 2016, yugioh.wikia.com/wiki/Card_Tips:Metamorphosis. Accessed 1 June 2017.

Castañeda López, Gabriela. "La frenología en México durante el siglo XIX." *Anales médicos (México)* vol. 54, no. 4, 2009, pp. 241–47.

Castro, Pedro. "The 'Return' of the Mennonites from the Cuauhtémoc Region to Canada: A Perspective from Mexico." *Journal of Mennonite Studies*, vol. 22, 2004, pp. 26–38.

Chávez Quezada, Martha. "La colonización menonita en el estado de Chihuahua." Lic. Thesis, UNAM, 1948.

Clark, J. Reuben. "Dear Mr. Ambassador." 14 June 1944. Departamento de Investigaciones Políticas y Sociales Collection. Archivo General de la Nación, Mexico City.

Cluff, Russell M. "Re: Mennonites and Mormons in Mexico." Email to author, 12 Aug. 2015.

"Código de moral eugénica: por una humanidad mejor." *Eugenesia*, vol. 2, no. 18, 1941, pp. 10–11.

Coerver, Don M. "Confederación Nacional Campesina (CNC)." *Mexico: An Encyclopedia of Contemporary Culture and History.* Edited by Don M.

Coerver, Suzanne B. Pasztor and Robert Buffington, ABC-CLIO, 2004, pp.114–17.

"Conferencia Menonita de México." Wix.com sites, 2015, www.conferenciamm. org. Accessed 1 July 2017.

"Constitución de los Estados Unidos Mexicanos." *Diario Oficial de la Federación* 1 Feb. 1917, pp. 1–13.

"Copia de la Solicitud de Tercera Ampliación de Ejido." *Periódico Oficial de Zacatecas*, vol. 82, no. 22, 17 Mar. 1976, pp. 597–98.

Corres, Manuel. Carta al Presidente de la República. "Se comunica en el asesinato de Victorio Ponce por los Mormones." 25 Apr. 1935. Dirección General de Gobierno collection, Archivo General de la Nación, Mexico City.

Cox, Christopher, Jacob M. Driedger and Benjamin V. Tucker. "Mennonite Plautdietsch (Canadian Old Colony)." *Journal of the International Phonetic Association*, vol. 43, no. 2, 2013, pp. 221–29.

Creechan, James H., and Jorge de la Herrán Garcia. "Without God or Law: Narcoculture and Belief in Jesús Malverde." *Religious Studies and Theology*, vol. 24, no. 2, 2005, pp. 8–13.

Cribb, Robert. "Introduction: Parapolitics, Shadow Governance and Criminal Sovereignty." Wilson, *Government of the Shadows*, pp. 1–9.

Cruz Gutierrez, Manuel, and Aurelio Lopez Quezada. "Relación de Colonos de la 'Colonia Pacheco' del Mpio. de Casas Grandes, Chih, que me fué proporcionada por los C. C. Manuel Cruz Gutiérrez y Aurelio Lopez Quezada, Presidente y Secretario respectivamente del Comité Ejecutivo Agrario de 'Col. Pacheco' y que actualmente se encuentran en posesion de terrenos de cultivo." 26 Mar. 1956. Ejido Colonia Pacheco Collection, Archivo General Agrario, Mexico City.

Cruz Gutierrez, Manuel, Aurelio Lopez Quezada, and Carlos Matas Provencio. "Observaciones hechas por los CC: Manuel Cruz Gutiérrez y Aurelio Lopez Quezada, Presidente y Secretario respectivamente del Comité Ejecutivo Agrario de 'Col. Pacheco,' a la lista de colonos de la colonia pacheco, presentada por el Sr. Melvin Turley, representante de la misma." 28 Mar. 1956. Ejido Colonia Pacheco Collection, Archivo General Agrario, Mexico City.

Cuerpo Consultivo Agrario. File on the Restitution of Land to the Population of Casas Grandes, in the Municipality of the Same Name in the State of Chihuahua. N. d. Ejido Casas Grandes Collection, Archivo General Agrario, Mexico City.

Dalton, David S. *Mestizo Modernity: Race, Technology, and the Body in Post-Revolutionary Mexico.* UP of Florida, 2018.

Dean, John E. *How Myth Became History: Texas Exceptionalism in the Borderlands.* U of Arizona P, 2016.

Debroise, Olivier. *Mexican Suite: A History of Photography in Mexico.* Translated and revised with Stella de Sá Rego. U of Texas P, 2001.

DeLamotte, Eugenia. "White Terror, Black Dreams: Gothic Constructions of Race in the Nineteenth Century." *The Gothic Other: Racial and Social Constructions in the Literary Imagination.* Edited by Ruth Bienstock Anolik and Douglas L. Howard, McFarland, 2004, pp. 17–31.

Denegri, Carlos. "29 Estados de Animo: III." *Excelsior*, 10 Aug. 1957, pp. 1, 10.

Departamento de Asuntos Agrarios y Colonización. "Plano Informativo La Batea." N. d. Map, scale 1:20 000. Ejido Niño Artillero Collection. Archivo General Agrario, Mexico City.

"Documentos originales de filiación." 1849–1850. Asuntos Criminales Collection. Archivo General de la Nación, Bogotá, Colombia.

Dormady, Jason H. "Mennonite Colonization in Mexico and the Pendulum of Modernization, 1920–2013." *Mennonite Quarterly Review*, vol. 88, no. 2, 2014, pp. 167–94.

———. *Primitive Revolution: Restorationist Religion and the Idea of the Mexican Revolution, 1940–1968.* U of New Mexico P, 2011.

Dormady, Jason H., and Jared M. Tamez. *Just South of Zion: The Mormons in Mexico and its Borderlands.* U of New Mexico P, 2015.

Driedger, Susan, and Katharina Redekop. Email to William Janzen. 20 June 2017.

Dyck, Andrea. " 'And in Mexico We Found What We Had Lost in Canada': Mennonite Immigrant Perceptions of Mexican Neighbours in a Canadian Newspaper, 1922–1967." MA thesis, U of Winnipeg, 2007.

Dyck, Isaak. Telegram to Lic. Augusto Gómez Villanueva, Jefe Departamento de Asuntos Agrarios y Colonización. Apr. 1973. Ejido Niño Artillero Collection, Archivo General Agrario, Mexico City.

Edgell, Amanda B. "The State of Exception, Sovereignty, and the National Emergencies Act." *A Crowing Hen*. Wordpress, 18 Sept. 2013,

acrowinghen.com/2013/09/18/the-state-of-exception-sovereignt
y-and-the-national-emergencies-act/. Accessed 1 Feb. 2017.

Epp, Frank H. *Mennonites in Canada, 1920–1940: A People's Struggle for Survival*. Macmillan, 1982.

Epplin, Craig. "Sacrifice and Recognition in Carlos Reygadas' *Japón*." *Mexican Studies/Estudios Mexicanos*, vol. 28, no. 2, 2012, pp. 287–305.

Escalante Gonzalbo, Fernando. "Homicidios 2008–2009: La muerte tiene permiso." *Nexos*, 1 Jan. 2011, www.nexos.com.mx/?p=14089. Accessed 1 June 2017.

Esplin, Scott C., E. Vance Randall, Casey P. Griffiths, and Barbara E. Morgan. "Isolationism, exceptionalism and acculturation: the internationalization of Mormon education in Mexico." *Journal of Educational Administration and History*, vol. 46, no. 4, 2014, pp. 387–404.

Fabila, Manuel. *Cinco siglos de la legislación agraria en México (1493–1940)*. Procuraduría Agraria, 2005.

"Facts and Statistics: Mexico." *The Church of Jesus Christ of Latter-Day Saints Newsroom*. Intellectual Reserve Inc, 2016, www.mormonnewsroom.org/facts-and-statistics/country/mexico. Accessed 1 July 2017.

"Farnsworth Bingham Brigham A." Servicio de Migración, Registro de Extranjeros. 18 Dec. 1933. Migración Collection, US Series. Archivo General de la Nación, Mexico City.

"Farnsworth Bingham Roien." Servicio de Migración, Registro de Extranjeros. 19 Dec. 1933. Migración Collection, US Series. Archivo General de la Nación, Mexico City.

"Farnsworth Nielson Douglas." Servicio de Migración, Registro de Extranjeros. 22 Apr. 1935. Migración Collection, US Series. Archivo General de la Nación, Mexico City.

"Farnsworth Nielson Elmo." Servicio de Migración, Registro de Extranjeros. 17 Oct. 1933. Migración Collection, US Series. Archivo General de la Nación, Mexico City.

"Farnsworth Nielson Leonora." Servicio de Migración, Registro de Extranjeros. 25 Dec. 1932. Migración Collection, US Series. Archivo General de la Nación, Mexico City.

Fast, Ben. "Mennonite Pioneer Funeral Practices." *Saskatchewan Mennonite Historian*, vol. 5, no. 1, 2000, pp. 13, 26.

Fierro Martínez, Santiago D. "Breve Estudio Económico de las Colonias Menonitas del Estado de Durango." *Ubamari: Revista del Instituto Tecnológico de Durango*, vol. 18, 1989, pp. 46–66.

Flores Vizcarra, David, and Fausto Flores Vizcarra. Letter to Gustavo Díaz Ordaz. 15 Feb. 1970. Ejido Casas Grandes Collection, Archivo General Agrario, Mexico City.

Flores, Judith. "México: 45 voces contra la barbarie. Un diálogo entre el dolor, la solidaridad y la esperanza." *Somos el Medio*. Somoselmedio.org, 2017, www.somoselmedio.org/article/mexico-45-voces-contra-la-barbarie. Accessed 1 July 2017.

Foltz, Jonathan. "Betraying Oneself: *Silent Light* and the World of Emotion." *Screen*, vol. 52, no. 2, 2011, pp. 151–72.

Foucault, Michel. *Power, Truth, Strategy*. Edited and translated by Paul Foss and Meaghan Morris, Feral Publications, 1979.

Friesen, Will. "Unjahoolinj met Alfredo Thiessen fonn Stellet Licht." ["Interview with Alfredo Thiessen about Silent Light"]. WilFriesen's channel. *Youtube*, 30 Jan. 2014. Accessed 1 Dec. 2016.

Gasiorowski, Dominika. "Bodies that do not Matter: Marginality in Maya Goded's Photographs of Sex Workers in Mexico City." *Journal of Latin American Cultural Studies*, vol. 24 no. 4, 2015, pp. 501–15.

Gerson, Jen. "Mennonites Linked to Mexican Cartels Established Cocaine Smuggling Pipeline Near Alberta Border: Police." *National Post*, 25 Sept. 2013, nationalpost.com/g00/news/canada/mennonites-link ed-to-mexican-cartels-established-cocaine-smuggling-pipeline-ne ar-alberta-border-police/wcm/3cf150ff-6164–441b-ac89–71b16f30 1e50?i10c.referrer=https%3A%2F%2Fwww.google.com%2F. Accessed 1 Feb. 2015.

Gesangbuch: Eine Sammlung geistlicher Lieder zur Allgemeinen Erbauung und zum Lobe Gottes [*A Collection of Spiritual Songs for Elevating the Community and Worshipping God*]. Mennonite Publishing House, 1974.

Glantz, Margo, coord. *La Malinche, sus padres y sus hijos*. Taurus, 2001.

Glaubitz, Charles, and Giancarlo Ruiz. "MacBurro: A Web Comic about Tijuana and Stuff!" *MacBurro*. Tumblr, 2011–2017, macburro.com. Accessed 1 Mar. 2017.

Goldman, Francisco. "Crisis in Mexico: The Disappearance of the Forty-

Three." *The New Yorker*, 24 Oct. 2014, www.newyorker.com/news/new s-desk/crisis-mexico-disappearance-forty-three. Accessed 1 Nov. 2015.

Gómez Robleda, José. *Pescadores y Campesinos Tarascos.* Secretaría de Educación Pública, 1940.

González Navarro, Gerardo N. *Derecho Agrario*, 2nd ed. Oxford UP, 2015.

González Navarro, Moisés. *Los extranjeros en México y los mexicanos en el extranjero, 1821–1970*, vol. 2. El Colegio de México, 1994.

González, Daniel Infante. "Colonia 4, con 24 lotes, correspondiente a la sub-división de 4 fracciones numeradas del 62 al 65, y comprendidas dentro de las 72 pequeñas propiedades que señala la resolución presidencial del NCPE [Nuevo Centro de Población Ejidal] El Niño Artillero, Mpio. de Sombrerete, Estado de Zacatecas." 1965. Archivo General Agrario, Ejido Niño Artillero Collection.

Good Gingrich, Luann. *Out of Place: Social Exclusion and Mennonite Migrants in Canada.* U of Toronto P, 2016.

Good Gingrich, Luann, and Kerry Preibisch. "Migration as Preservation and Loss: The Paradox of Transnational Living for Low German Mennonite Women." *Journal of Ethnic and Migration Studies*, vol. 36, no. 9, 2010, pp. 1499–1518.

Goodman, Tim. "The Bridge: TV Review." *The Hollywood Reporter* 26 June 2013, www.hollywoodreporter.com/review/bridge-tv-review-717459. Accessed 1 Feb. 2017.

Groys, Boris. *Under Suspicion: A Phenomenology of Media.* Translated by Carsten Strathausen, Columbia UP, 2012.

Hales, Brian C. "Chronology." *Mormon Polygamy and Mormon Fundamentalism.* Beaver Builder, 2016, www.mormonfundamentalism.com/basics/chronology/. Accessed 1 July 2017.

———. "The Beginnings of Mormon Polygamy." *Joseph Smith's Polygamy.* Summerwood Media, 2017, josephsmithspolygamy.org/beginnings-mormon-polygamy/. Accessed 1 July 2017.

———. "The LeBarons." *Mormon Polygamy and Mormon Fundamentalism.* Beaver Builder, 2017, www.mormonfundamentalism.com/polygamous-groups/the-lebarons. Accessed 1 July 2017.

Hancock, Brian C. "Reason and Revelation." *Encyclopedia of Mormonism.* Ed. Daniel H. Ludlow. Macmillan, 1992, pp. 1193–94.

Hansen Park, Lindsay. "Episode 76: The LeBarons." *Year of Polygamy.* Wordpress, 22 Feb. 2015. www.yearofpolygamy.com/year-of-polygamy/ episode-76-the-lebarons/. Accessed 1 Nov. 2016.

———. "Episode 121: Daughter of a Prophet, an Interview with Anna LeBaron." *Year of Polygamy.* Wordpress, 3 July 2017, www.yearofpolygamy.com/year-of-polygamy/episode-121-daughter-of-a-prophet/. Accessed 1 July 2017.

———. "Episode 128: Denver Snuffer, The Remnant Movement, and Polygamy." *Year of Polygamy.* Wordpress, 26 June. 2017, www.yearofpolygamy.com/year-of-polygamy/episode-128-denver-snuffer-the-remnant-movement-and-polygamy/. Accessed 1 Nov. 2017.

———. "Episode 129: Apostle vs. Apostle, the 1900–1920 Transition." *Year of Polygamy.* Wordpress, 1 July 2017, www.yearofpolygamy.com/uncategorized/episode-129-apostle-vs-apostle-the-1900–1920-transition/. Accessed 1 Aug. 2017.

Hardy, B. Carmon. *Solemn Covenant: The Mormon Polygamous Passage.* U of Illinois P, 1992.

Hernández, Silvia. "*Menonitas* de Quintana Roo, un viaje al siglo XIX." *El Universal* 28 Apr. 2014, archivo.eluniversal.com.mx/estados/2014/ menonitas-de-quintana-roo-un-viaje-al-siglo-xix--1006454.html. Accessed 1 Aug. 2017.

Herrera Bocardo, Antonio. Carta a Joel Luevanos Ponce y Arturo Medrano Cabral. 2 Apr. 1979. Ejido J. Santos Bañuelos Collection, Archivo General Agrario, Mexico City.

———. Carta a los CC: Joel Luevanos Ponce y Arturo Medrano Cabral, Comisionados de la Comisión Agraria Mixta en el Estado. 2 May 1979. Ejido J. Santos Bañuelos Collection, Archivo General Agrario, Mexico City.

———. Carta a los CC. Joel Luevanos Ponce y Arturo Medrano Cabral, Comisionados de la Comisión Agraria Mixta en el Estado. 24 Apr. 1979. Ejido J. Santos Bañuelos Collection, Archivo General Agrario, Mexico City.

Herrera H., Juan Manuel. Colaboración de Alfonso Quiroz, Luis Argoytia, Antonio Elizalde, Adán Mercado, Guillermo Fuentes y Liborio Martínez. "Informe sobre el Grupo documental: Departamento de

Migración; Registro de Extranjeros." [1989]. Mennonite Heritage
Centre, Winnipeg, Canada.

———. Letter to the Librarian at Canadian Mennonite Bible College. 17
Nov. 1989. Mennonite Heritage Centre, Winnipeg, Canada.

Hind, Emily. Femmen*ism and the Mexican Woman Intellectual from Sor Juana to
Poniatowska: Boob Lit.* Palgrave-Macmillan, 2011.

———. " 'Provincia' in Recent Mexican Cinema, 1989–2004." *Discourse*, vol.
26, no. 1–2, 2004, pp. 26–45.

"Historia del Ejido Casas Grandes." *Ejido Casas Grandes website.* Google.com
sites, 2013, sites.google.com/site/ejidocasasgrandes/historia-del-ejido.
Accessed 1 Dec. 2016.

*Holy Bible: New Revised Standard Version Containing the Old and New Testaments
and the Deuterocanonical Books.* Oxford UP, 2005.

Horowitz, Sara R. "The Paradox of Jewish Studies in the New Academy." Biale,
Galchinsky and Heschel, pp. 116–29.

Hunter, J. Michael, ed. *Mormons and Popular Culture: The Global Influence of an
American Phenomenon*, vol. 1. Praeger; ABC-CLIO, 2013.

Ibarra Chávez, Lic. José Antonio. Copia certificado de la "Carta al C.
Gobernador Const. Del Estado del 9 de enero [Solicitud de
Ampliación]." 4 Mar. 1976. Ejido J. Santos Bañuelos Collection,
Archivo General Agrario, Mexico City.

Islas-Salinas, P, A. Pérez-Piñón, and G. Hernández-Orozco. "Rol de enfermería
en educación para la salud de los menonitas desde el interaccionismo
simbólico." *Enfermería Universitaria*, vol. 12, no. 1, 2015, pp. 28–35.

"Itali Heide." *La Voz de México.* Televisa, 2014, especiales.televisa.com/
la-voz/2016/equipos/940279/itali-heide/. Accessed 1 Dec. 2016.

Janzen, Rebecca. "Plurinational Bolivia Protects Low German Mennonites:
Reading the Ghost Rapes." *A contracorriente*, vol. 13, no. 3, 2016,
acontracorriente.chass.ncsu.edu/index.php/acontracorriente/article/
view/1401. Accessed 1 Feb. 2017.

Jiménez Burillo, Pablo and Miguel Fernández Félix. *México a través de la
fotografía, 1839–1910.* Taurus; Fundación Mapfre, 2013.

"José Flores Ramos." Pasaportes del Estado Libre y Soberano de Coahuila
y Zaragoza. 20 May 1919. Archivo de la Secretaría de Relaciones
Exteriores, Mexico City.

Kaplan, Louis. *The Strange Case of William Mumler, Spirit Photographer.* U of Minnesota P, 2008.

Kaplan, Temma. "Final Reflection: Gender, Chaos and Authority in Revolutionary Times." Olcott, Vaughan and Cano, pp. 261–76.

Kelly, James J. "Article 27 and Mexican Land Reform: The Legacy of Zapata's Dream." *Columbia Human Rights Law Review* no. 25, 1994, pp. 541–70.

Knight, Alan. "Racism, Revolution, and *Indigenismo*: Mexico, 1910–1940." *The Idea of Race in Latin America, 1870–1940.* Ed. Richard Graham. U of Texas P, 1990, pp. 71–113.

———. "Narco-Violence and the State in Modern Mexico." *Violence, Coercion and State-Making in 20th Century Mexico: The Other Half of the Centaur.* Ed. Wil G. Pansters. Stanford UP, 2012, pp. 115–34.

Krahn Thiessen, Cornelius. "Carta al Ing. Vicente Fox Quezada, asunto: electrificación." 4 Apr. 2002. Archivo General de la Nación, Peticiones Presidenciales, 2000–2001 collection, Mexico City.

Kraybill, Donald. *Concise Encyclopedia of Amish, Brethren, Hutterites and Mennonites.* Johns Hopkins UP, 2010.

Krehbiel, Stephanie. "Pacifist Battlegrounds: Violence, Community, and the Struggle for LGBTQ Justice in the Mennonite Church USA." Dissertation, U of Kansas, 2015.

Kulig, Judith C., Margaret Wall, Shirley Hill, and Ruth Babcock. "Childbearing Beliefs among Low-German-Speaking Mennonite Women." *International Nursing Review*, vol. 55, 2008, pp. 420–26.

Kulig, Judith C., Ruth Babcock, Margaret Wall, and Shirley Hill. "Being a Woman: Perspectives of Low-German-Speaking Mennonite Women." *Health Care for Women International*, vol. 30, 2009, pp. 324–38.

"La exposición Tiempos de Sol: comunidad menonita en Chihuahua, reúne a más de 48 mil personas." *El Día* 13 Feb. 2015, periodicoeldia. mx/2015/02/13/la-exposicion-tiempos-de-sol-comunidad-menonita-en-chihuahua-reune-a-mas-de-48-mil-personas/. Accessed 1 Nov. 2017.

"la Sra. Agatha Banman Thiessen." Servicio de Migración, Registro de Extranjeros. 22 Feb. 1937. Migración Collection, Canadian Series. Archivo General de la Nación, Mexico City.

"la Srta. Farnsworth Call Ivis." Servicio de Migración, Registro de Extranjeros. 27 June 1940. Migración Collection, US Series. Archivo General de la Nación, Mexico City.

Langston, Joy. *Democratization and Authoritarian Party Survival: Mexico's PRI.* Oxford UP, 2017.

Laurell, Asa Cristina. "Three Decades of Neoliberalism in Mexico: The Destruction of Society." *International Journal of Health Services*, vol. 45, no. 2, 2015, pp. 246–64.

Legislación de terrenos baldíos ó sea completa colección de leyes, decretos, ordenes, circulares, reglamentos, contratos y demás disposiciones supremas relativas a terrenos baldíos de la república publicadas hasta el mes de setiembre de 1885. Chihuahua: Imprenta y librería de Donato Miramontes, 1885.

"Les bonbons." *Lyrics Translate.* Lyricstranslate.com, 3 Dec. 2008, lyricstranslate.com/en/Les-Bonbons-Les-Bonbons.html. Accessed 1 Oct. 2015.

"Letra 'No volveré'." *Música.com.* Musica.com, www.musica.com/letras.asp?letra=916600. Accessed 10 Dec. 2015.

"Ley de Migración de los Estados Unidos Mexicanos." *Diario Oficial de la Federación*, 2nd section, 19 Apr. 1926, pp. 1–8.

"Ley General de Población." *Diario Oficial de la Federación,* 1st section, 27 Dec. 1947, pp. 3–10.

Living in a Perfect World. Directed by Diego D'Innocenzo and Marco Leopardi, National Geographic Channel International, 2006.

Llewellyn, Nigel. *The Art of Death: Visual Culture in the English Death Ritual, c. 1500–1800.* Victoria and Albert Museum; Reaktion Books, 1992.

"Loeppky Funk Johann." Servicio de Migración, Registro de Extranjeros. 1 July 1933. Migración Collection, Canadian Series. Archivo General de la Nación, Mexico City.

Loeppky, Johann. "Journal on A Trip to Mexico." Translated by anon., *Preservings*, vol. 26, 2006, pp. 37–44.

Loewen, Royden. *Village Among Nations: "Canadian" Mennonites in a Transnational World, 1916–2006.* U of Toronto P, 2013.

Lomnitz, Claudio. *Death and the Idea of Mexico.* The MIT P; Zone Books, 2005.

———. *Deep Mexico, Silent Mexico: An Anthropology of Nationalism.* U of Minnesota P, 2001.

Loza, Gustavo, creator. *Los héroes del norte: Primera temporada.* Adicta Films; Televisa, 2011.

———. *Los héroes del norte: Segunda temporada.* Adicta Films; Televisa, 2013.

Luca, Tiago de. "Carnal Spirituality: The Films of Carlos Reygadas." *Senses of Cinema*, vol. 55, 2010, sensesofcinema.com/2010/feature-articles/carnal-spirituality-the-films-of-carlos-reygadas-2/. Accessed 1 Aug. 2016.

Luna Elizarrarás, Sara Minerva. "Corrupción, legitimidad y género en el México del 'Milagro': Discursos públicos en torno a la figura del Presidente Adolfo Ruiz Cortines. MA Thesis, UNAM, 2012.

Luna, Ilana Dann. *Adapting Gender: Mexican Feminisms from Literature to Film.* State U of New York P, 2018.

Lund, Joshua. *The Impure Imagination: Toward a Critical Hybridity in Latin American Writing.* U of Minnesota P, 2006.

———. *The Mestizo State: Reading Race in Modern Mexico.* U of Minnesota P, 2012.

Mariscal Moreno, Francisco. "Memorandum sobre la Restitución de Tierras 'Casas Grandes'." 1961. Ejido Casas Grandes Collection, Archivo General Agrario, Mexico City.

———. Memorandum to the Delegate for the Department of Agrarian Matters and Colonization. 19 Sept. 1963. Ejido Casas Grandes Collection, Archivo General Agrario, Mexico City.

Martínez García, Ing. Donaciano, and Antonio García Ramos. Carta a la Secretaría de la Reforma Agraria, Subsección de tierras y aguas. Attn: Ing. Mauricio Moreno F. 15 July 1980. Ejido Galeana Collection. Archio General Agrario, Mexico City.

Matas Provencio, Carlos. Resolución en primera instancia, dictada en el expediente de dotación de Ejidos, promovido por los vecinos del Poblado de Colonia Pacheco, del Municipio de Casas Grandes, Chih. N. d. Ejido Colonia Pacheco Collection, Archivo General Agrario, Mexico City.

McCloud, Scott. *Understanding Comics: The Invisible Art.* HarperCollins, 1994.

McNeil, Byron James. *The History of the Church of Jesus Christ of Latter-Day Saints in Mexico.* MA Thesis, San Jose State U, 1990.

Medrano Cabral, Arturo. Informe al C. Lic. Arturo J. Real Martínez. 1 Aug. 1979. Ejido J. Santos Bañuelos Collection, Archivo General Agrario, Mexico City.

Mennonite Mob. Directed by The Fifth Estate, *CBC*, 1992, www.youtube.com/watch?v=6Buf-yaN_tE. Accessed 1 Feb. 2015.

"Mexico." *Committee to Protect Journalists,* 2017, cpj.org/americas/mexico/. Accessed 1 June 2017.

"Mexico: EMMC Mexico." *EMMC*, Radiant WebTools, 2017, www.emmc.ca/missions/mexico/about. Accessed 1 July 2017.

Miller, Glenda Evon. *A Comparison of the Mennonite and Mormon Colonies in Northern Mexico*. MA Thesis, U of Texas-El Paso, 1993.

Miranda Madrid, José. "Renuncia Alex Lebarón en Conagua y va por diputación." *El Diario* 19 Feb. 2015, diario.mx/Nvo_Casas_Grandes/2015–02–19_680a430f/renuncia-alex-lebaron-en-conagua-y-va-por-diputacion/. Accessed 1 Dec. 2016.

Mirzoeff, Nicholas. *An Introduction to Visual Culture*. Routledge, 1999.

Mitrovica, Andrew, and Susan Bourette. "The Mennonite Mob: An Unholy Alliance of Drug Traffickers, Contract Killings, Corrupt Mexican Police and the Brethren." *Saturday Night* Apr. 2004, pp. 32–38.

Moguel, Julio, coord. *Historia de la cuestión agraria mexicana*. 8. Política estatal y conflictos agrarios 1950–1970. Siglo XXI; CEHAM, 1989.

Moguel, Julio. "La cuestión agraria en el período 1950–1970." Moguel, pp. 103–221.

Moreno G., Enrique, Julián Márquez E. Y Esteban Saucedo. "Carta al C. Gobernador Const. Del Estado [Solicitud de Ampliación]." 9 Jan. 1976. Ejido J. Santos Bañuelos Collection, Archivo General Agrario, Mexico City.

Morgan, Brandon. "Columbus, New Mexico, and Palomas Chihuahua: Transnational Landscapes of Violence, 1888–1930." Dissertation, U of New Mexico, 2013.

Morris-Reich, Amos. *Race and Photography: Racial Photography as Scientific Evidence, 1876–1980*. U of Chicago P, 2016.

Mraz, John. "Technologies of Seeing: Photography and Culture." Tinajero and Freeman, pp. 73–89.

———. *Photographing the Mexican Revolution: Commitments, Testimonies, Icons*. U of Texas P, 2012.

Muñoz Salcido, Velia. Letter to Dn. Antonio Toledo Corro. 15 Jan. 1980. Ejido Casas Grandes Collection, Archivo General Agrario, Mexico City.

Nelli, M. Florencia. "Usted está aquí: Antigone against the Standardization of Violence in Contemporary Mexico." *Romance Quarterly*, vol. 59, no. 1, 2012, pp. 55–65.

Niessen, Neils. "Miraculous Realism: Spinoza, Deleuze, and Carlos Reygadas's *Stellet Licht*." *Discourse*, vol. 33, no. 1, 2011, pp. 27–54.

Noble, Andrea. *Mexican National Cinema*. Routledge, 2005.

Nordstrom, Carolyn. *Global Outlaws: Crime, Money and Power in the Contemporary World*. U of California P, 2007.

"Now Counted by their Country, Afro-Mexicans Grab Unprecedented Spotlight." *All Things Considered*. NPR, 6 Feb. 2016, www.npr.org/2016/02/06/465710473/now-counted-by-their-country-afro-mexicans-grab-unprecedented-spotlight. Accessed 11 Jan. 2017.

Nugent, Daniel. *Spent Cartridges of Revolution: An Anthropological History of Namiquipa, Chihuahua*. U of Chicago P, 1993.

Olcott, Jocelyn H., Mary K. Vaughan and Gabriela Cano, eds. *Sex in Revolution: Gender, Politics, and Power in Modern Mexico*. Duke UP, 2006.

Olivares Arellano, Roberto. "Reporte del Consejero Agrario en el Estado sobre Amplificación del Ejido Napavechic de Abajo." 11 Feb. 1981. Ejido Napavechic de Abajo Collection, Archivo General Agrario, Mexico City.

Oman, Nathan B. "International Legal Experience and the Mormon Theology of the State, 1945–2012." *Iowa Law Review*, vol. 100, 2015, pp. 715–50.

Ordet. Directed by Carl Theodor Dreyer, performances by Henrik Malberg, Emil Hass Christensen, Preben Lerdoff Rye, Palladium Film, 1955.

Ortega Urquidi, Javier. *Los Güeros del Norte*. Chihuahua: CONACULTA Chihuahua; INAC; Gobierno del Estado de Chihuahua, [2010].

———. *Tierra de siete culturas*. 3ª ed. México, DF; Chihuahua, Chihuahua: CONACULTA, Instituto Chihuahuense de la Cultura, 2012.

Osuna Reyes, Héctor Manuel. Carta al Lic. Gonzalo Gómez Flores. 21 May 1980. Ejido Casas Grandes Collection, Archivo General Agrario, Mexico City.

Otero, Gerardo. "Agrarian Reform in Mexico: Capitalism and the State." *Searching for Agrarian Reform in Latin America*. Edited by William C. Thiesenhusen, Unwin Hyman, 1989, pp. 276–304.

Our Heritage: A Brief History of The Church of Jesus Christ of Latter-day Saints. The Church of Jesus-Christ of Latter-Day Saints, 1996, www.lds.org/manual/our-heritage-a-brief-history-of-the-church-of-jesus-christ-of-latter-day-saints?lang=eng. Accessed 1 July 2017.

Palomares Peña, Noé G. *Propietarios norteamericanos y reforma agraria en Chihuahua, 1917–1942.* Universidad Autónoma Ciudad Juárez, 1991.

Palou, Pedro Ángel. *El fracaso del mestizo.* Ariel, 2014.

Pansters, Wil G. "Zones of State-Making: Violence, Coercion, and Hegemony in Twentieth-Century Mexico." *Violence, Coercion and State-Making in 20th Century Mexico: The Other Half of the Centaur.* Ed. Wil G. Pansters. Stanford: Stanford UP, 2012, pp. 3–42.

Pegler-Gordon, Anna. *In Sight of America: Photography and the Development of US Immigration Policy.* U of California P, 2009.

Peña, Alfredo and Mark Stevenson. "Mexico's Drug War Marks a Decade amid Doubts, Changes." *AP News,* 10 Dec. 2016, apnews.com/edf2fe18fe-534c3a9e62badb7aee2492/mexicos-drug-war-marks-deca de-amid-doubts-changes. Accessed 1 Feb. 2017.

Penn, Sean. "El Chapo Speaks: A Secret Visit with the Most Wanted Man in the World." *Rolling Stone* 9 Jan. 2016, www.rollingstone.com/culture/features/el-chapo-speaks-20160109. Accessed 1 May 2016.

Pérez Aldama, César and Miguel Ángel Rivera. "Carta al Jefe del Departamento de Investigaciones Políticas y Sociales." 22 June 1944. Departamento de Investigaciones Políticas y Sociales Collection. Archivo General de la Nación, Mexico City.

"Peter Braun Thiessen." Servicio de Migración, Registro de Extranjeros. 30 Mar. 1940. Migración Collection, Canadian Series. Archivo General de la Nación, Mexico City.

Piñon Cordoba. Elfego. Letter to the Head of the Agrarian Department. Asunto: "Exp. 'Colonia Pacheco', Mpio. Casas Grandes, Chih." 7 Jan. 1959. Ejido Colonia Pacheco Collection, Archivo General Agrario, Mexico City.

Polanco Hernández, Alfredo. Carta a Víctor Manuel Torres, el Secretario General de Asuntos Agrarios. 11 Abr. 1973. Ejido Niño Artillero Collection, Archivo General Agrario, Mexico City.

Pratt, Mary Louise. *Imperial Eyes: Travel Writing and Transculturation,* 2nd ed., Routledge, 2008.

Quiring, David M. *The Mennonite Old Colony Vision: Under Siege in Mexico and the Canadian Connection.* 2003. DF Plett Historical Research Foundation, 2009.

"Ralph Clarence Farnsworth." Servicio de Migración, Registro de Extranjeros. 10 Jan. 1947. Migración Collection, US Series. Archivo General de la Nación, Mexico City.

Ramírez Villareal, Fco. Carta al Goberador del Estado de Chihuahua. 20 May 1935. Dirección General de Gobierno collection, Archivo General de la Nación, Mexico City.

———. Carta al Gobernador del Estado de Chihuahua. "Suplicándole practicar una investigación en el asunto de que se trata." 18 May 1935. Dirección General de Gobierno collection, Archivo General de la Nación, Mexico City.

Redekop, Calvin Wall. *The Old Colony Mennonites: Dilemmas of Ethnic Minority Life.* Johns Hopkins UP, 1969.

Regehr, T. D. "Of Dutch or German Ancestry? Mennonite Refugees, MCC and the International Refugee Organization." *Journal of Mennonite Studies,* vol. 13, 2005, pp. 7–25.

Reimer, George. "Noch nichts „Stilles" bei „Stellet Licht"!" ["Nothing 'Silent' about *Silent Light*"]. *Kurze Nachrichten aus Mexiko [Brief News from Mexico],* 19 Oct. 2007, p. 4.

Rempel, Gerhard and Franz Rempel. *75 Jahre: Mennoniten in Mexico [75 Years: Mennonites in Mexico].* Comité Pro Archivo Histórico; Museo Menonita, 1998.

"Resolución en el expediente de dotación de ejidos al poblado Galeana, Estado de Chihuahua." *Diario Oficial de la Federación,* 21 June 1939, pp. 10–11.

"Resolución en el expediente de restitución de ejidos, promovida por vecinos del pueblo de Galeana, Estado de Chihuahua." *Diario Oficial de la Federación,* 2nd section, 19 Apr. 1927, pp. 1–9.

"Resolución sobre ampliación de ejido al poblado Colonia Pacheco y sus anexos Corrales y El Molino, en Casas Grandes, Chih." *Diario Oficial de la Federación,* 17 March 1965, p. 9.

"Resolución sobre dotación de ejido al poblado Colonia Pacheco y sus anexos Corrales y El Molino, en Casas Grandes, Chih." *Diario Oficial de la Federación,* 20 Aug. 1956, p. 13.

"Resolución sobre dotación de tierras, solicitada por vecinos del poblado denominado El Lagunero, ubicado en el Municipio de Mapimí, Dgo. (Reg.-331)." *Diario Oficial de la Federación,* 30 Aug. 1983, p. 24.

"Resolución sobre el nuevo centro de población agrícola denominado El Niño Artillero, en Sombrerete, Zac." *Diario Oficial de la Federación*, 11 Oct. 1962, pp. 14–16.

"Resolución sobre privación de derechos agrarios y nuevas adjudicaciones de unidades de dotación y confirmación de Derechos Agrarios, a Ejidatarios del N. C. P. E. Denominado El Niño Artillero, Municipio de Sombrerete, Zac." *Diario Oficial de la Federación,* 1st section, 11 June 1979, pp. 9–11.

"Resolución sobre privación de derechos agrarios y nuevas adjudicaciones de unidades de dotación, en el ejido del poblado denominado J. Santos Bañuelos (antes Col. González Ortega) Municipio de Sombrerete, Zac. (Registrada con el número 6604)." *Diario Oficial de la Federación*, 3 Oct. 1979, pp. 16–17.

"Resolución sobre privación de derechos agrarios y nuevas adjudicaciones de unidades de dotación, en el ejido del poblado denominado J. Santos Bañuelos, ubicado en el Municipio de Sombrerete, Estado de Zacatecas." *Diario Oficial de la Federación,* 27th section, 6 Jan. 1985, dof.gob.mx/nota_detalle.php?codigo=4647082&fecha=06/01/1984. Accessed 1 July 2017.

"Restitución 1927: Ejido Casas Grandes." *Ejido Casas Grandes website.* Google. com sites, 2013, docs.google.com/viewer?a=v&pid=sites&src id=ZGVmYXVsdGRvbWFpbnxlamlkb2Nhc2FzZ3JhbmRlc3xneDo xZGIxOTZlYTc1ZGI0ZDI1. Accessed 1 Dec. 2016.

Robles B., Rosario. "La participación estatal en la agricultura: veinte años de irrigación y crédito." *Historia de la cuestión agraria mexicana: política estatal y conflictos agrarios 1950–1970.* Siglo XXI, 1989.

Rodarte Solis, Juventino. "SRA al cuerpo consultivo agrario." 28 Feb. 1985. Archivo General Agrario, Mexico City. 25–483–6.

Rodríguez, Jaime Javier. *The Literatures of the U. S.–Mexico War: Narrative, Time, and Identity.* U of Texas P, 2010.

Rodríguez, José de la Luz. Letter to the Director de Land and Water, Department of Agrarian Matters and Colonization. 10 Oct. 1972. Ejido Casas Grandes Collection, Archivo General Agrario, Mexico City.

———. Letter to the Director de Land and Water, Department of Agrarian Matters and Colonization. 2 May 1972. Ejido Casas Grandes Collection, Archivo General Agrario, Mexico City.

Romney, Joseph Barnard. "The Exodus of the Mormon Colonists from Mexico, 1912." MA Thesis, U of Utah, 1967.

Romney, Thomas C. *The Mormon Colonies in Mexico*. 1938. Revised with new introduction. U of Utah P, 2005.

Rubalcava, Boanerges. "Mexico and Central America, the Church in." *Encyclopedia of Mormonism*. Edited by Daniel H. Ludlow, Macmillan, 1992, pp. 897–902.

Rubenstein, Anne. *Bad Language, Naked Ladies and Other Threats to the Nation*. Duke UP, 1998.

Ruiz Castro, Fernando. Informe sobre la colonia en la ex hacienda La Honda. N. d. Ejido J. Santos Bañuelos Collection, Archivo General Agrario, Mexico City.

Ruiz, Giancarlo. "Re: Macburro." Email to author, 17 Mar. 2015.

Ryan, Maureen. " 'The Bridge' Review: A Compelling Look at Complex Border Cops." *The Huffington Post* 9 July 2013, updated 8 Sept. 2013, www.huffingtonpost.com/maureen-ryan/the-bridge-fx_b_3567345.html. Accessed 1 Feb. 2017.

Ryskamp, George. "Mormon Colonists in the Mexican Civil Registration: A Case Study in Transnational Immigrant Identity." Dormady and Tamez, pp. 39–54.

Salomán Meraz, Liliana. *Historia de los menonitas radicados en Durango*, 2nd ed. Programa de Apoyo a Comunidades, 2010.

Sánchez Prado, Ignacio. *Screening Neoliberalism: Transforming Mexican Cinema, 1988–2012*. Vanderbilt UP, 2014.

Sawatzky, Harry Leonard. *They Sought a Country: Mennonite Colonization in Mexico*. U of California P, 1971.

Sawatzky, Roland. "Mennonite Funerals in Manitoba." *Preservings*, vol. 30, 2010, pp. 72–76.

Schell, Patience A. "Gender, Class, and Anxiety at the Gabriel Mistral Vocational School, Revolutionary Mexico City." Olcott, Vaughan and Cano, pp. 112–26.

Schmiedehaus, Walter. *Ein feste Burg ist unser Gott: Der Wanderweg eines christlichen Siedlervolkes* [*A Mighty Fortress is Our God: The Wanderings of a Group of Christian Settlers*]. G. J. Rempel, 1948.

Schmitt, Carl. *Political Theology: Four Chapters on the Concept of Sovereignty*. Translated by George Schwab, U of Chicago P, 2005.

"Secretaría de Agricultura y Fomento: Resolución en el expediente de resti-
    tución de ejidos promovida por vecinos del pueblo de Casas Grandes,
    Estado de Chihuahua." *Diario Oficial de la Federación*, 12 May 1927,
    pp. 1–10.
Secretaría de Cultura. "Biblioteca Vasconcelos y Editorial Océano invitan a
    la presentación del libro *México: 45 voces contra la barbarie,* de Lolita
    Bosch," *Secretaría de Cultura de México*, 2015, www.bibliotecavascon-
    celos.gob.mx/detalle-convocatoria/?id=1953., 2013. Accessed 1 Mar
    2016.
Secretaría de Fomento. "Sección Primera. Contrato." *Diario Oficial de la
    Federación*, 12 Oct. 1893, pp. 3–4.
Sepinwall, Alan. "How *The Bridge* Rebuilt Itself into the Best Show You're Not
    Watching." *Uproxx*, 10 Sept. 2014, uproxx.com/sepinwall/how-the-
    bridge-rebuilt-itself-into-the-best-show-youre-not-watching/. Accessed
    1 July 2017.
Serrano Palomino, Víctor Manuel. "Carta al C. Ing. Efrén González Mendoza."
    22 May 1980. Ejido Galeana Collection, Archivo General Agrario,
    Mexico City.
Slomp, Gabriella. *Carl Schmitt and the Politics of Hostility, Violence and Terror.*
    Palgrave-Macmillan, 2009.
Smith, Paul Julian. *Mexican Screen Fiction: Between Cinema and Television.*
    Polity, 2014.
"Solicitud de Pasaporte o Documento de Viaje: Chaviva Kreiner Gasman."
    11 Feb. 1956. México en Italia Collection, Archivo de la Secretaría de
    Relaciones Exteriores, Mexico City.
Sontag, Susan. *On Photography.* Picador/Farrar, Straus and Giroux, 1977.
Soriano Duarte, Rodolfo. "Relación de las propiedades rústicas ubicadas en el
    predio denominado "La Batea" de este municipio, que aparecen inscri-
    tas a nombre de los menonitas que a continuación se detalle." 26 Jan.
    1971. Archivo General Agrario, Mexico City. Ejido Niño Artillero
    Collection.
Sotero-Galindo, Rodolfo. "Resultados de la colonización extranjera en México:
    La colonización menonita en Chihuahua." Lic. en derecho thesis,
    UNAM, 1956.
Soto Laveaga, Gabriela. *Jungle Laboratories: Mexican Peasants, National Projects,
    and the Making of the Pill.* Duke UP, 2009.

Stellet Licht [*Silent Light*]. Directed by Carlos Reygadas, performances by Cornelio Wall, Maria Pankratz, Miriam Toews, Mantarraya, Bac and No Dream Films, 2007.

Stern, Alexandra Minna. "Eugenics and Racial Classification in Modern Mexican America." *Race and Classification: The Case of Mexican America.* Edited by Ilona Katzew and Susan Deans-Smith, Stanford UP, 2009, pp. 151–73.

———. "From Mestizophilia to Biotypology: Racialization and Science in Mexico, 1920–1960." *Race & Nation in Modern Latin America.* Edited by Nancy P. Applebaum, Anne S. Macpherson and Karin Alejandra Rosemblatt, U of North Carolina P, 2003, pp. 187–210.

———. "Responsible Mothers and Normal Children: Eugenics, Nationalism, and Welfare in Post-revolutionary Mexico, 1920–1940." *Journal of Historical Sociology,* vol. 12, no. 4, 1999, pp. 369–97.

Stjerna, Kirsi I. "Grace Only? Or, All is Grace?" *Dialog: A Journal of Theology,* vol. 54, no. 3, 2015, pp. 260–68.

Stoesz, Conrad. "Krause, Cornelius, 1886–1986." *Mennonite Heritage Centre.* Mennonite Church Canada, 17 July, 2006, www.mennonitechurch.ca/ programs/archives/holdings/papers/Krause,%20Cornelius%20fonds. htm. Accessed 1 Aug. 2017.

Stover, Philip R. *Religion and Revolution in Mexico's North: Even Unto Death . . . Tengamos Fe.* Rio Vista P, 2014.

Tejada, Roberto. *National Camera: Photography and Mexico's Image Environment.* U of Minnesota P, 2009.

"Temple Garments." *The Church of Jesus Christ of Latter Day Saints | Newsroom: The Official Resource for News Media, Opinion Leaders and the Public.* Intellectual Reserve, 2017, www.mormonnewsroom.org/article/temp le-garments. Accessed 23 Apr. 2017.

The Bridge: The Complete Second Season. Directed by Elwood Reid, 20th Century Fox; FX, 2014.

The Church of Jesus Christ of Latter Day Saints | Newsroom: The Official Resource for News Media, Opinion Leaders and the Public. Intellectual Reserve, 2017, www.mormonnewsroom.org/topics-and-background/. Accessed 23 July 2017.

Tinajero, Araceli and J. Brian Freeman, eds. *Technology and Culture in Twentieth-Century Mexico.* U of Alabama P, 2013.

Toews, Miriam. *Irma Voth*. Harper, 2011.

Tompkins, Cynthia. *Experimental Latin American Cinema: History and Aesthetics*. U of Texas P, 2013.

Towell, Larry. *The Mennonites: A Biographical Sketch*. Phaidon, 2000.

Tullis, F. LaMond. *Mormons in Mexico: The Dynamics of Faith and Culture*. U of Utah P, 1987.

Turley I., Melvin I. "Lista de Propietarios de Terrenos de Cultivo de la Colonia Pacheco." 27 Mar 1956. Ejido Colonia Pacheco Collection, Archivo General Agrario, Mexico City.

"Turley Wilson Tenna Augusta." Servicio de Migración, Registro de Extranjeros. 14 Dec. 1932. Migración Collection, US Series. Archivo General de la Nación, Mexico City.

"Últimos Acontecimientos en el Ejido Casas Grandes." *Ejido Casas Grandes website*. Google.com sites, 2013, sites.google.com/site/ejidocasasgrandes/ultimos-acontencimientos. Accessed 1 Aug. 2016.

U.S. Department of State. "Merida Initiative." *U.S. Department of State: Diplomacy in Action*, n. d. www.state.gov/j/inl/merida/. Accessed 1 Feb. 2017.

Valenzuela, Samuel. Memorandum to Lic. Augusto Gomez Villanueva. 19 Feb. 1971. Letter. Ejido Colonia Casas Grandes Collection, Archivo General Agrario, Mexico City.

Vargas, Carolina and Martha García Ortega. "Vulnerability and Agriculture Among Old Colony Mennonites in Quintana Roo, Mexico: A Research Note." Translated by Ben Nobbs-Thiessen. *Journal of Mennonite Studies*, vol. 35, 2017, pp. 329–37.

Vasconcelos, José. *The Cosmic Race: A Bilingual Edition*. Translated and edited by Didier T. Jaén, Johns Hopkins UP, 1997.

Villalón Valencia, Faustino. "Inafectabilidad Ganadera." *Semanario de la Suprema Corte de Justicia*, sexta época, segunda sala, tercera parte, vol. 66, p. 10, 3 Dec. 1962. www.jurisconsulta.mx/index.php/JurisprudenciaSCJN/ViewTesis?iD=126775. Accessed 1 Aug. 2016.

Wald, Elijah. *Narcocorrido*. HarperCollins, 2001.

Walsh Sanderson, Susan R. *Land Reform in Mexico: 1910–1980*. Academic P, 1984.

Warner, Rick. "Filming a Miracle: *Ordet, Silent Light,* and the Spirit of Contemplative Cinema." *Critical Quarterly*, vol. 57, no. 2, 2015, pp. 46–71.

Wariner, Ruth. *The Sound of Gravel: A Memoir.* Flatiron Books, 2016.

Weaver-Zercher, David. *The Amish in the American Imagination.* Johns Hopkins UP, 2001.

Weaver-Zercher, Valerie. *Thrill of the Chaste: The Allure of Amish Romance Novels.* Johns Hopkins UP, 2013.

Whetten, LaVon B. "Las Colonias: Once a Haven, Still a Home." Photographs by Don L. Searle. *Ensign* August 1985. Intellectual Reserve, 2016, www.lds.org/ensign/1985/08/las-colonias-once-a-haven-still-a-home?lang=eng. Accessed 1 Aug. 2016.

———. *Colonia Juarez: Celebrating 125 Years of the Mormon Colonies in Mexico.* AuthorHouse, 2010.

Wiebe, Franz. Telephone conversation with William Janzen. 21 July 2017.

"Wiebe Justina." Servicio de Migración, Registro de Extranjeros. 24 Dec. 1949. Migración Collection, Canadian Series. Archivo General de la Nación, Mexico City.

Will, Martina E. "The Mennonite Colonization of Chihuahua: Reflections of Competing Visions." *The Americas*, vol. 53, no. 3, 1997, pp. 353–78.

Williams, Gareth. *The Mexican Exception: Sovereignty, Police and Democracy.* Palgrave, 2012.

Wilson, Eric, ed. *Government of the Shadows: Parapolitics and Criminal Sovereignty.* Pluto P, 2009.

———. *The Dual State: Parapolitics, Carl Schmitt and the National Security Complex.* Ashgate, 2012.

Wright, John B. "Mormon Colonias of Chihuahua." *Geographical Review*, vol. 91, no. 3, 2001, pp. 586–96.

Yehya, Naief. "*Silent Light* (Mexico, 2007) Carlos Reygadas's Meditation on Love and Ritual." *The Ten Best Latin American Films of the Decade (2000–2009).* Edited by Carlos A Gutiérrez, Cinema Tropical; Jorge Pinto, 2010, pp. 19–26.

Zavala, Oswaldo. "Imagining the US-Mexico Drug War: The Critical Limits of Narconarratives." *Comparative Literature*, vol. 66, no. 3, 2014, pp. 340–60.

Žižek, Slavoj. *Violence: Six Sideways Reflections.* Picador, 2008.

Zuk, Tanya D. " 'Proud Mormon Polygamist': Assimilation, Popular Memory, and the Mormon Churches in Big Love." *Journal of Religion and Popular Culture*, vol. 26, no. 1, 2014, pp. 93–106.

INDEX